THE POETRY OF JUAN RAMÓN JIMÉNEZ

THE POETRY OF JUAN RAMÓN JIMÉNEZ
An Example of Modern Subjectivity

JULIO JENSEN

MUSEUM TUSCULANUM PRESS
UNIVERSITY OF COPENHAGEN
2012

The Poetry of Juan Ramón Jiménez:
An Example of Modern Subjectivity

© Museum Tusculanum Press and Julio Jensen, 2012
Consultant: Richard Cardwell
Copy editor: Jordy Findanis
Cover design: Pernille Sys Hansen, Damp Design
Set in Palatino and printed by Tarm Bogtryk
ISBN 978 87 635 3647 9

This book is published with financial support from
Birthe og Knud Togebys Fond
Kirsten Schottlænders Fond
Landsdommer V. Gieses Legat
Knud Henders Legatfond

Museum Tusculanum Press
126 Njalsgade
DK-2300 Copenhagen S
Denmark
www.mtp.dk

But if I got my being from myself, I would not doubt, nor would I desire, nor would I lack anything at all. For I would have given myself all the perfections of which I have some idea; in so doing, I myself would be God!

René Descartes

CONTENTS

	Acknowledgements	ix
	Introduction	1
1	Earthly and Heavenly: Mythical Spatiality	11
2	Infinite Longing as a Dynamic Spatial Force	37
3	Pantheistic and Textual Space	63
4	Poetic Time and Eternal Return	93
5	Poetic Memory	117
6	The *Obra* as Subjective Memory	143
	Conclusion	161
	Notes	167
	Abbreviations	195
	Bibliography	197
	Index	207

ACKNOWLEDGEMENTS

Many persons have contributed to the realization of this book. Among these are Marianne Alenius, Jørn Erslev Andersen, Rocío Bejarano, Javier Blasco, Richard Cardwell, Martin Chase sj, José Domínguez Caparrós, Trevor Curnow, Jesper Fich op, Jordy Findanis, Susanne Hoyos csj and the community of Stella Matutina in Kokkedal, Mogens Chrom Jacobsen, Jonna Kjær, Hans Peter Lund, Miguel Ángel Márquez Guerrero, Morten Nøjgaard, Berta Pallares, Poul Rasmussen, Esteban Torre, Frederik Tygstrup, and many more whom I fail to remember. Special thanks are due to my colleagues at the Department of English, Germanic and Romance Studies, University of Copenhagen. The department has provided me with the necessary support in order to finish this study, for which I am grateful.

The book has received financial support, without which it could not have been published, from the following foundations: Birthe og Knud Togebys Fond, Kirsten Schottlænders Fond, Knud Henders Legatfond, and Landsdommer V. Gieses Legat. I want to express my deepest gratitude for their support. Thanks are also tendered to Carmen Hernández-Pinzón for the permission to reproduce Jiménez's texts and the graphic material used in the cover page.

Finally, to my wife and children, as well as to my parents, I owe a debt which I cannot hope to repay.

Grateful acknowledgement is made to the following for permission to reproduce copyrighted material: Antonio T. de Nicolás for permission to quote from Juan Ramón Jiménez, *God Desired and Desiring*, translated by Antonio T. de Nicolás (New York: Paragon House, 1987) and *Time and Space: A Poetic Autobiography*, translated by Antonio T. de Nicolás (New York: Paragon House, 1988); Associated University Presses for permission to quote from Juan Ramón Jiménez, *Diary of a Newlywed Poet*, translated by Hugh A. Harter (Selinsgrove: Susquehanna University Press, 2004); The Edwin Mellen Press for permission to quote from Juan Ramón Jiménez, *Spiritual Sonnets / Sonetos espirituales*, translated by Carl W. Cobb (Lewiston, Queenston and Lampeter, 1996); Joseph A. Roach III for permission to quote from Juan Ramón Jiménez, *Three Hundred Poems*, translated by Eloïse Roach (Austin: University of Texas Press, 1962); and to Farrar, Straus & Giroux, Inc. for permission to quote from *Selected Writings of Juan Ramón Jiménez*, translated by H.R. Hays (New York: Farrar, Straus and Cudahy, 1957).

Portions in the Introduction and Chapter 3 have appeared in a different form in respectively "The Face of the Author: A Sample of the History of the Humanities", in *The Object of Study of the Humanities: Proceedings from the Seminar at the University of Copenhagen, September 2001* (Copenhagen: Museum Tusculanum Press, 2004) and "Antropomorfismens reversibilitet. Perception og tekstualitet i lyrikken", *K&K* no. 91 (2001). Chapter 6 is a revised version of "La Obra de Juan Ramón Jiménez como elaboración vivida del concepto del absoluto", in *Revue Romane* 37.2 (2002). The material has been reprinted with kind permission.

INTRODUCTION

This study is an interpretation of the lyrical output of one of the most important twentieth-century Spanish poets, Juan Ramón Jiménez (1881–1958). The work of this author covers the first half of the twentieth century and develops from Symbolism to abstract, quasi-religious poetry at the end of his life. The aim here is to explain this evolution from the perspective of modern subjectivity, that is, by analyzing the articulation of the lyrical subject that appears in Jiménez's poetry in the context of the philosophy of the subject. This speculative tradition is in the following understood as the paradigm that sets the consciousness as the primordial philosophical principle.

A key presupposition underlying this work is that, although each discourse develops within its own generic rules, literature and philosophy hold a historical correlation, as they, respectively, represent and conceptualize the prevailing understanding of the human being at a given moment. The present book aims at displaying this correlation, assuming that such a perspective will cast light on both literature and speculative thought. At the same time, since literature has its own generic presuppositions, it is essential to consider these in order to do justice to literary discourse.[1] Jiménez's poetry can justifiably be related to notions and questions belonging to philosophical discourse if an awareness of the specificity of the literary tradition is maintained. For this reason the main part of this study will consist of textual analyses of Jiménez's poems, as it is through close readings that their distinctiveness as literature is best preserved. On the other hand, these readings of relatively few poems (or fragments of poems) from Jiménez's vast output are to be regarded as representative for his whole lyrical output.[2] It is thereby implied that it is possible to categorize a given text as paradigmatic or exemplary within a wider body of texts. The same assumption is taken when Jiménez's poetry is regarded as exemplary with respect to the notion of modern subjectivity. To work with a notion of representativity means that a given example contains a series of central traits that are shared by a larger number of texts or by a paradigm of thought. This book, then, can be regarded as the display of one long example that sets a philosophical paradigm before the reader's eyes. In other words, Jiménez's prolific work is regarded as a laboratory producing representations of modern subjectivity.[3]

The emergence of the modern notion of subjectivity can be outlined with the figures of William of Ockham, Descartes and Kant. Modern thought begins to appear with the figure of William of Ockham.[4] In contrast to St Thomas Aquinas, who taught that it is possible to know the essence of things, Ockham maintained that outside the mind only individual things and qualities exist. Universal notions can only be found in the mind, they do not have reality status, neither in a Platonic fashion – as transcendent ideas – nor in an Aristotelian way – as essential properties immanent in things. The abstract and the universal do not exist in nature, only in the individual's consciousness. In this way appears the problematic relationship between mind and exterior reality that will characterize modern subjectivity.[5] Descartes's intention was to reach a fixed point that could give understanding a firm basis. The methodical doubt in the *Meditations on First Philosophy* (1641) puts the evidence of the senses into question, but certitude can be reached thanks to the *cogito*. Understanding belongs to the *res cogitans*, to the thinking subject that has reason as its principal faculty, while both the external world and the human body are physical entities (any body is a *res extensa*). The comprehension of reality is possible because Descartes operates with a necessary link between human and divine. The human subject bears the stamp of its Creator and even if there is a difference between divine and human reason (because God's intellect is infinite and mankind's finite), the analogy between the two endows the subject with the foundations required for knowledge of exterior reality. In this way, Descartes's philosophy is epistemologically subject-centred but gives ontological priority to God (cf. Taylor 1989: 157).

The change to a thoroughly anthropocentric paradigm takes place with Kantian thought. Kant cuts the link between God and man because he considers that the finite condition of the human subject entails the impossibility of attaining knowledge about the divine subject. In Kant the subject is split in a transcendental and an empirical subjectivity. The transcendental subject is a self-founded self-consciousness. At the same time, the I finds its determination in the world of objects, and is thus also an empirical and finite subjectivity. This entails that anything the subject can know about the world necessarily bears the marks of its perspective. We can never know anything in-itself, because that would require that we observed the world from no (or every) point of view, from a divine omniscient perspective. At the same time, Kant wished to refute a sceptical position like Hume's, which threatened to undermine the objectivity of scientific thought. A central claim in the *Critique of Pure Reason* (1781/87) is that even if anything we know about the world is always dependent on our own perspective upon it, it is still possible to obtain universally and necessarily valid knowledge.[6]

This subjectivity, split between an empirically given subject (which can thus be regarded as an object in a world of objects) and a self-founded transcendental consciousness, is a fundamental part of the modern paradigm. The human subject becomes the foundation of knowledge, and this means that man must – with the consciousness of his own finite forces – carry out a task that would require infinite strength. This characterization of Modernity is one of Foucault's central ideas in *The Order of Things* (1966). According to Foucault, Modernity is the anthropocentric age when the subject posits itself as a sovereign and absolute I, and at the same time vainly attempts to let this empty self-consciousness be the founder of the world it inhabits. Modern subjectivity is furthermore destined to be split between being, on the one hand, the source of understanding and, on the other hand, an object for itself in order to gain clarity about the epistemological process as such. Commenting on Foucault, Habermas has noted in *The Philosophical Discourse of Modernity* (1985) how the modern understanding of the subject produces a series of efforts in the nineteenth and twentieth centuries to overcome the opacity inherent in this self-founding subject. In this period the idea emerges that the I can only arrive at itself through establishing a non-I that then is to be conquered by the I.[7] This dialectic is due to a constitutive trait of modern subjectivity: the self-absolutization of a finite being. Throughout Modernity the subject oscillates between aiming for an absolute – which if attained would be a self-conquest that would confirm the subject's absolute being – and regarding itself as an empty subjectivity.

This study holds as a key assumption that modern literature can be regarded as vitally conditioned by this oscillation, and one manifestation of it is the literary production of variations upon a subjectivity split between an empirical (finite and contingent) I, and a self-posited absolute subject. In the following the expression "absolute subject" will be used not only in the sense of a transcendental consciousness but also in that of an almighty subject. A self-founding subjectivity has a divine characteristic, and this trait is unfolded, experimentally as it were, in the literary texts. It is undeniable that when subjectivity becomes the foundation of knowledge, a metaphysical consequence is that consciousness becomes the ground of being.[8] The alternation between absolutization and contingency of the subject will be exemplified in the following lines with the author-figure in modern literature. In turn, in the subsequent chapters this oscillation will be further developed through the analysis of Jiménez's poetry.

With Idealism and Romanticism the idea of the author-god emerged, an idea that can be illustrated through the concept of the organic work of art.[9] The notion of a perfectly homogeneous work where every part is connected to the whole in a harmonic and necessary way is sanctioned by figures such as Kant, Goethe, Schelling and Hegel, and runs into the twentieth century, either as an active ideal or as a conceptual ghost that must be exorcized again and again. Since modern thought cannot dispense with the notion of an absolute, absolute ideas (such as that of the organic work of art) keep reappearing throughout Modernity.[10] Within the sphere of literature, demonstratively anti-organic works such as those of James Joyce, Marcel Duchamp and Raymond Roussel testify to what could be called the absent presence of the organic work of art in the twentieth century. In the domain of aesthetic theory, thinkers such as Lukacs, Adorno and Barthes exhibit the same urge to refute this notion. The first systematic rejection of the organic work of art appears in the first decades of the twentieth century, when the historical Avant-Gardes deconstruct this idea. If the organic work of art receives a perfect form through the divine force of the artist, the Avant-Garde work emphasizes its condition as an elaborated and crafted work, as can be seen in the collage technique or, taken to its limit, in Duchamp's readymades. In the case of the organic work of art the authorial figure that underlies it is a god-like individual endowed with the capacity to create a perfect and self-sufficient universe. Conversely the Avant-Garde author negates such a subjectivity since in the most radical Avant-Garde manifestations, the author obliterates himself by leaving the work to be constituted by chance (Dadaism, Queneau) or by letting industrial objects appear as works of art (Duchamp, Warhol). The philosophical correlate of such a literary practice that vehemently negates an absolute is the tradition of negative metaphysics from Nietzsche to Derrida.

Between Romanticism and the Avant-Gardes – between the author-genius who with the inner forces creates a perfect universe and the anti-author of Dadaism and Surrealism – the autotelic practice crystallizes in modern literature. This mode of writing tends toward displaying a purely linguistic play that suspends reference. Mallarmé has been identified as the paradigmatic figure of this literary tendency.[11] According to the present hypothesis, this literary practice can be related to the endeavour of allowing absolute subjectivity to act as the uttering voice in the poetic text, even if not in the same way as in organicist aesthetics. If the Romantic artist creates a perfect totality in the work of art, Aestheticism eliminates any reference to empirical circumstances. A Symbolist poem is a purely self-referential linguistic surface uttered by a voice freed from its ties to the empirical world. Such a voice is not linked to a body, and for this reason it does not refer to the world of physical entities. This is a way of transcending the corruptible and transitory nature of our empirical self, and represents an access to an unconditioned sphere. Ultimately, however, the recourse to a purely linguistic universe means that the subject becomes dissolved in the immateriality of syntax. Certain manifestations of the Avant-Gardes can be interpreted as an ironic corollary to the attempt to express absolute subjectivity through nonreferential language. The Dadaist recipe for making a poem by cutting a newspaper article into bits and pasting them onto a piece of paper in a random order, or Raymond Queneau's text, *Cent mille milliards de poèmes* (1961), guided by mathematical principles, can be regarded as the ultimate logical consequence of the wish to develop a pure linguistic utterance. Anything that remains of syntactical order could be regarded as a reference to the actual use of language in the empirical world, and for this reason the destruction of syntax represents the last step in the direction of a nonreferential absolute enunciation. In Queneau's text the authorial figure has vanished in an anonymous mathematical play, and the only task of the author is the suicidal activation of a system that gradually erases any trace of an empirical subjectivity.

Similarly, an author-figure arises that can be characterized as an entirely empirical subject. If empirical subjectivity is to appear as the origin of the enunciation, the subject will tend to disappear into the diversity of its representations – as can be observed in the synaesthetic perception of Symbolism. The lyrical subject is dissolved into the plurality of its sense-impressions, causing a perceptual stream without a sharp delimitation between each perception. Such a lyrical subjectivity becomes god-like when it is inserted into a pantheistic worldview (as will be shown in Chapters 3 and 4 below). Then the subject becomes the self-consciousness of the universe, since it is dissolved and transformed into an impersonal voice expressing the cosmic rhythm of death and rebirth. In a similar way as with respect to absolute subjectivity, a parodical account of the empirical subject is given by a particular thread of modern literature. A chaotic stream of things, words and persons, as in the *nouveau roman* or in some of James Joyce's works, could be regarded as the reduction of the individual to the simplest form of consciousness, one that perceives the surroundings without any synthetic processing. Another representation of empirical subjectivity can be found in Marcel Duchamp's celebrated *Fountain* (1917). This work can be regarded as a monument of empirical subjectivity since it, like Andy Warhol's movie *Sleep* (1963), only represents the pure physicality of a corporeal necessity. In these works, the hand of the artist is absent except for the act of presenting metonymically (in the case of Duchamp) or in a direct representation (in the case of Warhol) a given corporeal function. The opposite of an absolute subjectivity emerges as the author-subject of works like the mentioned ones, since no form-giving force has been activated in the "creation" of the works. In the *Fountain* a signature (which is not Duchamp's) is the only ironic reference to an authorial figure. In a similar way, in *Sleep* the domination of form is practically absent. The movie is silent, and the first shot, which lasts about 45 minutes, is a close-up of a sleeping man's abdomen. The introduction of these objects into the art institution is only meaningful if an historical perspective is adopted, as they can be considered to constitute the strongest possible emphasis on the empirical side of subjectivity, one that has renounced the slightest epistemological or creative ambition.

Less radical works, nonetheless pointing in the same direction, can also be mentioned. The (in principle) endless series of images in the surrealist texts or the collage technique in the plastic arts as well as in literature refer to an authorial function that does not aim at a masterful synthesis of forms in an aesthetic whole but to a more or less elaborated *bricolage*, a gathering of individual elements that, taken separately, could just as well be absent from the work without significantly changing the whole. A negative metaphysics is thus expressed that has its roots in precisely the same paradigm as the idealist notion of the work of art, i.e. in the historical break that can be related to Kant's Copernican turn. From the understanding of subjectivity as self-founded follows the dream of omnipotence – which in turn is frustrated by the subject's knowledge of its finitude. The notion of *modern literature* could from this perspective be understood as the period when the idea of a self-founding subject was exposed to a series of literary experiments.

With respect to Jiménez's work, the leading hypothesis of this study is that the change in style and motifs that his poetry undergoes from the early to the mature period is a consequence of precisely the oscillation between empirical and absolute subjectivity described above. In the Aestheticist poetry written in the period 1900–12 the contemplation and creation of beauty is endowed by the mind, and at the same time the mood is mainly elegiac because of the pervasive consciousness of the transience of life and beauty. Beauty is the creation of the lyrical subject, it is the product of the infinite depths of his inner world,[12] and for this reason the asymmetry between the contemplation of perfect beauty and the consciousness of its transience and contingency causes an intense feeling of pain. In turn, the mature poetry – *poesía pura* or *desnuda* (*pure* or *naked poetry*) – can be regarded as a logical consequence of the first part of his output because it aims at eliminating any reference to exterior reality. In this way, the lyrical subject is able to create an autonomous poetic world without being troubled by the condition of corruptibility and finitude. Beauty, the product of the infinite inner world of the lyrical subject, is now given a sphere entirely of its own.

In the following, Jiménez's poetry will be seen as an exploration of the paradigm of the modern subject, and the perspective chosen will be to focus on the articulations of space and time in his works.[13] Jiménez's lyrical subject is fundamentally a Romantic one,[14] and for this reason an important part of the theoretical and philosophical framework used in the analyses – especially in the first chapters – belongs to Romantic thought. At the same time, given that Jiménez's poetry develops within the same literary historical frame as the one described above, from Romanticism to the Avant-Gardes, also theory posterior to Romanticism will be applied. Jiménez's output exhibits Romantic subjectivity, Symbolist textuality and Avant-Garde self-parody as different facets of the same paradigm. Chapters 1 to 3 analyze the representation of space. The first chapter shows how Jiménez, as a coherent consequence of his absolutization of the lyrical subject, constitutes spatiality in the same way as mythical thought. The second chapter analyzes how Jiménez's spatial representation is inherently dynamic due to the Romantic motif of infinite longing. The third chapter discusses how empirical subjectivity can, by means of a pantheistic worldview in which inner and outer space blend, appear to express a cosmic self-consciousness. Chapters 4 to 6 elaborate on the treatment of time in Jiménez's poetry. The fourth chapter discusses the creation of a *monadic temporality* (Walter Benjamin) separated from objective, historical time. In Chapter 5 it is considered to what extent the thematization of memory is used for the constitution of an autobiographical identity based upon the actual, lived experiences of the historical person Juan Ramón Jiménez. Such an identity would amount to the articulation of a *self*. As will be seen, however, the remembrances expressed by Jiménez's lyrical subject do not primarily have the function of creating an identity but rather of relating to the supra-individual cosmic rhythm of eternal return, that is, to a sense of belonging to a pantheistic absolute. The achievement of an autobiographical identity is further discussed in Chapter 6, where Jiménez's ideas of his *Work*, the *Obra*, as a self-conquest are discussed. A certain progression can thus be followed throughout the chapters, from the mythologized absolute subject to the discussion of whether a self is articulated in the poetic texts on the basis of the lived experiences. It is important to emphasize that while this progression informs the structure of this book, it is not thereby implied that Jiménez developed in the same way himself. Each chapter addresses both a facet of his poetry and a specific aspect of modern subjectivity.

One last introductory remark concerns a methodological aspect. The division of the subject into empirical and transcendental can also be related to the domain of literary criticism. The widespread methodological prohibition against including biographical information in the interpretation of literary texts eventually has its origins in this dual subjectivity and the epistemological conditions connected to it. Since in Modernity the subject is the foundation of knowledge, the aim for objective knowledge and the acknowledgment of the finitude of our faculties of understanding creates a state of tension between desire for epistemological certainty and sceptical disillusionment. Positivism, Formal Logic or Structuralism are theoretical currents that lay claim to the possibility of attaining objective knowledge. Conversely, Poststructuralism in its various manifestations sustains the impossibility of achieving any stable insight into the world. The suppression of the author in the interpretation of literary texts, as is prescribed by theories such as the New Criticism and Structuralism, is caused by the wish to produce an interpretation that is as objective as possible. In these theoretical schools the biographical context of the literary works is considered contingent in relation to the formal and thematic aspects of literature. The desire to produce objective readings of the literary texts contrasts with the fact that interpretation is unavoidably linked to a series of factors that escape from the domain of definite knowledge (understood to mean knowledge of the kind found in Formal Logic or mathematics). Apparently the formal features or semiotic structures of a text represent a pure form of knowledge, but at the same time it is impossible to isolate this sphere completely from the circumstances surrounding the production of the specific works. References to the historical period, to the literary traditions, to genre conventions, and sometimes also to biographical information about the author, are in practice unavoidable for the understanding of literature. Since it is impossible to attain pure knowledge within literary analysis (something which this discipline has in common with vast fields of the humanities), reference will be made to the author Juan Ramón Jiménez whenever it is relevant, rather than trying to avoid biographical information in order to reach a supposedly more objective understanding.[15] Any literary text obeys a system or a grammar and is *also* related to a series of particularities that may be indispensable for its understanding. Both particularity and universality are vital parts of a literary text and can work together in the interpretation.

At the same time, it is clear that the lyrical subject cannot be regarded as solely an autobiographical testimony. The present approach – and the following analyses will prove this – considers Jiménez's lyrical subject a constructed subjectivity. The main hypothesis that guides this study, to regard Jiménez's poetry as the elaboration of variations of modern subjectivity, entails precisely the separation of lyrical subject and biographical person. This separation has a basis in Jiménez's output, since his poetic work can be regarded as a series of endeavours to, within the modern paradigm, elevate the individual existence from contingency to necessity. This takes place by only representing the absolute side of subjectivity, thereby leaving empiricity behind. At the same time, the literary tradition to which Jiménez belongs entails that autobiographical and lyrical subject coincide to a certain extent given that the overcoming of contingency can only be carried out by a poet-subject (a Romantic idea that will be treated in the first chapter). For this reason, the lyrical subject appearing in Jiménez's poetic texts is a poet who sometimes is explicitly identified as the individual Juan Ramón Jiménez. In some poems Jiménez aims at overcoming and deleting his individual features – when he separates the self-founded and world-generating aspect of the subject from its empirical sides – while in others he tries to fuse life and work in order to reach a totality of both in his *Obra*. This ambiguity is part of the modern notion of subjectivity, as will be further developed in the following.

CHAPTER ONE

Earthly and Heavenly: Mythical Spatiality

> *The manifestation of the sacred ontologically founds the world. In the homogeneous and infinite expanse, in which no point of reference is possible and hence no orientation can be established, the hierophany reveals an absolute fixed point, a center.*
>
> Mircea Eliade

Modernity can be defined as the historical period when humanity tried to understand itself exclusively on the basis of its own forces. Central to this philosophical and political project is a thoroughly anthropocentric rationality that displaces mythical and religious beliefs. In his philosophy of religion, Kant considers the moral law – what we ought to do – as the essence of religion. According to Kantian philosophy, religion is an articulation of practical reason that should be divested of external rituals and precepts. Philosophy must carry out this task by determining what can be accepted of the content of religious traditions.[1] Furthermore, Kant inverts the Judaeo-Christian notion that it is God's commands that bind us to morality. Instead Kant maintains that it is morality that points to a divine will, whereby the reverence owed to God is changed into devotion to moral law. In a similar way, Kant argues that in the experience of natural beauty we feel nature as created and sense its transcendent origin. This feeling, however, is not a theoretical proof of the existence of God, only an intimation that induces us to believe in a divine order. As a consequence of this entirely anthropocentric understanding of religion, in Romantic thought the poet becomes a central figure: "[e]l poeta desaloja al sacerdote y la poesía se convierte en una revelación rival de la escritura religiosa"

(Paz 1981: 75) ([t]he poet replaces the priest, and poetry becomes a revelation rivalling the Scriptures) (Paz 1991a: 46).² The creative imagination of the poet becomes identified as the origin of all myths and religious thought, and consequently the poetic word becomes the word of foundation, a primordial access to the absolute. As the substitute of God, the artist's mind has the power to produce epiphanies.³

This suggests that a constitutive similarity can be found between the spatiality articulated by Romantic and post-Romantic poetry on the one side and mythical thought on the other, since the opening towards an absolute reality is thematized in both. In fact Jiménez's poetry represents a world ruled by a basic mythical dichotomy: earthly-heavenly.⁴ The earthly-heavenly duality in Jiménez's poetic output corresponds precisely with what Cassirer calls the "primary spatial difference" in mythical thought (Cassirer 1955: 85), which is between two ontologically different regions, the profane and the sacred: "a common, generally accessible province and another, sacred, precinct which seems to be raised out of its surroundings, hedged around and guarded against them" (Cassirer 1955: 85). The sky as the place where the sacred resides, in contrast to the imperfect and corruptible being that characterizes earthly existence, is both a Greek and a Biblical conception, appearing in the whole body of Western thought and literature. Cassirer considers this division, however, a universal perception: "by a primal and basic religious intuition the heavens [der Himmelsraum] as a whole appear as just such an enclosed, consecrated zone; as a temple inhabited by one divine being and governed by one divine will" (Cassirer 1955: 100).⁵

In the present chapter the analyses will focus on the constitution of a specific spatial duality running throughout Jiménez's poetic output: the earthly, profane realm and the heavenly, sacred realm. This dichotomy can furthermore be applied to the duality absolute-empirical subject, because the former is identified with the sacred and with poetry whereas the latter is related to finitude and transience. This tension generates two basic moods in Jiménez's poetic writing. On the one side a melancholy expression caused by the experience of individual finitude and contingency appears because, even if a fleeting consolation can be found in beauty and poetry, the sense of the elevated and sacred is ultimately overshadowed by the subject's consciousness of his mortality. On the other side appears the triumphant mood that is expressed in the mature phase of Jiménez's work, the *segunda época*, where the divine poet-subject possesses an unconditioned kingdom in his *Obra*

(*Work*), a kingdom that will endure by being handed over to the future readers. In this way the duality of the "above" and the "below" is, at the level of representation, a basic trait of Jiménez's poetic world, while it also relates to the thematic level of ontological and existential presuppositions.

Earthly and Heavenly in Jiménez's Early Poetry
The earth-sky dichotomy is clearly present in the first two collections of poems, *Ninfeas* (*Water Lilies*) and *Almas de violeta* (*Violet Souls*) – both from 1900. The "high" elements of this duality appear valued positively while the "low" manifestations are given a pejorative accent. In the poem "Nochebuena" (Christmas Eve) from *Almas de violeta*, the falling snow is presented as pure and unsoiled in its descent from the celestial sphere:

> Del empañado cielo
> la nieve cae, quejándose con fúnebre amargura
> al ver en la inmundicia manchada su blancura,
> al verse desterrada desde la gloria al suelo…
> (*Plp*: 1537)

> From the misty sky
> the snow falls, lamenting with gloomy bitterness
> when it sees its whiteness stained in the filth,
> when it sees itself exiled from the glory to the ground…

A strong feeling of despair of the earthly existence pervades the poems in the first books, underscoring the perfection of the celestial realm in contrast. At the same time, the heavenly is recurrently identified with the realm of fantasy and dream, "ensueño", as in the following verses from the poem "Extasis":

> Como adoro un sublime Idëal azulado,
> y la Vida es muy roja y es muy negra la Vida;
> de la Vida mi alma sollozante se olvida
> y llorando se eleva al Ensueño dorado…
> (*Plp*: 1474)

> Since I adore a sublime and bluish Ideal,
> and Life is very red and very black is Life;

Life my sobbing soul forgets
and crying it rises to the golden Dream…

Heaven and earth confront each other in these verses by means of a colour symbolism. Red and black refer to terrestrial life, metonymically signifying that illness, suffering and death are the basic conditions of human existence. Conversely, "un sublime Idëal azulado" (a sublime and bluish Ideal) relates to the heavenly domain.[6] In the last verse it is stated with the verb "elevar" (to rise) how the lyrical subject ascends to a higher realm, "al Ensueño dorado" (to the golden Dream), whereby the celestial and the inner realms are conflated, identifying the ascending movement with the act of dreaming.

Both the earth-heaven duality and the conflation inner-celestial are constants in the poetical books that follow after *Ninfeas* and *Almas de violeta*, as can be observed in the following examples from *Rimas* (*Rhymes*, 1902) and *Arias tristes* (*Sad Airs*, 1903):

Siento frío… ¡Quién pudiera
dormitar eternamente en un ensueño,
olvidarse de la tierra
y perderse en lo infinito de los cielos!
(*Op*, I, 1: 41)

I feel cold… Who could
doze eternally in a dream,
forget the earth
and disappear in the infinite of the heavens!

Los gusanos de la muerte
harán su nido en mi pecho,
donde el corazón un día
alzó fragancia de ensueños,
    y mis ojos que miraron
tantas veces a los cielos,
se pudrirán en la tierra
del cerrado cementerio.
(*Op*, I, 1: 225)

The worms of death
will make their nest in my bosom,

where the heart one day
raised a fragrance of dreams,
   and my eyes that looked
so many times to the heavens,
will rot in the earth
of the closed cemetery.

In the first example the loss of the I in a dream sends the lyrical subject to the domain of the heavens, that is, the transition from the inner world to the infinite celestial space is seamless. In the second example the earth-heaven duality is the structuring thematic nucleus, as it is possible to analyze the cited stanzas on the basis of two thematic fields or isotopies[7] corresponding with this duality. The elements "gusanos", "muerte", "pudrirán", "tierra" and "cementerio" (worms, death, rot, earth, cemetery) constitute the isotopy of earth and mortality. Conversely the isotopy of inner and celestial realms counts the following words: "pecho", "corazón", "alzó", "ensueños" and "cielos" (bosom, heart, raised, dreams, heavens). In particular the verb "alzar" (to raise) in verse 4 expresses the continuity from the inner domain to the realm of the heavens. As will be shown below, dreaming is equated with poetic creation given that both are products of the imagination. And yet, as is expressed in these texts, poetry is ultimately experienced as empty. In the first example the impossibility of attaining an enduring dwelling in the celestial realm is denoted by the expression "¡Quién pudiera […]!" (Who could […]!), while in the second example the finality of death is directly expressed. The consciousness of death is clearly stronger than the sense of the heavenly realm.[8]

The background for this weak faith in the salvific function of art can be found in the position assigned to the religious in modern thought. The modern paradigm displaces the religious world understanding, either from a naturalistic perspective (Marx, Nietzsche, Freud) or from a more or less explicitly agnostic attitude that considers it impossible to attain theoretical knowledge about the divine subject (Kant). Since the religiosity of modern poetry is based on a sceptical attitude, a logical consequence is to consider the poetic mind as the generator of wonderful but eventually arbitrary mythical configurations. In modern thought, art is given the task of reminding us of the numinous, but at the same time we must consider this latter realm a fenced domain for our logical capacities. For this reason, modern art oscillates between the desire for religious plenitude and its denial and parody; by not admitting any deity other than the artist, only a fictional or subjectively conditioned notion of the sacred is established. Since the modern subject is empirical and contingent, a defeatism arises with respect to the value of the poetic creations. This can be observed in ideas such as Schlegel's notion of *romantic irony* or Ruskin's *pathetic fallacy*. What should be a communion with the absolute is eventually understood as the creation of a linguistic room of mirrors.[9] This limitation of poetry leads in many cases to a self-enclosure that is epitomized in Mallarmé's texts, but that appears throughout Modernity as the self-reflexivity of the poetic expression. Whether stress is laid on the positive and creative aspect of the aesthetic activity or on the disillusioned understanding of it, art is turned against itself. Poetry becomes self-reflexive and self-referential, and the motif of the poetic creation becomes a *topos* of modern poetry.

This notion of poetry as enclosed in an autonomous sphere, mirroring its own emergence from the depths of the poet-subject's soul, is a constant in Jiménez's poetry, appearing both in the early and in the mature works.[10] The divergence in mood between Jiménez's early and mature poetry can be explained by a difference of accent on the understanding of the creative activity. If a perspective of nihilism and sense of ontological contingency dominates Jiménez's early poetry, his mature work tends to stress the demiurgic and self-assertive facet of modern subjectivity.

Earthly and Heavenly in Jiménez's Mature Poetry

Jiménez himself assigned to the *Diario de un poeta recién casado* (*Diary of a Newlywed Poet*, 1917) the position of the work that initiated his *segunda época*. This interpretation has subsequently been accepted by the criticism.[11] Even if a shift in style and, to a certain degree, in thematics with respect to his early work can be observed in this book, an analysis of the mythical patterns and themes that appear in the *Diario* will show the continuity with the early poetry. The *Diario* is a poetic diary recording Jiménez's impressions of his travel to the United States with the object of marrying his fiancé, Zenobia Camprubí Aymar.[12] The marriage took place in New York on 2 March 1916 in the church of St Stephen, and the book is structured in six parts corresponding to the phases of the trip: "Hacia el mar" (Toward the Sea), "El amor en el mar" (Love at Sea), "América del Este" (Eastern United States), "Mar de retorno" (The Return Voyage's Sea), "España" (Spain) and "Recuerdos de América del Este escritos en España" (Memories of Eastern United States Written in Spain).

The conception of the soul as the *locus* of the divine is stated in the introductory note at the beginning of the *Diario*:

No el ansia de color exótico, ni el afán de «necesarias» novedades.
La que viaja, siempre que viajo, es mi alma entre almas.

Ni más nuevo, al ir, ni más lejos; más hondo. Nunca más diferente, más alto siempre. (*Op*, I, 2: 55)

Neither the longing for exotic color nor the desire for something "necessarily" new. What travels, whenever I travel, is my soul, among souls.

Neither newer, on going, nor farther; deeper. Never more different, always higher. (*DNP*: 84)

In these lines the idea of poetry as emerging from the depths of the poet's soul is formulated. The parallelism of the two last sentences indicates the connection between the inner and the celestial realm, since the deepest (inner realm) and the highest (celestial realm) converge and are at the same time opposed to the physical world (neither newness nor remoteness is pursued). Inner world and heavenly realm are inherently connected and represent the sphere of the ideal and the eternal in the *Diario* too. A few examples will corroborate this:

Cuando, dormida tú, me echo en tu alma,
y escucho, con mi oído
en tu pecho desnudo,
tu corazón tranquilo, me parece
[…]
que legiones de ángeles,
en caballos celestes
[…]
vienen por ti, de lejos,
a traerme, en tu ensueño,
el secreto del centro
del cielo.
(*Op* I, 2: 121)

With you asleep, when I cast myself into your soul,
and I listen, with my ear
against your naked breast,
to your quiet heart, it seems to me
[…]

that legions of angels
on celestial steeds
[…]
come in search of you, from afar,
to bring to me, in your slumber,
the secret of the center
of heaven.
(*DNP*: 232)

Enclavado [el cielo] a lo eterno eternamente
por las mismas estrellas,
¡qué tranquilos sentimos, a su amparo,
el corazón, como en el sentimiento
de una noche, que siendo sólo nuestra madre,
fuera el mundo!
(*Op*, I, 2: 173-4)

[The sky is e]ternally bound to eternity
by the stars themselves,
how peaceful we feel, under its protection,
the heart, as in the feeling
of a night, that being only our mother,
were the world!
(*DNP*: 362; translation modified)

¡Qué contenta va el alma
porque torna a quemarse,
a hacerse esencia única,
a trasmutarse en cielo alto!
(*Op*, I, 2: 182)

How happy the soul is
because it is set afire again,
to become the single essence,
to be transmuted into lofty sky!
(*DNP*: 386)

In the first example one continuous movement leads from the lyrical subject's access to the beloved woman's soul – by the listening to her heart – to "el secreto del centro del cielo" (the secret of the centre of heaven); similarly, the second text expresses the intimate connection of the eternal (the sky) and the lyrical subject's inner domain (the heart); the last fragment, finally, asserts the conflation of the soul with the celestial realm in the same way as in the early poetry.

In "Partida" (Departure), poem no. 175, the contemplation of the sky is the main motif of the poem:

> Sí, sí, así era, así empezaba
> aquello, de este modo lo veía
> mi corazón de niño, cuando, abiertos
> como cielos, los ojos,
> se alzaban, negros, desde aquellas torres
> cándidas, por el iris, de su sueño,
> a la alta claridad del paraíso.
> Así era aquel pétalo de cielo,
> en donde el alma se encontraba,
> igual que en otra ella, sola y pura.
> Este era, esto es, de aquí se iba,
> como esta noche eterna, no sé a donde,
> a la tranquila luz de las estrellas;
> así empezaba aquel comienzo, gana
> celestial de mi alma
> de salir, por su puerta, hacia su centro…
>   ¡Oh blancura primera, sólo y siempre
> primera!
> …¡Blancura de esta noche, mar, de luna!
> (*Op* I, 2: 176)

> Yes, yes, that is how it was, how that
> began, in that way my child's heart
> saw things when my eyes,
> open like vast skies,
> looked up, black, from those bright
> towers, through the iris of its dream,
> to the lofty brilliance of paradise.
> That is how that petal of the sky was,
> in which the soul, as if in another self,
> found itself to be alone and pure.
> This it was, this it is, from here it was departing,
> like this eternal night to unknown destinations,

under the peaceful light of the stars;
That is how that commencement began,
a celestial yearning of my soul
to escape, through the portal, toward its center...
   Oh primal whiteness, only and
always primal!
...Whiteness of this night, moonlit sea!
(*DNP*: 369–70)

Given the autobiographical referentiality[13] inherent in the *Diario*, this poem describes Jiménez's feeling of ecstasy while he contemplates the night sky from the deck of the ship that will bring him and his wife back to Spain. Regarding the sky brings up a memory of the desire for eternity that he had experienced as a child. Since his childhood the poet has looked up to the sky and wished to reach "la alta claridad del paraíso" (the lofty brilliance of paradise) (verse 28). Continuity is thus stated to run from the earliest experience of the world to the contemplation of the sky on this night of 15 June 1916: "así empezaba aquel comienzo, gana / celestial de mi alma / de salir, por su puerta, hacia su centro..." (That is how that commencement began, / a celestial yearning of my soul / to escape, through the portal, towards its centre...").[14] Just as in the early poetry, the idea of the inner world as the domain where the absolute can be grasped is expressed as the continuity between interiority and the celestial realm, that is, the inner realm is an infinite and sacred sphere.

Within Jiménez's production, *Animal de fondo* (*Animal of Depth*, 1949[15]) and *Espacio* (*Space*, 1943-44-54) are considered the peak of his output of maturity. The former work presents a parallel to the *Diario* in the autobiographical reference underlying it. As has been mentioned above, the *Diario* refers to Jiménez's transatlantic voyage to New York in order to marry Zenobia Camprubí Aymar. Similarly, the inspiration for *Animal de fondo* also came from a sea journey, this time in 1948, from Jiménez's North American exile to Argentina and Uruguay where he had been invited to lecture.[16] *Animal de fondo* consists of a series of hymnic poems with a common theme, the celebration of the lyrical subject's encounter with an absolute poetic consciousness – designated by the term "god".[17] The *Diario* describes the stages of the trip through day to day annotations just as it represents a world with recognizable features, whereas *Animal de fondo* is a hermetic work devoid of both narrative and mimetic representation of the world. However, despite the breakdown of representation, the basic spatial duality that has been analyzed still appears. The vertical polarity is present throughout *Animal de fondo* in various forms, as in the following fragment of the poem "Todas las nubes arden" (All the Clouds are Burning) where it is represented by means of a dynamic ascending movement. The last verse conflates the altitude of the celestial with the profundity of the inner realm in a similar way to the introductory note to the *Diario*:

> Todas las nubes que existieron,
> que existen y que existirán,
> me rodean con signos de evidencia;
> ellas son para mí
> la afirmación alzada de este hondo
> fondo de aire en que yo vivo;
> el subir verdadero del subir,
> el subir del hallazgo en lo alto profundo.
> (*Op*, I, 2: 1149–50)

> All the clouds that were,
> that are, that will be,
> surround me with signs;
> they are to me
> the high affirmation of this deep
> depth of air within which I live;
> the true climb of climbing,
> the climb of the discovery made in the highest depth.
> (*GDD*: 11)

The following examples also express the continuum of the ascending movement that connects inner realm and heavenly sphere:

> qué elevación de ti en nosotros
> hasta llegar a ti,
> a este tú que te pones sobre ti
> para que todos lleguen por la escala
> de carne y alma
> a la conciencia desvelada que es el astro
> que acumula y completa, en unificación,
> todos los astros en el todo eterno!
>   El todo eterno que es el todo interno.
> (*Op*, I, 2: 1161–2)

what an uplifting of you in us
to make us reach you,
this you you cover yourself with
so that all may ascend by the stairs
of flesh and soul
to the awakened consciousness that is the star
that accumulates and completes, in unification,
all the stars in the eternal whole!
    The eternal whole is the internal all.
(*GDD*: 43)

The conflation of heavenly and inner realms also appears in the poem "Soy animal de fondo" (I Am Animal of Depth), number 29 in the collection and the text that closes the edition of *Animal de fondo* published in 1949:

SOY ANIMAL DE FONDO

«En el fondo de aire» (dije) «estoy»,
(dije) «soy animal de fondo de aire» (sobre tierra),
ahora sobre mar; pasado, como el aire, por un sol
que es carbón allá arriba, mi fuera, y me ilumina
con su carbón el ámbito segundo destinado.
    Pero tú, dios, también estás en este fondo
y a esta luz ves, venida de otro astro;
tú estás y eres
lo grande y lo pequeño que yo soy,
en una proporción que es ésta mía,
infinita hacia un fondo
que es el pozo sagrado de mí mismo.
    Y en este pozo estabas antes tú
con la flor, con la golondrina, el toro
y el agua; con la aurora
en un llegar carmín de vida renovada;
con el poniente, en un huir de oro de gloria.
En este pozo diario estabas tú conmigo,
conmigo niño, joven, mayor, y yo me ahogaba
sin saberte, me ahogaba sin pensar en ti.
Este pozo que era, sólo y nada más ni menos,
que el centro de la tierra y de su vida.

Y tú eras en el pozo májico el destino
de todos los destinos de la sensualidad hermosa
que sabe que el gozar en plenitud
de conciencia amadora,
es la virtud mayor que nos trasciende.
    Lo eras para hacerme pensar que tú eras tú,
para hacerme sentir que yo era tú,
para hacerme gozar que tú eras yo,
para hacerme gritar que yo era yo
en el fondo de aire en donde estoy,
donde soy animal de fondo de aire
con alas que no vuelan en el aire,
que vuelan en la luz de la conciencia
mayor que todo el sueño
de eternidades e infinitos
que están después, sin más que ahora yo, del aire.
(*Op*, I, 2: 1169–70)

I Am Animal Of Depth

"Upon a depth of air" (I said) "I am"
(I said), "I am animal of depth of air" (upon the earth),
now upon the sea; crossing, like the air, through a sun
that is red hot coal up there, my outside, and it lights up
with its hot coals the second fated space.
    You, god, are also in this depth
and you see by this light coming from another star;
and you are here and are
the great and the small that I am,
in the exact proportion that is my own,
infinite towards the depth,
the sacred well of myself.
    You were here before in this well
with the flower, the swallow, the bull
and the water; with the dawn
in a crimson arrival of renewed life;
with the setting sun in a flight of heavenly gold.
In this daily well you were with me,
with me as a child, young, old, and I was drowning

not knowing you, drowning not thinking of you.
This well, by itself, was no more and no less
than the center of the earth and of life.
    You were in the magic well the fate
of all the fates of the beautiful sensuality
that knows that pleasure is plenitude
of loving consciousness,
the greatest virtue that transcends us.
    You were so to make me think that you were you,
to make me feel that I was you,
to make me enjoy your being me,
to make me shout that I was I
upon the depth of the air I am standing on,
where I am animal of the depth of air
with wings that do not fly in the air,
but fly in the light of consciousness,
larger than any dreams of eternities and infinities
that arrive, with no more than I have now, later than the air.
(*GDD*: 61–3)

The first five verses effect an estrangement of the spatial order, only the four elements ("aire, tierra, mar, sol" (air, earth, sea, sun)) appear as a recognizable reference to everyday life. The lyrical subject claims to have been in contact with the four elements and is now illuminated by the sun in "el ámbito segundo destinado" (the second fated space) (verse 5), whereby a narrative of evolution and fulfilment is suggested. The second stanza identifies the lyrical subject with the invoked god: "tu estás y eres / lo grande y lo pequeño que yo soy" (you are here and are / the great and the small that I am) (verses 8–9). Through this "proporción que es ésta mía, / infinita" (exact proportion that is my own, / infinite), reference is made to the inner realm of the poet, to "el pozo sagrado de mi mismo" (the sacred well of myself). In this way the conflation of inner and sacred realm is expressed once more. The inner realm of the poet-subject is as vast as the cosmos while his empirical being is small as an individual. In the final verses of the poem a motif of flying, a pair of wings, is introduced (verse 34), but these wings are clearly metaphorical, since they are flying in "la luz de la conciencia" (the light of consciousness) (verse 35). The wings belong to the "animal de fondo de aire" (animal of the depth of air) that was presented both in the first verse and in verse 33, now identified as the lyrical subject flying in the light of poetic consciousness: "Soy animal de fondo de aire / con alas [...] / que vuelan en la luz de la conciencia" (I am animal of the depth of air / with wings that [...] / fly in the light of consciousness). Just as in the early poetry, the poetic imagination is identified with the realm of the heavens, to which the semantics of flying is evidently connected.[18] In this way the central images of the poem – the "animal de fondo" (animal of depth), the "aire" (air), the "luz de la conciencia" (light of consciousness) – are revealed as representing the inner world of the lyrical subject.[19]

Even if the spatial representation in these texts from *Animal de fondo* is highly abstract, as no specific setting is described, the vertical structure keeps reappearing with the ascending movement symbolizing the access to the sacred realm. In *Animal de fondo* the representation of elements belonging to the physical world is used only figuratively, as metaphors of the poetic mind. In this way the notion of the absolute lyrical subject is coherently developed from its presuppositions, since the world represented is a wholly interior one, an expression of the poetic imagination. This means the separation of language from its reference to the physical world: a wholly textual universe is created. Nonetheless, the vertical structure common to mythical thought keeps pervading the texts, whereby a primary perception of the world in keeping with a mythical form of experience lies at the base of such a thoroughly modern text as *Animal de fondo*.

The Symbolism of the Sun and the Moon

As a further step along the analytic path given by the representation of space in mythical thought, the symbolism of the sun and the moon in Jiménez's poetry will now be considered. The analysis of the earthly-heavenly duality has, up to this moment, focused on the absolute subject and the sacred domain founded by the poetic imagination, but the fact that this majestic consciousness is also rooted in an empirical, bodily being, is expressed by means of a central symbol from mythical thought, that of the sun.

The opposition of day and night, light and darkness, is fundamental for any mythology. Cassirer thus describes the meaning assigned in myths to the cardinal points where dawn and dusk appear: "The east as the origin of light is also the source of life – the west as the place of the setting sun is filled with all the terrors of death" (Cassirer 1955: 98). Just as the earth-heaven duality pervades Jiménez's entire work, the sun is identified as the life-giving principle of the universe in both the early and late poetry. For this reason, the motif of the sunset with its connotations of death is related to the finitude of all things. In sum, the sun is an ambivalent symbol in Jiménez's work, associated with both life and, through the motif of the setting sun, death.

The Sun and the Moon in the Early Works
In "¡Solo!" (Alone!) from *Almas de violeta*, the sun appears in a rural setting with the natural elements in bloom:

> La primavera reía,
> reía en el cielo expléndido,
> reía en los verdes prados
> de amarillas flores llenos…;
> con sus besos febrecientes
> inflamaba el sol de fuego
> el alma de la Natura
> en amores y en deseos…
> (*Plp*: 1531)

> Spring laughed,
> laughed in the splendid sky,
> laughed in the green meadows
> with yellow flowers filled…;
> with its feverish kisses
> the fiery sun inflamed
> Nature's soul
> with loves and desires…

Litvak has noted, with respect to Jiménez's early poetry, how the sun is related to sexuality (Litvak 1981: 90),[20] which is also the case in this poem since the sun is represented as a lover who awakens the desire of personified nature. As an element of vitality, the sun is related to the reproductive force of nature, showing in this way coherence with its identification as the well of life in mythical thought. However, in the same poem the vital force represented by the sun is contrasted with the human subject's finitude. This is the reason why the lyrical subject perceives the blooming of nature with an incurable melancholy:

> Con la alegría del campo
> no se curó mi alegría…,

y todo, todo cantaba
un himno blanco a la Risa;
¡el mundo entero gozaba!
¡tan sólo mi alma sufría!
(*Plp*: 1532)

With the joy of the countryside
my joy was not cured…,
and everything, everything sang
a white hymn to Laughter;
the whole world was relishing!
Only my soul was suffering!

It has been noted that the reason why Jiménez's early poetry often displays a rejection of the vital force of nature is to be found in the loss of religious meaning. In *fin de siècle* literature, the sense of missing values and the absence of a finality of existence determines the melancholic and nihilistic outlook on the world (Cardwell 1977: 63). This outlook is anti-vitalistic due to the absurdity of life; the superiority of suffering and death explains the inability to participate in nature's spring festival. In a poem from *Ninfeas*, "La cremación del sol" (The Cremation of the Sun) (*Plp*: 1482–3), the victory of death over life is expressed as the killing of the sun by the night, in turn personified as "sarcásticos Gigantes" (sarcastic Giants). Cassirer's remark cited above, identifying the place of the setting sun with "all the terrors of death," is unfolded in this poem in a most exact way.

In the poem "Crepúsculo de abril" (April Dusk), which will be analyzed in its totality in the next chapter, the dying sun is represented ambivalently since it is associated with death but at the same time represented as beautiful. A sick woman dies during a sunset:

Por el cielo, una nube (concepción fabulosa)
se teñía de sangre y de oro; en su espléndida
luz de vida flotaban mil auroras divinas:
apoteosis sublime de la púrpura regia
de los soles, sus flores incendiadas mandaron
un reflejo de llama celestial a la tierra.
    Las mejillas de lirio de la enferma tuvieron
ilusiones de vida en su frío de muertas:
se tiñeron de un rosa dulce y vago…; diríase

que en su nieve crecía una lumbre secreta.
Se apagó lentamente la magnífica nube;
se apagaron las rosas de la pálida enferma.
Resonaban distantes las esquilas; temblaban
en el cielo profundo las divinas estrellas;
empezaron las flores a dormirse... Moría
uno de esos crepúsculos de la azul primavera.
(*Op*, I, 1: 50–1)

In the sky a cloud (fabulous conception)
was dyed in blood and gold; on its splendid
light of life a thousand divine dawns floated:
Sublime apotheosis of the royal purple
of the suns, their burning flowers sent
a reflection of heavenly flame to the earth.
   The sick woman's lily cheeks had
illusions of life on their deadly coldness:
they became coloured with a sweet and vague pink...; one
would say that on their snow a secret fire grew.
Slowly the magnificent cloud burned out;
the roses of the pale sufferer burned out.
The sheep bells sounded in the distance; the divine
stars trembled in the deep sky;
the flowers began to fall asleep... One
of these dusks of the blue spring was dying.

Although she is dying the woman is immersed in the beauty of the chromatic play of the evening sky, whereby the sadness inherent in the *memento mori* is sweetened. The reason why the sunset can be identified with the aesthetic experience is because it represents a temporal suspension between day and night.[21] Both the sunset and the aesthetic experience represent the rapture of a moment where a transport to a different sphere, other than that of earthly corruption, takes place. At the same time, no claim is made about having overcome human contingency; on the contrary, the despair and finitude of existence is strongly emphasized.

The exaltation of the moment of the dying sun can be related to Romantic and *fin de siècle* aesthetics. Richard Cardwell has noted the aesthetic proximity of Edgar Allan Poe's works to Jiménez's early poetry (Cardwell 1977: 110). In his essay "The Philosophy of Composition", Poe regards melancholy as "the most legitimate of all the poetical tones" (Poe 1946: 981), just as the celebrated assertion "the death […] of a beautiful woman is unquestionably the most poetical topic in the world" (ibid.: 982) appears in the same text. An array of interpretations could be given of the motif Poe considers to be the most poetic, but in the present context the juxtaposition of death and beauty can be related to the opposition between empirical subject and the sense of the absolute. The subject is finite and lives in the shadow of its mortality, but it is also capable of attaining a sense of the absolute. The death-beauty duality represents the asymmetry of modern subjectivity: a finite individual endowed with a feeling of the absolute.

Although the sun is related to life and causes Jiménez's lyrical subject to reflect upon his mortality, the moon is not associated with death, as one might reason in a strictly symmetrical way. The moon and the night illuminated by the moon are related to the feminine and to the imaginary realm of pure beauty. This is clearly expressed in the poem "El alma de la luna" (The Soul of the Moon) from *Ninfeas*:

> El pöeta que sueña Amores imposibles,
> mujeres de almas de oro y carnes intangibles;
> en la escala celeste del alma de la Luna
> sube a los áureos reinos en donde la Fortuna
> lo estrechará en su pecho…;
> (*Plp*: 1489)

> The poet who dreams impossible Loves,
> women with souls of gold and untouchable flesh;
> in the heavenly ladder of the soul of the Moon
> he climbs to the golden kingdoms where Fortune
> will hold him in her bosom…;

The ending of the poem unequivocally relates the moon to poetic creation:

> …El pöeta refleja en su lago, en su Alma,
> la tristeza solemne de la solemne Calma
> del Alma de la Luna, en que nacen los lirios
> que embriagarán su pecho de fragantes Delirios…
> (*Plp*: 1489–90)

> ...The poet mirrors in his lake, in his Soul,
> the solemn sadness of the solemn Calm
> of the Soul of the Moon, in which the lilies are born
> that will enrapture his bosom with fragrant Deliria...

The oneiric "soul of the moon" represents, in a self-reflective way that prefigures the I-god duality of *Animal de fondo,* the absolute realm of beauty. This second poetic reality is nonetheless unsubstantial, and this is the reason why the duality of the profane world and poetic heavenly realm is perceived with sadness. The absolute subject does not in the end overcome its finite and contingent being: "El pöeta refleja en su lago, en su Alma, / la tristeza solemne de la solemne Calma / del Alma de la Luna" (The poet mirrors in his lake, in his Soul, / the solemn sadness of the solemn Calm / of the Soul of the Moon).

The Sun and the Moon in the Mature Poetry

Jiménez's mature output often shows a different sense assigned to the motif of the sunset with respect to the early work:

> TARDE
>
> El oro chorreante
> de hoy, puro y claro.
> ¡Oh, siempre presente, siempre
> este sol de este árbol!
>   Cenizas de mi cuerpo,
> debajo, en el pasado.
> ¡Pero en la tarde, mi alma
> sin final, goteando!
>   Y el libro, trasparente
> siempre, fresco e ingrávido.
> ¡Cristal por el que se vea
> futuro tras futuro májico!
> (*Op*, I, 2: 535)

> EVENING
>
> The pouring gold
> of today, pure and clear.

Oh, always present, always
this sun of this tree!
   Ashes of my body,
below, in the past.
But in the evening, my endless
soul, dripping!
   And the book, transparent
always, fresh and weightless.
Glass through which may be seen
magical future after future!

As in the early texts, in this poem from *Piedra y cielo* (*Rock and Sky*, 1919), the lyrical subject contemplates the sunset and expresses the emotions it stirs within him. However, the elegiac mood has been replaced by a victorious achievement of eternity. In the first stanza the light of the evening sun is metaphorically expressed as "oro" (gold), which in turn is a pervasive symbol in Jiménez's poetry.[22] Sabine Ulibarri (1962) devotes a chapter to the gold symbolism in Jiménez, identifying it with "la plenitud y realización de la vida humana en el momento justo cuando la vida alcanza su punto más alto y se detiene momentáneamente, en toda su gloria de oro, en el umbral de la eternidad" (the plenitude and realization of human life in the precise moment when life reaches its highest point and stops momentarily, in all its golden glory, on the threshold of eternity) (Ulibarri 1962: 208). Precisely such a moment of plenitude is described in the first stanza of this poem, an eternal moment as those Jiménez described with the word-play *éstasis dinámico* (dynamic ecstasy/stasis). In this stanza, the unification of eternity and "now" appears through a series of spatiotemporal motifs. The setting sun is described as "chorreante" (pouring) in the first verse. This is an adjective that indicates a continuous activity that on the other side is located in time by the temporal adverb "hoy" (today) in the second verse. In turn, this temporal fixation is contrasted with the syntagma "siempre presente, siempre" (always present, always) in verse 3, whereby the sunset appears as a moment of pure beauty that unifies temporal flow, present and perennial being. If the sunset was associated with an acute consciousness of death in the early poetry, in the mature works the temporal suspension of the dusk is related to eternity.

   In the second stanza the lyrical subject is presented first in his mortal manifestation, as the syntagma "Cenizas de mi cuerpo" (Ashes of my body) refers to his empiricity. While the first two verses relate to empirical subjectivity and its transience, the two last verses of this stanza relate to absolute subjectivity and infinity: "en la tarde, mi alma / sin final, goteando" (in the evening, my endless / soul, dripping). In the final stanza poetic creation, "el libro" (the book), is the central motif. Three metaphors define the poetic work; it is "transparente", "fresco" and "ingrávido" (transparent, fresh, weightless). The book is fresh, suggesting a semantics of life and growth. It is also weightless, that is, it does not belong to the physical realm where things have a weight pulling them to the ground but belongs instead to the elevated sphere of poetry. The transparency of the book is explained in the last two verses, where it is called "cristal por el que se vea / futuro tras futuro májico" (glass through which may be seen / magical future after future). This expression recalls a passage from Ortega y Gasset's *La deshumanización del arte* (*The Dehumanization of Art*, 1925) where the classical metaphor of the painting as a window is re-elaborated:[23]

> Imagínese el lector que estamos mirando un jardín al través del vidrio de una ventana. Nuestros ojos se acomodarán de suerte que el rayo de la visión penetre el vidrio, sin detenerse en él, y vaya a prenderse en las flores y frondas. Como la meta de la visión es el jardín y hasta él va lanzado el rayo visual, no veremos el vidrio, pasará nuestra mirada a su través, sin percibirlo. Cuanto más puro sea el cristal menos lo veremos. Pero luego, haciendo un esfuerzo, podemos desentendernos del jardín y, retrayendo el rayo ocular, detenerlo en el vidrio. Entonces el jardín desaparece a nuestros ojos y de él sólo vemos unas masas de color confusas que parecen pegadas al cristal. [...]
> Del mismo modo, quien en la obra de arte busca el conmoverse con los destinos de Juan y María o de Tristán e Iseo y a ellos acomoda su percepción espiritual, no verá la obra de arte. La desgracia de Tristán sólo es tal desgracia, y, consecuentemente, sólo podrá conmover en la medida en que se la tome como realidad. Pero es el caso que el objeto artístico sólo es artístico en la medida en que no es real. Para poder gozar del retrato ecuestre de Carlos V, por Tiziano, es condición ineludible que no veamos allí a Carlos V en persona, auténtico y viviente, sino que, en su lugar, hemos de ver sólo un retrato, una imagen irreal, una ficción. El retratado y su retrato son dos objetos completamente distintos; o nos interesamos por el uno o por el

otro. En el primer caso, «convivimos» con Carlos V; en el segundo, «contemplamos» un objeto artístico como tal. (Ortega y Gasset 1957: 357–8)

> Take a garden seen through a window. Looking at the garden we adjust our eyes in such a way that the ray of vision travels through the pane without delay and rests on the shrubs and flowers. Since we are focusing on the garden and our ray of vision is directed toward it, we do not see the window but look clear through it. The purer the glass, the less we see it. But we can also deliberately disregard the garden and, withdrawing the ray of vision, detain it at the window. We then lose sight of the garden; what we still behold of it is a confused mass of color which appears pasted to the pane. [...]
> Similarly a work of art vanishes from sight for a beholder who seeks in it nothing but the moving fate of John and Mary or Tristan and Isolde and adjusts his vision to this. Tristan's sorrows are sorrows and can evoke compassion only in so far as they are taken as real. But an object of art is artistic only in so far as it is not real. In order to enjoy Titian's potrait of Charles the Fifth on horseback we must forget that this is Charles the Fifth in person and see instead a portrait – that is, an image, a fiction. The portrayed person and his portrait are two entirely different things; we are interested in either one or the other. In the first case we "live" with Charles the Fifth, in the second we look at an object of art. (Ortega y Gasset 1948: 10–11)

The change of focus from what is behind the window and to the pane, represents for Ortega the correct attitude with respect to the contemplation of art (and is at the same time the modern inversion of a classical, mimetic notion of art). In this sense, Ortega is entirely in line with Jiménez's idea of a *pure poetry* in which representation of reality is eliminated in order to set free the play of the aesthetic elements.[24] Furthermore, this passage explains the characterization of the book in the poem "Tarde" as a window opened on a plurality of futures, that is, on the readers who will relive Jiménez's poetry. The self-referentiality of this poem, representing the aesthetic experience as transitory but destined to be re-enacted by coming readers, is emblematic of the triumphant expression of Jiménez's *segunda época*. From this perspective, the absolute poet-subject is life-giving like the sun, and has left his light in the form of a poetic legacy that will survive his empirical being.

As in the early poems, it is possible to find the moon associated with femininity and poetic creativity also in the later works, as can be seen in the following poem from *La estación total* (*The Total Season*, 1946):

Luna del hombre

La hermosa luna llena
de esta noche profunda y conseguida,
levanta en rapto blanco,
redonda donación,
la desnudez total de la mujer pasada,
del oriente cercano y duro.
    Una plena alegría,
desde el este de la marmórea espuma,
se derrama por todo en marea de gloria;
y las rosas alertas
reciben en su fresca boca unánime
a su divina reina humana.
    ¡Y cómo sale el hombre
a esta luna de carne de mujeres!
¡Cómo la coje en él
definida y rotunda, neta y suave,
de la concavidad radiante del azul
de primavera verdadera!
(*Op*, I, 2: 977)

Man's Moon

The magnificent full moon
of this profound and achieved night,
rises in white rapture,
round gift,
the total nakedness of the past woman,
of the near and harsh east.
    A full joy,
from east of the marmoreal foam,
is poured everywhere in a tide of glory;
and the alert roses
receive in their unanimous fresh mouth

their divine human queen.
   And how the man comes out
to this moon of women's flesh!
How he takes it in him
clear and full, distinct and gentle,
from the radiant concavity of the blue
of true spring!

Apparently a considerable difference is to be found between this poem and "El alma de la luna", discussed above (p. 29), since the melancholic tone of the latter seems to be at a vast distance from the expression of plenitude of this text. Both poems share, however, a theme of erotic tension between the masculine and feminine principles.[25] In "Luna del hombre", the moon is conflated with the feminine aspect ("esta luna de carne de mujeres" (this moon of women's flesh), verse 15), whereas the masculine is represented by the general idea of man, "el hombre" (verse 14). The man taking possession of or conquering the moon can – in an entirely similar way as in the celebrated poem "Vino, primero, pura" (She came, first, pure) from *Eternidades* (*Eternities*, 1918) – be regarded as the achievement of a fulfilled lyrical expression by the poet-subject.[26] The mature Jiménez rejected an important part of his early poetry as he considered it excessively rhetorical and ornate, and for this reason he termed his late production *poesía pura* or *desnuda*. As in "Vino, primero, pura", in "Luna del hombre" a narrative of achievement is displayed, an ecstatic encounter with the accomplished poetic expression. In this way, poetic creativity fuses both the vitalistic and the imaginative.

However, in the same collection, *La estación total*, the poem "Los esclavos" (The Slaves) (*Op*, I, 2: 973) makes exactly the opposite claim from the one found in "Luna del hombre": the lyrical subject's belonging to the earthly realm and the impossibility of reaching the ideal beauty of the moon. This suggests that the plenitude achieved is not a stable one (a question that will be discussed in the next chapter). In this way a romantic irony appears in Jiménez's work that is also characteristic of modern poetry as a whole. Even if the thematization of the subject's mortality undergoes a change from his early to his late poetry, this is not due to a change of paradigm. It should rather be regarded as a change of emphasis within the same paradigm: if the early poetry stressed the futility of poetry in the face of death, the later texts underscore the autonomy of poetic creativity and its permanence through the readers. There is no change of paradigm, however, because the renewal of Jiménez's writing – the *poesía pura* – is based on stressing the absolute side of subjectivity rather than the empirical aspect. The duality remains, however, unchanged, just as the understanding of the absolute subject as the source of poetic creation is the same in both periods.

The analyses carried out up to this point have shown that the spatial representation in Jiménez's texts is very similar to that in mythical discourse. The perception of the sky as the realm of the sacred, the sun as the life-giving force of nature and the sunset as related to death, are all significations originating in mythical thought. Even if the early poetry is dominated by a nihilistic and melancholic mood and the mature poetry by the sense of fulfilment, the vertical spatial structure, just as its signification, is the same throughout. The expression of plenitude in the mature poetry should not be seen as an overcoming of the sense of finitude, but rather as a change of emphasis within a poetic paradigm that can focus on the finite and contingent conditions of the subject as well as on the vision of the absolute that this same subject can leave to posterity. In the mature poetry the consciousness that the poetic texts will be relived by future readers – as was shown with the poem "Tarde" – brings a certain reconciliation with the finitude of empirical subjectivity. Similarly, "Luna del hombre" unfolds a triumphant overcoming of empirical subjectivity in the realm of poetry, since the lyrical subject accomplishes plenitude within the textual universe. The stability of this poetic fulfilment will be the object of analysis of the following chapter.

CHAPTER TWO

Infinite Longing as a Dynamic Spatial Force

Despite the fact that Jiménez in his mature poetry frequently asserts having achieved a poetic plenitude, longing or desire is an essential theme throughout his work – also in the later texts.[1] The aim of the present chapter is to show how space in Jiménez's poetry is intrinsically dynamic because of the projection of longing upon the spatial representations. In modern literature the presence of infinite longing can be understood as the literary elaboration of a philosophical question. According to Kantian and post-Kantian philosophy the totality of the world can never be a given for human epistemological faculties, but it is a task assigned to thought that it must work towards grasping the whole of nature even if this is impossible.[2] For this reason, this paradigm can also be called that of the fragmented absolute. To know all facets of the world has become an unreachable ideal in the modern period – but nonetheless thought continues to proceed in terms of totality. One version of this condition is the typically modern notion of *infinite perfectibility*, the idea that reason is infinitely advancing towards an end-goal that never will be reached.[3] A similar figure of thought appears with respect to the status of a transcendent creator God in modern thought. In Kantian philosophy, God cannot be the object of theoretical knowledge, but, at the same time, Kant finds that the work of art may, to some degree, give a sensory form to ideas of reason such as God or eternity.[4] In the modern paradigm, then, absolute notions become a kind of absent presences that nourish infinite longing. When modern aesthetic expression oscillates to the side of the absolute, this necessity of making an ambiguous and vague reference to the numinous is carried out. At the same time the sceptical attitude towards human epistemological faculties entails the impossibility of satisfying this longing.

Octavio Paz has unfolded an interpretation of the modern poetical tradition from Romanticism to the Avant-Gardes which includes the notion of desire or longing as a central trait. Paz operates with a notion he terms *analogía universal* (universal analogy), and which he considers to be one of the features of modern poetry:

> Es una tradición antiquísima, reelaborada y transmitida por el neo-platonismo renacentista a diversas corrientes herméticas de los siglos XVI y XVII y que, después de alimentar a las sectas filosóficas y libertinas del XVIII, es recogida por los románticos y sus herederos hasta nuestros días. Es la tradición central, aunque subterránea, de la poesía moderna, de los primeros románticos a Yeats, Rilke, los surrealistas. (Paz 1990: 35–6)

> This is a very old idea, re-elaborated and transmitted by Renaissance Neoplatonism through various Hermetic traditions of the sixteenth and seventeenth centuries. After having nourished the philosophical and libertine sects of the eighteenth century, it was taken up by the Romantics and their followers and passed on to our own era. It is the central, yet underground, tradition of modern poetry, from the first Romantics to Yeats, Rilke, and the Surrealists. (Paz 1991b: 37)

The principle of the universal analogy is an archaic world-view (very similar to Foucault's description of the Renaissance episteme in *The Order of Things*) that regards the universe as a totality in which all its entities are interrelated and interdependent:

> El mundo no es un conjunto de cosas, sino de signos: lo que llamamos cosas son palabras. Una montaña es una palabra, un río es otra, un paisaje es una frase. Y todas esas frases están en continuo cambio: la correspondencia universal significa perpetua metamorfosis. El texto que es el mundo no es un texto único: cada página es la traducción y la metamorfosis de otra y así sucesivamente. (Paz 1981: 108)

> The world is not an ensemble of things but of signs; or, rather, what we call things are in fact words. A mountain is a word, a river is another, a landscape is a sentence. And all these sentences are in continual change: universal correspondence means perpetual metamorphosis. The text which is the world is not one but many: each page is

the translation and the metamorphosis of another page which is the same in relation to another, and so on ad infinitum. (Paz 1991a: 71)

The notion of the universal analogy regards the universe as a system of hidden correspondences. Every entity is connected to every other in an arcane communication, and it is the task of poetry to reveal these exchanges. The paradigmatic expression of this idea appears in Baudelaire's sonnet "Correspondances". In this poem the lyrical subject senses the "vague words" of the natural world. According to the principle of the universal analogy, poetic language is a duplication of the cosmic order. The analogical communication means that the universe is structured linguistically, as everything can be connected through the comparative particle: "La analogía es el reino de la palabra *como*, ese puente verbal que, sin suprimirlas, reconcilia las diferencias y las oposiciones" (Paz 1981: 102, author's emphasis) (Analogy is the kingdom of the word *as*, that verbal bridge that, without abolishing them, reconciles the differences and oppositions).

Furthermore, this notion contains a bodily-erotic aspect that is regarded as a cosmological law:

> La creencia en la analogía universal está teñida de erotismo: los cuerpos y las almas se unen y separan regidos por las mismas leyes de atracción y repulsión que gobiernan las conjunciones y disyunciones de los astros y de las sustancias materiales. Un erotismo astrológico y un erotismo alquímico; asimismo, un erotismo subversivo: la atracción erótica rompe las leyes sociales y une a los cuerpos sin distinción de rangos y jerarquías. (Paz 1981: 103)

> The belief in the universal analogy is tainted of eroticism: the bodies and the souls unite and separate ruled by the same laws of attraction and repulsion that rule the conjunctions and disjunctions of the stars and of the material substances. An astrologic eroticism and an alchemistic eroticism; likewise, a subversive eroticism: the erotic attraction breaks the social laws and unites the bodies without the difference of ranks and hierarchies.

The universal analogy is, then, a mythical or archaic thought that regards the universe as intrinsically governed by an unending dynamism of desire. It is important to note that this system of hidden correspondences never refers to a transcendent Signifier that eventually unites and reconciles the differences. This is the reason why in Baudelaire's poem "Correspondances" nature's words are vague ("confuses" in the original). Intimation of a hidden universal meaning can be sensed but modern thought rejects the idea of reaching the final meaning of cosmic totality. For this reason, Paz posits an "adversary twin" to the notion of the universal analogy, his concept of *irony*. Together, these two notions represent the above described modern oscillation between myth and scepticism:

> Doble transgresión: la analogía opone al tiempo sucesivo de la historia y a la beatificación del futuro utópico, el tiempo cíclico del mito; a su vez, la ironía desgarra el tiempo mítico al afirmar la caída en la contingencia, la pluralidad de dioses y de mitos, la muerte de Dios y de sus criaturas. (Paz 1990: 36)

> A mutual transgression: analogy replaces the linear time of history and the canonization of the utopian future with the cyclical time of myth; irony, in turn, shreds mythical time in order to affirm the fall into accident, the plurality of gods and myths, the death of God and of his creatures. (Paz 1991b: 38)

The idea of the universal analogy represents the drive towards the numinous, and the notion of irony the impossibility of accomplishing this desire. At the same time, the universal analogy also has another function. Modern anthropocentric thought has a strong tendency towards solipsism, but thanks to the idea of the universal analogy, inner and outer nature become connected. Modernity offers two versions of interiority:

> Kant offers one form of modern internalization, that is, a way of finding the good in our inner motivation. Another comes with that family of views in the late eighteenth century that represents nature as an inner source. I am speaking about views which arise with the German Sturm und Drang and continue developing thereafter through the Romantic period, both English and German. Rousseau is naturally its point of departure, and its first important articulation comes perhaps in the work of Herder; thereafter it is taken up not only by Romantic writers but by Goethe and, in another way, by Hegel and becomes one of the constituent streams of modern culture. (Taylor 1989: 368)

Nature as an inner source is precisely what is expressed through the notion of the universal analogy. In this way, anthropocentrism is preserved and at the same time extended to an ontological level. Since the subject carries within itself the same principle as that which governs the totality of nature – *natura naturans* – idealism and pantheism can be conflated. Finally, it can be noted that the principle of the universal analogy shows the strong tendency of aesthetic Modernity to relapse to archaic or mythical motifs when the numinous or an absolute principle is to be suggested.

In the following it will be shown how the lyrical subject in Jiménez's texts expresses the desire to access the plenitude of the absolute through the vertical structure that was analyzed in the previous chapter. This desire to reach the sacred realm is often represented by an erotic desire between earthly and heavenly realms – a manifestation of the universal analogy. Thematically, then, the present chapter will continue to explore the earthly-heavenly duality in Jiménez's poetry by adding to it the dynamic spatiality that the motif of infinite yearning provides.

Rimas, 26 / *Rhymes*, 26 (1902)

In the poem "Crepúsculo de abril" (April Dusk), from the collection *Rimas* (*Rhymes*), a sick woman directs her longing towards the evening sky because of the both sensory and imaginative relief it can give her:

CREPÚSCULO DE ABRIL

A Juan Héctor

El sol puro y magnífico de la tarde, arrastraba
tras su espalda de oro, a través de la tierra,
los suavísimos rayos moribundos.
                            Volviendo
sus mejillas al beso de occidente, la enferma
deseó las caricias del suave crepúsculo;
quiso luz, quiso cantos y colores y esencias;
y anhelando embriagarse con la tibia dulzura
de esas tardes que mata la oriental primavera,
quedó muda, soñando lejanías fantásticas
y misterios floridos y alboradas quiméricas;
en el ansia infinita de los tristes ensueños

las nostalgias ahondaron sus azules ojeras;
y el postrero carbunclo que dejó el sol vencido,
a sus ojos profundos dio una chispa sangrienta.
   Declinaba la tarde. Sobre un cielo de rosa
sus dorados verdores reposó la arboleda
y empezaron las flores a dormirse; fluían
en el aire ternuras de fragancia serena;
desde el valle llegaba un sonar melancólico
de canciones y esquilas, y la rítmica y quieta
placidez de los campos, anunciar parecía
que en el cielo empezaban a entreabrir las estrellas.
   Una fuente de mármol elevaba la lluvia
diamantina del fondo de su cáliz de piedra,
y por cauces cubiertos de florido heliotropo,
iba el agua fragante, saturando de frescas
ascensiones el sueño del jardín; sobre el musgo,
moribundas acaso, las tardías violetas
esfumaban la triste vaguedad de sus tonos,
y los rojos geranios, ascuas vivas, más cerca,
el aliento exhalaban de sus secos olores,
agria nota en el coro de las ricas esencias.
   Por el cielo, una nube (concepción fabulosa)
se teñía de sangre y de oro; en su espléndida
luz de vida flotaban mil auroras divinas:
apoteosis sublime de la púrpura regia
de los soles, sus flores incendiadas mandaron
un reflejo de llama celestial a la tierra.
   Las mejillas de lirio de la enferma tuvieron
ilusiones de vida en su frío de muertas:
se tiñeron de un rosa dulce y vago…; diríase
que en su nieve crecía una lumbre secreta.
Se apagó lentamente la magnífica nube;
se apagaron las rosas de la pálida enferma.
Resonaban distantes las esquilas; temblaban
en el cielo profundo las divinas estrellas;
empezaron las flores a dormirse… Moría
uno de esos crepúsculos de la azul primavera.

Arcachon.
(*Op*, I, 1: 49–51)

April Dusk

To Juan Héctor

The pure and magnificent evening sun dragged
behind its gold back, over the earth,
the softest moribund rays.
                    Turning
her cheeks towards the kiss of the west, the sick woman
desired the caresses of the gentle dusk;
she wanted light, she wanted chants and colours and essences;
and yearning for the bliss of the balmy sweetness
of these evenings that the eastern spring kills,
she became mute, dreaming of fantastic distant places
and flowery mysteries and chimaeric dawns;
in the infinite longing of the sad dreams
nostalgia deepened her blue sleepless eyes;
and the dying ruby that the vanquished sun left,
to her profound eyes gave a bloody spark.

    The evening was falling. On a rosy sky
the grove rested its golden greenness
and the flowers started to sleep; in the air
flowed caresses of calm fragrance;
from the valley arrived a melancholic ringing
of songs and sheep bells, and the rhythmic and still
peacefulness of the fields seemed to announce
that in the sky the stars were beginning to open up.

    A marble fountain was raising the diamond
rain from the bottom of its stone chalice,
and along beds covered by flowery heliotropes,
the fragrant water ran, saturating with fresh
ascensions the garden's dream; over the moss,
dying perhaps, the belated violets
blurred the sad vagueness of their tones,
and the red geraniums, living embers, closer by,
emitted the breath of their dry smells,
a sour note in the choir of the rich essences.

    In the sky a cloud (fabulous conception)
was dyed in blood and gold; on its splendid
light of life a thousand divine dawns floated:
Sublime apotheosis of the royal purple

of the suns, their burning flowers sent
a reflection of heavenly flame to the earth.
   The sick woman's lily cheeks had
illusions of life on their deadly coldness:
they became coloured with a sweet and vague pink...; one
would say that on their snow a secret fire grew.
Slowly the magnificent cloud burned out;
the roses of the pale sufferer burned out.
The sheep bells sounded in the distance; the divine
stars trembled in the deep sky;
the flowers began to fall asleep... One
of these dusks of the blue spring was dying.

Arcachon.

A pictorial spatial representation can be observed in this poem. As in a painting, foreground and background are clearly differentiated. The sick woman's face is described in detail twice, as in a close-up (verses 3–14 and 39–44). She is in a garden with a fountain (verses 23–32), presumably a sanatorium.[5] In the background a valley is to be found (verses 15–22), and behind it are the sunset and the evening sky. The "ensueño" (dream) momentarily allows the sick woman to forget her suffering, as the contemplation of the beauty of the sky triggers her imaginative flight. The conflict between absolute and empirical subject can be observed in the mortality of the body and its discordance with the powers of the mind. Imagination and corporeity, absolute and empirical subject, are experienced as asymmetrical, since the former is able to grasp infinity and absolute beauty while the latter provides illness and death. The knowledge of this asymmetry is the source of a desire that cannot be fulfilled, as can be inferred from verses 9–10: "quedó muda, soñando lejanías fantásticas / y misterios floridos y alboradas quiméricas" (she became mute, dreaming of fantastic distant places / and flowery mysteries and chimaeric dawns).

The central correspondence between a subject and the celestial realm in "Crepúsculo de abril" takes place between the woman and the sun, as their deaths are simultaneous (verses 43–44): "Se apagó lentamente la magnífica nube; / se apagaron las rosas de la pálida enferma" (Slowly the magnificent cloud burned out; / the roses of the pale sufferer burned out). As in the analyses of the previous chapter, the sun is presented as a vitalistic element (it is "puro y magnífico" (pure and magnificent) verse 1, and it shows its "espalda de oro" (gold back), verse 2). At the same time, through its death, it enacts the theme of subjective finitude. The analogy between the woman and the sun is stated explicitly in verses 13–14: "el postrero carbunclo que dejó el sol vencido, / a sus ojos profundos dió una chispa sangrienta" (the dying ruby that the vanquished sun left, / to her profound eyes gave a bloody spark). The bloody spark in the woman's eyes has a double signification. The spark is on the one hand a reflection of the last sunbeams. On the other, symbolically, it stands for the death that is taking hold of both the sun and the woman. The relation between the woman and the sun is extended further than the coincidence of their deaths, since also an erotic correspondence is suggested. In verses 3 and 4 the woman moves her cheeks towards "el beso de occidente" (the kiss of the west), as she "deseó las caricias del suave crepúsculo" (desired the caresses of the gentle dusk) (verse 5). The development of the poem is structured in keeping with this correspondence between the earthly and the heavenly.

The poem can be divided into three parts according to this alternation between the elevated and the low. The first part runs from verses 1 to 14 (stanza one) and depicts the correspondence between the sun and the woman that has just been presented. The second part, which begins in verse 15 and ends in verse 38 (stanzas two, three and four), describes a cosmic harmony, a fulfilled correspondence between heavenly and earthly realms. This part of the poem can be further divided as regards the represented settings: stanza two is a depiction of the landscape and the communication between the earth and the stars, the third stanza describes the garden sending floral scents to the heavens, while stanza four pictures the colours of the sunset and the sending of "un reflejo de llama celestial a la tierra" (a reflection of heavenly flame to the earth). The last part of the poem (stanza five, verses 39–48) returns to the woman as she now becomes the figurative stage for the correspondence between heaven and earth. A more detailed analysis of stanzas two to five will reveal the spatial dynamism pervading the text.

A pastoral setting is suggested in stanza two: from the valley arrive songs and the sound of sheep-bells. In verses 15 and 16 the sky becomes a metaphorical resting place for the grove ("Sobre un cielo de rosa / sus dorados verdores reposó la arboleda" (On a rosy sky / the grove rested its golden greenness); the colour of the grove is "dorados verdores" (golden greenness), meaning that the heavenly realm (the rays of the falling sun) reaches down to the earthly realm (the trees) and produces the golden-green colour of the scenery. But the protagonists in this part of the poem with respect to the exchange between terrestrial and celestial are the flowers and the stars, since they establish the main contact between the two realms. The falling asleep of the flowers and of the entire landscape[6] "anunciar parecía / que en el cielo empezaban a entreabrir las estrellas"(seemed to announce / that in the sky the stars began to open up). The analogy between the flowers and the stars – the flowers as the stars of the earth and the stars as the flowers of heaven – is a topos that can be traced back to medieval literature, and its importance for modern poetry starts with its recuperation by Romanticism.[7]

The correspondence between flowers and stars is introduced in the second stanza in the verses just cited, and continues in the third stanza through the ascending perfumes emanated from heliotropes, violets and geraniums, since the perfume works as a mediating element between earthly and heavenly.[8] The fourth stanza, describing the evening sky and its profusion of colours, lets the correspondence work the opposite way, from heaven to earth: "sus flores incendiadas mandaron / un reflejo de llama celestial a la tierra" (their burning flowers sent / a reflection of heavenly flame to the earth) (verses 37–38). Finally, the mentioned topos reappears in the last verses of the poem, just before the death of the woman occurs: "temblaban / en el cielo profundo las divinas estrellas; / empezaron las flores a dormirse…" (the divine / stars trembled on the deep sky; / the flowers began to fall asleep) (verses 45–47). The correspondence between celestial and terrestrial is, then, primarily actualized by the flowers and the stars, but it is also – through a different motif – represented by the dying woman. In the final stanza the woman has "mejillas de lirio" (lily cheeks) (verse 39), and they become coloured "de un rosa dulce y vago" (with a sweet and vague pink) (verse 41). The latter is the colour of the sky in verse 15, whereby the connection between flowers and heavens is represented in the cheeks of the woman. Furthermore, the metaphor cheek : rose appears in verse 44: "se apagaron las rosas de la pálida enferma" (the roses of the pale sufferer burned out). In this way the woman's cheeks unify heaven and earth by relating at the same time to the sky (through the colour), and to the flowers (cheeks : lilies/roses).

Within a *fin de siècle* framework of interpretation, this poem can be related to the theme of the search for an aesthetic ideal which ends in the death of the artist or his other I, a beggar or another broken individual (Cardwell 1977: 116) – in this case the sick woman. Mortality is emphasized as the final condition of the human being, which is particularly tormenting for the artist who strives for the realm of eternal beauty. The metaphor of the beggar or the sick illustrates the condition of spiritual penury that is experienced by the individual who is able to sense the absolute but is at the same time conscious of its unattainability. The asymmetry between absolute and empirical subject causes the desire for the sphere of the absolute, and it is this desire that enacts the imaginative correspondence between heaven and earth. If the woman is considered an *alter ego* of the poet, then the poet's desire to reach the celestial realm of absolute beauty is represented as the dying woman's desire for the personified sun ("Volviendo / sus mejillas al beso de occidente, la enferma / deseó las caricias del suave crepúsculo / quiso luz, quiso cantos y olores y esencias" (Turning / her cheeks towards the kiss of the west, the sick woman / desired the caresses of the gentle dusk), verses 3–6). The death of the woman at the end of the poem can be interpreted as the impossibility of obtaining the fulfilment of desire.

At the same time, the desire can, in a certain sense, be regarded as accomplished within the text, since the wish expressed in verse six, "quiso *luz*, quiso *cantos* y *colores* y *esencias*" (she wanted *light*, she wanted *chants* and *colours* and *essences*) coincides with the represented scenery of the poem, and is thereby satisfied within the margins of the text. *Luz*: the light is endowed by the sun, and stanza four is almost exclusively a description of a luminous and chromatic play that ends with the arrival on earth of "un reflejo de llama celestial" (a reflection of heavenly flame) (verse 38). *Cantos*: the singing appears in verses 19–20 as the songs of the shepherds. *Colores*: the chromatic dimension appears continuously throughout the poem, but especially in stanzas two, three and four with the description of the landscape. *Esencias*: the presence of scents also pervades the poem; their connecting role between heaven and earth has already been commented on.

The desire for beauty beyond corruptibility can, then, be considered fulfilled within the poetic play of language, but it is only a virtual fulfilment. The display of the universal analogy is a kind of *stade du miroir* (Lacan) where the subject sees itself and its desire in all things. With the death of the poet's double, the mirror is broken, and with it the ontology of the universal analogy. This consciousness can be observed also at another level. The fact that a geographic location is paratextually stated as the setting of the poem, and that this place has an autobiographical reference for Juan Ramón Jiménez, represents the marking out of a position for the poet-subject. The voice uttering this poem must, through the toponym at the end of the poem, be traced back to Jiménez, whereby lyrical and autobiographical subject coincide. This authorial subject inscribed into the text who is conscious of his belonging to the paradigm of the fragmented absolute is – as will be seen – the same who lends voice to the poems of *Animal de fondo*.

Estío, 73 / Summer, 73 (1916)

Sólo mi frente y el cielo.
¡Los únicos universos!
¡Mi frente, sólo, y el cielo!
   –Entre ellos, la brisa pura,
caricia fiel, mano única,
para tantas plenitudes…
La brisa, que baja y sube…–
   Arriba, todo lo vivo,
todo el sueño en mi sentido,
poblando a aquél de las alas
que a su armonía él le baja.
   Nada más.
            –¿Acaso eres
tú la brisa que va y viene
del cielo, amor, a mi frente?–
(*Op*, I, 1: 1446–7)

Only my forehead and the sky.
The only universes!
My forehead, only, and the sky!
   – Between them, the pure breeze,
fond caress, unique hand
that brings so much plentifulness;
the breeze, always falling and rising… –
   Above, all that is life,
the entire dream in my senses,
settling him with the wings,
that he brings down to its harmony.
   Nothing else.
            – Are you perhaps
the breeze that comes and goes
from the sky, love, to my forehead? –

This poem (number 73 in the collection *Estío* (*Summer*), 1916) apparently displays the ideal, spiritual fulfilment that characterizes the mature Jiménez's poetry. *Estío* is a central work in Jiménez's production with respect to the crystallization of the *poesía pura* since it represents, together with the *Sonetos espirituales* (*Spiritual Sonnets*), the first work of the *segunda época*. The departure from Symbolism can be observed to begin around 1911–12, when Jiménez started to explore new creative paths (Palau de Nemes 1974: 456–98). However, a central cause for the change of style and mood in Jiménez's poetic production is to be found in his acquaintance with the woman who would become his wife, Zenobia Camprubí Aymar, as she expressed her dislike for his aestheticist and decadent poetry at an early stage of their relationship (Palau de Nemes 1974: 525–9).[9] *Estío* is a poetic diary that refers to the encounter with the person who would be the poet's wife. Jiménez met her in the autumn of 1913. In 1915 she agreed to marry him, but towards the end of that year her mother removed her to the USA in order to avoid that marriage (in vain, as it turned out). Palau de Nemes describes the troubles of the *noviazgo*, and it is the ups and downs of this period that are represented in *Estío* (Palau de Nemes 1974: 585).

Formally the poem "Sólo mi frente y el cielo" consists of four stanzas, the first and last ones have three verses, while the two central stanzas are made up of four verses; the rhymes are assonant throughout.[10] Thus, it appears as a symmetrical and self-enclosed poem expressing both in form and content the artistic and existential plenitude of the author – as should be expected in Jiménez's mature poetry. Thematically the seamless connection between poetic imagination and the sky that was analyzed in the previous chapter is present here as well. In this poem, the desire to belong to the absolute realm of poetry is claimed with the strongest emphasis to be fulfilled, since reference to the earthly realm has apparently been expelled from the text: the forehead (metonym for the inner world) and the sky are "¡Los únicos universos!" (The only universes!) (verse 2). The first stanza makes this claim with a strong determination, since each verse is a nominal sentence asserting the inner world and the heavenly domain as the only reality to which the lyrical subject belongs. As a means of emphasizing this claim, the first and third verse only differ by a hyperbatonic structure in the latter. The second stanza seems to corroborate the claim made in the first one. Here the breeze, "que baja y sube...–" (always falling and rising), connects the inner life of the lyrical subject with the heavenly realm. In addition, an amorous metaphor for the breeze is displayed, "caricia fiel, mano única" (fond caress, unique hand) (verse 5), whereby the cosmic eroticism belonging to the notion of the universal analogy is enacted – just as was the case in "Crepúsculo de abril". Nonetheless, the following analysis will show that in the present poem the appearance of the love theme has a most disturbing effect.

Stanza three continues the transport between the imaginative and the heavenly realms, although a syntactic and semantic complication makes it impossible to overcome ambiguity. The reference of "aquél" (him) in verse 10 is uncertain, as it may relate to "sueño" (dream), to "todo lo vivo" (all that is life) or, as has been proposed,[11] to the god Eros if the syntagma "aquél de las alas" (him with the wings) is read as an allusion to this mythological character. In the same way, the reference of the personal pronoun "él" (he) in verse 11 is equivocal: is it the same as "aquél" of verse 10 or another person? The syntagma "todo lo vivo" can be a verbal as well as a nominal syntagma; only the parallel construction with the beginning of the following verse, "todo el sueño" (the entire dream), is a pointer to identifying it as a nominal syntagma, but this cannot be determined definitely. If it is identified as a nominal syntagma then a verb is omitted at the beginning of the stanza; it could be "estar" whereby the phrase would say: "Arriba [está] todo lo vivo" (above [is] all that is life), instead of regarding "vivo" as the first person form in present tense of the verb "vivir" (to live). Neither of this, however, clarifies the two last verses of the stanza.

Instead of trying to work out an explanation that would force a univocal sense upon a sentence that evidently cannot have it, a semantic grouping of the words appearing in the stanza will provide a reasonable understanding. The stanza begins with the adverb "arriba" (above) and ends with the verbal syntagma "le baja" (brings down). This semantic framing of the stanza by the vertical structure indicates that the rest of the elements are likely to be integrated into it. To this structure "las alas" (the wings), "sueño" (dream) and "armonía" (harmony) will also belong. The elements "sueño" and "armonía" belong to the domain of poetic imagination and thus also to the heavenly realm. This part of the poem would then represent the vertical correspondence that appeared to have been overcome in the first stanza.

The first verse of stanza four is *escalonado*, that is, graphically divided into two lines. The verse starts with the words "nada más" (nothing else), and continues on the next line with the question that finishes the poem – as if the lyrical subject at this moment reflected upon and doubted his initial self-assurance. The expression "nada más" is likely to leave the reader puzzled given the syntactical ambiguity of stanza 3. The meaning of this expression must be related to the exclusivity of poetic imagination and celestial realm asserted in stanza one, in turn ambiguously repeated in stanza three through the elements belonging to the vertical structure. In stanza four, syntax is restored, but thematically an otherness, the breeze that first appeared in stanza two, intrudes into the exclusiveness of the spiritual and the imaginative realms: "tú [...], amor" (you [...] love). In this way the text reveals its condition of being a love poem where the breeze lending dynamism to the imaginative flight could be a metaphor for the beloved woman, the *you* that opposes the *I*. If this were the case, then the initial self-enclosure would be broken by the appearance of the beloved person, that is, the virtual fulfilment is substituted by a specific love for another person.

The initial isolation is challenged as the poem progresses since in each stanza a different expressive register is presented. Stanza one states its semantic content with a marmoreal definiteness, emphasized by the elision of the verb in all three verses, thereby asserting the content of the stanza with an atemporal determination. Stanza two turns to a standard syntactical expression (the only irregularity can be found in the final words of the stanza where the idiom "sube y baja" is changed to "baja y sube" (always falling and rising)). The syntactic breakdown of the third stanza leaves only a ravaged semantics of the determination of the first stanza, as if the appearance of an amorous theme – the "caricia fiel" (fond caress) of the second stanza – completely undermined the self-enclosed determination that opened the poem. Stanza four begins with a colloquial expression, "nada más", followed by a question directed to a *tú* in an uncomplicated syntax. A stylistic pattern thus appears questioning the plenitude of the subject, apparently fully constituted and self-sufficient. In stanza one the subject asserts to have attained a total I, that is, rather than being longed for, the absolute is said to have been attained. The verisimilitude of this claim is, however, undermined as the text develops because if stanza three is regarded as an attempt to return to the self-sufficiency of the first three verses, after the appearance of a love motif in stanza two, then this effort clearly fails since syntax and semantics break down. Finally, in stanza four, the restoration of a proper syntax coincides with the explicit invocation of the beloved *tú*, whereby the lyrical subject definitively acknowledges his belonging to the empirical order, where the *yo* is opposed to the *tú*. Complementing the linear progression of the text, a symmetrical structure, marked by the dashes that frame the two stanzas referring to the *you*, exhibits graphically the duality which in fact governs the poem.

This poem can be related to the philosophy of love that emerges with Romanticism, since the historical background for the loving subject that appears in "Sólo mi frente y el cielo" can be found in the incorporation of love into transcendental subjectivity by Romantic thought.[12] Instead of understanding subjectivity as based on the self-reflective *cogito*, the subject becomes connected to an existential I through its constitution by an emotion related to the bodily – empirical – experience of the world. The inclusion of love in transcendental subjectivity entails regarding a bodily and emotional aspect as part of the absolute subject. Falling in love means seeing the absolute in another person, who thus becomes the cipher of the universe.[13] Love is the experience of the absolute, but since the beloved one is, as an empirical subject, a finite being, falling in love means envisaging a precarious absolute. The entire collection where "Sólo mi frente y el cielo" is found, *Estío*, is characterized by the display of a wide variety of moods. Jiménez himself described *Estío* as a poetic diary, and in fact it alternates between enthusiasm, hope and happiness on one side and anguish and scepticism on the other. In this way a consciousness of belonging to the paradigm of the fragmented absolute is expressed in the sense that the plenitude is constantly challenged by the emotional tides. Furthermore, the projection of the absolute onto the beloved one suggests how Romantic philosophy remains within the paradigm of the philosophy of the subject. The elevation of the beloved one to the absolute is not equivalent to a paradigm of intersubjective rationality, since the adored one is idealized into an absolute object rather than being approached as another subject who might have a world-understanding that should be contrasted with that of the loving subject. The absolute is transferred to the beloved other, but in fact the centre remains the loving subject and its feeling of unlimited striving towards this finite absolute. The subject is in no way decentred and part of a dual (or multi-polar) communicative relationship but remains the metaphysical principle of this paradigm.

Animal de fondo / *Animal of Depth* (1949)
The criticism has often described Jiménez´s *segunda época* as the attainment of an artistic and spiritual plenitude culminating in the collection *Animal de fondo*.[14] Yet the thematics of an arrival pervades his whole mature output, and its expression as a triumphant encounter is already

thematized in the *Sonetos espirituales* (1917) – as will be shown below in Chapter 5. From the perspective taken in this chapter the poems of *Animal de fondo* are, rather than the attainment of a long pursued plenitude, the expression of infinite longing as a force driving poetic creativity. *Animal de fondo* was in fact planned by Jiménez to be part of the work *Dios deseado y deseante* (*God Desired and Desiring*), a volume only posthumously published (in different versions depending on the edition) on the basis of material found in the Jiménez archives. Already the title of the projected version, which includes the notion of desire, points to the opposite of a self-enclosed and fully finished work. The open-ended character of the work is also supported from a biographical viewpoint, since Jiménez never considered it finished. This is a pointer to the thematization of infinite desire in the work, since if closed formal perfection suggests accomplishment, the fragment relates to a process and unfinished work.

In the *Notes* at the end the first edition of the book, which appeared on 4 July 1949, Jiménez calls this collection of poems "una anticipación de mi libro «Dios deseante y deseado»" (*Op*, I, 2: 1232) (an anticipation of my book *God Desiring and Desired*, GDD: 127). In a letter to Lysandro Galtier, the translator of the first edition of this work into French, dated 5 November 1949, Jiménez mentioned that "[e]l libro completo *Dios deseado y deseante* tiene ahora 57 poemas" (Jiménez 1977: 178) (the complete book *God Desired and Desiring* has now 57 poems), in contrast to the 29 that appeared in the first edition of the work. On 20 February 1953, he offers Max Aub (another exiled Spanish writer) the publication of the "edición completa de *Animal de fondo*" (complete edition of *Animal of Depth*) which now has "tres veces más poemas que el anterior" (Jiménez 1977: 278) (three times more poems than the previous one) – that is, 87 poems. In a conversation with the critic Ricardo Gullón, dated 17 December 1953, Jiménez considered the book to be still incomplete, as he at that moment planned for it to contain 80 poems in its final version.[15] In the *Tercera antolojía poética* (*Third Poetic Anthology*) (1957), seven poems that did not appear among the 29 of the first edition are included as belonging to this collection. Since no final edition of this work appeared in the poet's lifetime, we must regard *Animal de fondo* as a torso, and, consequently, the understanding of it as the culmination of his whole poetic output becomes paradoxical. Nonetheless, from the perspective sketched out in the present chapter it is possible to see *Animal de fondo* as representative of a central aspect of Jiménez's work: the unfulfillable desire to reach the absolute.[16]

Even if it is an unfinished work, there is certainly a basis in the text for understanding *Animal de fondo* as an expression of plenitude, since a feature of the work is the lyrical subject's claim of having reached a "tierra de llegada" (place of arrival) (*Op*, I, 2: 1161/ *GDD*: 43):

Todas las nubes arden
porque yo te he encontrado,
dios deseante y deseado;
(*Op*, I, 2: 1149)

All the clouds are burning
because I found you,
god desiring and desired;
(*GDD*: 11)

ahora yo sé ya que soy completo,
porque tú, mi deseado dios, estás visible,
estás audible, estás sensible
en rumor y en color de mar, ahora;
porque eres espejo de mí mismo
en el mundo, mayor por ti, que me ha tocado.
(*Op* I, 2: 1148-9)

now I know that I am complete,
for you, my desired god, are visible,
audible, touchable
within the sound and the color of the sea, right now;
for you are the mirror of myself
in the world, made larger because of you, that I live in.
(*GDD*: 9)

By means of the motif of the encounter, Jiménez is referring to a topos from mystical poetry, a tradition with a very strong presence in Spanish literary history. In the mystical tradition two stages have to be passed through before the encounter with God can be reached: *purgatio* and *illuminatio* precede *unio*. The mystical tradition has been referred to in the criticism about *Animal de fondo,* just as Jiménez himself was explicit about his inscription in this tradition: "Por eso la mejor lírica española ha sido y es fatalmente mística, con Dios o sin él, ya que el poeta, vuelvo a decirlo de otro modo, es un místico sin dios necesario" (For this reason the best Spanish poetry has been and is fatefully mystical, with God or without him, since the poet, I repeat it in a different way, is a mystic without a necessary god) (*Tg*: 41). The difference of religious and historical horizon between the Christian poets of the sixteenth century and Jiménez is levelled in this citation, but the relation to the mystical tradition should obviously be understood from the intellectual horizon of the Spanish *fin de siglo*. Art was regarded – as mentioned above – as the source of spirituality, which is an idea that Jiménez still builds upon in his mature poetry. This faith in the poetic word is Jiménez's poetological background for his "dios deseado y deseante".[17]

Despite the solemn and religious mood of the poems, the lyrical subject that appears in them is not unlimited, but a subject reaching out towards omnipotence, that is, a subject conscious of his finitude. In *Animal de fondo* modern fragmentation is represented through the desire for totality, as can be seen in the following poem:

CONCIENCIA HOY AZUL

(Dios está azul…
Antes)

Conciencia de hondo azul del día, hoy
concentración de trasparencia azul;
mar que sube a mi mano a darme sed
de mar y cielo en mar,
en olas abrazantes, de sal viva.
    Mañana de verdad en fondo de aire
(cielo del agua fondo
de otro vivir aún en inmanencia)
esplosión suficiente (nube, ola, espuma
de ola y nube)
para llevarme en cuerpo y alma
al ámbito de todos los confines,
a ser el yo que anhelo
y a ser el tú que anhelas en mi anhelo.
    Conciencia hoy de vasto azul,
conciencia deseante y deseada,
Dios hoy azul, azul, azul y más azul,
igual que el Dios de mi Moguer azul,
un día.
(*Op*, I, 2: 1153)

CONSCIOUSNESS TODAY BLUE

("God is blue..."
Before)

Consciousness of deep blue of the day, today
concentration of blue transparency;
sea that climbs to my hand to make me thirsty
for the sea and the sky on the sea,
in embracing waves of living salt.
    Morning of truth against a depth of air
(sky of the water, depth
of a different life still in immanence)
sufficient explosion (cloud, wave, foam
of wave and cloud)
to carry me in body and soul
to the threshold of all boundaries,
to become the I I long for
and to become the you you long for in my longing,
consciousness of vast blue today,
consciousness desiring and desired,
god today blue, blue, blue and more blue,
just like the god of my blue Moguer,
once.
(*GDD*: 21)

The epigraph of the poem and the mention of Moguer at the end of it are, respectively, a textual and an autobiographical self-reference. Moguer is Jiménez's beloved hometown, often evoked in his texts. The epigraph refers to the early poem "Balada de la mañana de la cruz" (Morning of the Cross), the text opening the book *Baladas de primavera* (*Spring Ballads*) of 1907.[18] In this way the continuity of life and work across time is suggested. A repetition of the experience recorded in "Balada de la mañana de la cruz" is sustained, implying that throughout the course of Jiménez's life, his writing has been guided by the same poetic consciousness directed towards the absolute.

Now, at this moment in Jiménez's life, the absolute seems to have been reached. Apparently the lyrical subject is an unlimited I since the experience of the morning is "esplosión suficiente [...] para llevarme en cuerpo y alma / al ámbito de todos los confines, / a ser el yo que anhelo" (sufficient explosion [...] to carry me in body and soul / to the threshold of all boundaries, / to become the I I long for) (verses 9 and 11–13). These verses seem thus to express the fulfilment of desire. The lyrical subject experiences being a limitless I, represented by the breaking of dawn. The fact that the lyrical subject is split – the *I* is opposed to the poetic *god* that runs through the poems of *Animal de fondo* – is not in itself a reason to consider the encounter unfulfilled. In the mystical as well as in the metaphysical tradition, self-transcendence and affirmation of the individual are complementary.[19] And yet the unlimited I that is claimed to have been reached is expressed paradoxically, through the desire – both on part of the subject and of the god – to be such a limitless subject: "ser el yo que anhelo / y a ser el tú que anhelas en mi anhelo" (to become the I I long for / and to become the you you long for in my longing). It is furthermore remarkable that the plenitude and the longing are asserted in the present tense whereby fulfilment as well as desire are expressed as active. The reason for this may be found in the lyrical subject's consciousness of being a finite individual who aims for an impossible goal. The conquest of self-sufficiency through poetry is – given the belonging to the paradigm of the fragmented absolute – bound to remain envisaged.

As a logical consequence of the idea of self-conquest through poetic expression, the motif of the mirror is present in *Animal de fondo* in several poems, as in the following examples:

> Aquí estás en ejemplo y en espejo
> de la imajinación, de mi imajinación en movimiento,
> estás en elemento triple incorporable,
> agua, aire, alto fuego,
> con la tierra segura en todo el horizonte.
> (*Op*, I, 2: 1147–8)

> You are here as exemplar and mirror
> of the imagination, of my imagination in movement,
> you are in a triple embodiable element,
> water, air, high fire,
> with the firm earth circling the horizon.
> (*GDD*: 7)

> Dios, circula el amor gustador y oloroso,
> y cantando circula, tocante y mirador,
> porque eres mi flor y mi fruto en mi forma,

porque eres mi espejo en mi idea
(idea, forma, espejo, fruto y flor, y todo único)
porque eres mi música, dios, de todo el mundo,
toda la música de todo el mundo con la nada.
(*Op*, I, 2: 1169)

God, make love flow pleasurable and aromatic,
flow singing, touching, glancing,
for you are the flower and fruit in my form,
for you are the mirror in my idea
(idea, form, mirror, fruit and flower, each unique)
for you are my music, god, of the whole world,
the whole music of the whole world plus the nothingness.
(*GDD*: 59)

The former citation describes the attained god as a mirror-image of the lyrical subject's imagination,[20] which furthermore is asserted to be a dynamic element: "espejo / [...] de mi imajinación en movimiento" (mirror [...] of my imagination in movement). The second quotation represents the principle of universal correspondence as a pan-erotic force pervading the universe: "circula el amor gustador y oloroso, / y cantando circula, tocante y mirador" (make love flow pleasurable and aromatic, / flow singing, touching, glancing). At the same time, the consciousness that this universal erotic force is a subjective aesthetic creation is clearly expressed: "porque eres mi flor y mi fruto en mi forma, / porque eres mi espejo en mi idea [...] mi música, dios, de todo el mundo, / toda la música de todo el mundo con la nada" (for you are my flower and my fruit in my form, / for you are my mirror in my idea [...] my music, god, of the whole world, / the whole music of the whole world plus the nothingness). The singing of universal love is the poetry written by the lyrical subject, but this *music* and this *world* that joyfully interweave are ultimately connected with nothingness. The encounter with the absolute does not transcend the experience of absence and contingency but remains within the sphere of a fragmented being. The fragmented absolute is a contingent absolute; the loss of a transcendent signified is not overcome, and the cult of poetry becomes explicitly asserted as such:

¡Qué trueque de hombre en mí, dios deseante,
de ser dudón en la leyenda

del dios de tantos decidores,
a ser creyente firme
en la historia que yo mismo he creado
desde toda mi vida para ti!
(*Op*, I, 2: 1160)

What a transformation of the man in me, god desiring,
from being doubtful of the stories
about god of so many preachers,
to become a firm believer
in the story I have myself created
from the beginning of my life for you!
(*GDD*: 41)

The use of the religious terminology of faith relates to the Romantic sacralization of poetry and the poet – and at the same time poetic expression is acknowledged to be a purely subjective construct. The Romantic analogy between poets and priests is thus self-consciously elaborated: the religion that is founded through poetry is subjective in its essence, created and constituted on the basis of a subject's longing for the absolute. In one poem after another, the lyrical subject repeats the claim to be a self-sufficient I, and yet the fact that the claim has to be repeated again and again indicates that fulfilment is not attained. The desire of *Animal de fondo* is essentially unfulfilled, it is a modern desire for an absolute that can be thought but that cannot be appropriated. This was noted by Jiménez himself, who in several writings commented upon this paradoxical striving:

> Y la poesía no se «realiza» nunca, por fortuna para todos; escapa siempre, y el verdadero poeta, que suele ser un ente honrado porque tiene el hábito de vivir con la verdad, sabe dejarla escapar, ya que el estado de gracia poético, el éstasis dinámico, el embeleso rítmico embriagador, el indecible milagro palpitante, de donde sale el acento esencial, la queja amorosa feliz o melancólica, es forma de la huida, forma apasionada de la libertad. (*Tg*: 40)

> And poetry is never "realized", fortunately for everyone, it always escapes and the true poet, who is usually an honorable person because he has the habit of living with truth, knows how to let it escape since the state of poetic grace, the dynamic ecstasy[/stasis], the

rhythmic, drunken rapture, the unutterable, palpitating miracle from which the essential accent arises, is indeed a form of flight, a passionate form of liberty. (*SW*: 201)

In this quotation what is underscored is not the encounter but the search or the movement in itself.[21]

For this reason, the only coherent form *Animal de fondo* can have is that of the unfinished work or of the fragment. To finish the work would mean to give it a final form and thus to definitively terminate the search. Instead it seems that Jiménez envisaged the totality in the fragment, in a similar way as the Romantics:

> The fragment […] involves an essential incompletion. This is why, in *Athenaeum* fragment 22, it is identical to the *project*, a "fragment of the future," insofar as the constitutive incompletion of the project is its most valuable quality, "the ability to idealize and realize objects immediately and simultaneously." In this sense, every fragment is a project: the fragment-project does not operate as a program or prospectus but as the *immediate* projection of what it nonetheless incompletes. (Lacoue-Labarthe and Nancy 1988: 42–3, authors' emphasis)

The aesthetics of the fragment can thus be regarded a consequence of the paradox inherent in the representation of the absolute in the modern period. In the absence of an aesthetics capable – as Medieval or Renaissance art were – of representing the cosmic order, the Romantic fragment refers to the infinite search for an unrepresentable totality. In an entirely parallel way, *Animal de fondo* is a work that aims to express a sense of totality through a series of fragments. Each poem of *Animal de fondo* is a whole in itself that represents the desire for totality but, at the same time, it is necessary that these poems are fragments of a whole that remains to be finished. The intention behind *Animal de fondo* is to bring before the eyes of the reader the *vision* of self-fulfilment through poetry rather than its realization. In this way the metapoetic level that emerged in "Crepúsculo de abril" is continued and developed in *Animal de fondo*. If in the former text the consciousness of belonging to the paradigm of the fragmented absolute is asserted through the indirect inscription of the authorial I, in *Animal de fondo* it is expressed by the work's non-closure. The open-ended nature of this work appears both thematically – one text after the other claims the achieved fulfilment in a seemingly unending series – as well as by the fact that it never was finished by the author. Open-endedness is a feature shared by many modern literary texts because a closure could suggest a paradigm in which it is possible to refer to an absolute measure.[22]

The incompletion of *Animal de fondo* contrasts with its homogeneous style – the religious tonality of the poems – which does work as a unifying principle. The simultaneous cohesion and incompletion refers to a totalizing intention that at the same time is infinitely perfectible. In *Animal de fondo* the desired totality can be identified as the unity of Juan Ramón Jiménez's life and work. Jiménez pursued this fusion of life and poetry as a means to overcome contingency. In this way another facet of absolute subjectivity is presented, the wish to sublate, as it were, contingent individual existence by making it coalesce with an eternal and perfect work of art. This struggle represents the ambition Habermas has noted is a feature of nineteenth- and twentieth-century thought, to posit a non-I to be conquered by the I as a means of self-conquest that thus would corroborate the absolute status of the I. *Animal de fondo* is a product of the wish to accomplish what absolute subjectivity promises, complete self-sufficiency.[23] At the same time, the actual work exposes the impossibility of that wish within the modern paradigm. No omnipotent I is achieved through the fragments of *Animal de fondo*, only a series of texts that points to the striving for the absolute as a guiding principle in Jiménez's life and work.

CHAPTER THREE

Pantheistic and Textual Space

In the previous chapters the world-generating poetic consciousness, absolute subjectivity, has been identified as the principle by means of which Jiménez expected to overcome contingency. However, within a modern framework the empirical side of subjectivity can also be sacralized. If a pantheistic worldview is adopted then the empirical subject is part of cosmic totality and can become the medium of an anonymous voice expressing the self-consciousness of the universe.[1] In the following, three texts by Juan Ramón Jiménez will be analyzed: "Primavera y sentimiento" (Spring and Feeling) from *Rimas* (*Rhymes*, 1902), Poem 122 from *Eternidades* (*Eternities*, 1918) and the first and third fragments of *Espacio* (*Space*, 1943-1944-1954). The analysis of the poems will be guided by the question of the lyrical subject's relation to nature, since one main intention underlying the present chapter is to address the question of the adherence to a totalizing world-understanding by a modern subject. The principle of the universal analogy, that in the present context can be identified with pantheism, appears as a possible open-ended understanding of cosmic totality that could be adopted by a modern subject. Nonetheless, the analysis of the first poem, "Primavera y sentimiento", will show how the scepticism inherent in modern thought is also at work with respect to a pantheistic outlook. As if drawing the consequence of this disillusionment, the mature Jiménez displays a textual writing in which reference to the empirical world is eliminated, and correspondingly the lyrical subject becomes god in the textual realm. Poem 122 of the collection *Eternidades* presents such a textual notion of poetry in the sense of regarding a poem as a wholly self-referential entity. The first fragment of *Espacio* displays a rhapsodic representation of the universal analogy, whereas the third fragment exhibits a self-critique that reiterates the sceptical attitude intrinsic to Modernity.

Apparently the sacralized poet-subject becomes one with the universe. Eventually, however, the modern scepticism towards any totalizing principle causes the two mentioned outcomes: textuality or self-parody.

Rimas, 13 / *Rhymes*, 13 (1902)

PRIMAVERA Y SENTIMIENTO

Estos crepúsculos tibios
son tan azules, que el alma
quiere perderse en las brisas
y embriagarse con la vaga
tinta inefable que el cielo
por los espacios derrama,
fundiéndola en las esencias
que todas las flores alzan
para perfumar las frentes
de las estrellas tempranas.
　Los pétalos melancólicos
de la rosa de mi alma,
tiemblan, y su dulce aroma
(recuerdos, amor, nostalgia),
se eleva al azul tranquilo,
a desleirse en su mágica
suavidad, cual se deslíe
en un sonreír la lágrima
del que sufriendo acaricia
una remota esperanza.
　Está desierto el jardín;
las avenidas se alargan
entre la incierta penumbra
de la arboleda lejana.
Ha consumado el crepúsculo
su holocausto de escarlata,
y de las fuentes del cielo
(fuentes de fresca fragancia),
las brisas de los países
del sueño, a la tierra bajan
un olor de flores nuevas
y un frescor de tenues ráfagas…

Los árboles no se mueven,
y es tan medrosa su calma,
que así parecen mas vivos
que cuando agitan las ramas;
y en la onda transparente
del cielo verdoso, vagan
misticismos de suspiros
y perfumes de plegarias.
    ¡Qué triste es amarlo todo
sin saber lo que se ama!
Parece que las estrellas
compadecidas me hablan;
pero como están tan lejos,
no comprendo sus palabras.
¡Qué triste es tener sin flores
el santo jardín del alma,
soñar con almas floridas,
soñar con sonrisas plácidas,
con ojos dulces, con tardes
de primaveras fantásticas!…
¡Qué triste es llorar, sin ojos
que contesten nuestras lágrimas!
Ha entrado la noche; el aire
trae un perfume de acacias
y de rosas; el jardín
duerme sus flores… Mañana,
cuando la luna se esconda
y la serena alborada
dé al mundo el beso tranquilo
de sus lirios y sus auras,
se inundarán de alegría
estas sendas solitarias;
vendrán los novios por rosas
para sus enamoradas;
y los niños y los pájaros
jugarán dichosos… ¡Almas
de oro que no ven la vida
tras las nubes de las lágrimas!
    ¡Quién pudiera desleirse
en esa tinta tan vaga

que inunda el espacio de ondas
puras, fragantes y pálidas!
¡Ah, si el mundo fuera siempre
una tarde perfumada,
yo lo elevaría al cielo
en el cáliz de mi alma!
(*Op*, I, 1: 30–2)

Spring and Feeling

These balmy evenings
Are so blue, that the soul
Wants to be lost in the breezes
And become drunk with the vague,
Ineffable tint which the sky
Scatters throughout all of space,
Fusing it in essences
Which all the flowers lift up
To perfume the brows
Of the early stars.[2]
    The melancholic petals
Of the rose of my soul
Tremble, and their sweet aroma
(Remembrances, love, nostalgia),
Rises to the tranquil blue,
To be dissolved in its magical
Softness, like is dissolved
In a smile the tear
Of he who suffering keeps
A secret hope.
    The garden is deserted.
The avenues lead off to
The uncertain penumbra
Of far away foliage.
The twilight has consumed
Its holocaust of scarlet
And from the fountains of the sky –
Founts of blossoming waters –
Breezes from the countries

Of slumber bear down to earth
A fragrance of new flowers,
A coolth of tenuous airs…
The trees are not moving;
Their calm is so human
They seem more alive
Than when their branches are waving.
…And in transparent waves
Of the green zenith wander
Mysticisms of a sigh
and a perfume of prayers –
    How sad to love everything
And not to know what we love!
…It seems that the stars
Speak to me with pity
But are so far away
I cannot understand their words –
How sad to possess the sacred
Soul's garden, blossomless,
To dream of souls in flower,
To dream of gentle smiles,
Of sweet eyes, of evenings
In fantastic spring seasons!
How sad to weep without eyes
That answer our tears,
…Night has entered, the air
Bears a perfume of acacias
And of roses; the garden puts its flowers
To sleep… Tomorrow,
When the moon hides away
And serenity of dawn
Gives the world the soft kiss
Of its lilies and breezes,
These solitary paths
Will be flooded with joy;
Lovers coming for roses
To give to their sweethearts
And children and birds
Shall play gaily… Souls
Of gold who see no life

> Through a cloud of tears!
> ...Who could dissolve himself
> In this vague tint
> Which floods space with its waves,
> Pure, pale and fragrant!
> Ah if this world were but always
> A perfumed evening,
> I would lift it to the skies
> In the chalice of my soul!
> (SW: 3-5; translation modified)

As in "Crepúsculo de abril", the setting of this poem is a garden at dusk. At the same time that the lyrical subject wishes to be dissolved into the totality of nature – a wish expressed both at the beginning (verses 2–3) and at the end of the poem (verses 71–74) – a number of metaphors effect an exchange of human and natural features. As in "Crepúsculo de abril", the commonplace analogy between the stars and the flowers establishes the communication between heaven and earth: "las esencias / que todas las flores alzan / para perfumar las frentes / de las estrellas tempranas" (essences / which all the flowers lift up / to perfume the brows / of the early stars) (verses 7–10). The preposition "para" ([in order] to), in verse 9 denotes an intention on the part of the subject of the verb "alzar" (to lift up), that is, the flowers. Similarly, the expression "la frente de las estrellas" (the brows of the stars) suggests metonymically the capacity of thinking or creating on the part of the stars. In this way flowers and stars are anthropomorphized through the attribution of will and intelligence respectively. In the third stanza, the correspondence between the celestial and the terrestrial spheres continues. Now a fragrance of "flores nuevas" (new flowers) descends from the sky: "de las fuentes del cielo / (fuentes de fresca fragancia), / las brisas de los países / del sueño, a la tierra bajan / un olor de flores nuevas" (from the fountains of the sky – / Founts of blossoming waters – / Breezes from the countries / Of slumber bear down to earth / A fragrance of new flowers) (verses 28–32). The perfume is, as in "Crepúsculo de abril", the unifying principle between the terrestrial and the heavenly. It is into this correspondence that the lyrical subject wishes to enter, and this desire is the reason for the soul : rose metaphor that initiates the second stanza.

The anthropomorphosis of natural elements is reversible, and its other side has been termed "naturalization" (de Man 1984: 255).[3] Riffaterre has developed this idea and has called this correspondence or reversibility between natural and human spheres "the chiasmic structure of prosopopeia" because the animated object will gaze back "to the subject daydreaming a Narcissistic reflection of itself in things" (Riffaterre 1985: 112). This chiasmic structure is also at work in "Primavera y sentimiento", since – in an inversion of the anthropomorphosis of natural elements – the longings of the subject are represented as the perfume of a rose. In verses 13–14 it is stated that "recuerdos, amor, nostalgia" (Remembrances, love, nostalgia) are the soul's "dulce aroma" (sweet aroma), which is a development of the mentioned metaphor soul : rose. In this way a correspondence between subject and world is established where interiority and exteriority, subjectivity and nature, are not radically separated but intertwined.

In addition to the figurative reversibility of human and natural, Jiménez uses another technique to express the lyrical subject's relation with nature. It is a feature of *fin de siècle* poetry that sense-impressions are not expressed by means of an active and explicit subject but through the mention of the perception as such (Cardwell 1977: 154–9). Throughout the first three stanzas, the lyrical subject does not at any moment express his sensations in the first person. This impersonality is strengthened by the use of reflexive verbs ("perderse", "embriagarse", "elevarse", "desleírse", "alargarse", "moverse") which place the focus on the verbal act itself instead of on its subject or object. Similarly, the use of synaesthesia underscores the perceptive act in itself rather than its subject, as in verses 4–8 where colours and smells are intertwined. The lyrical subject is present mainly through his perceptions, that is, the aim is to express the dissolution of the subject in the natural world.

If the first three stanzas are a representation of the principle of the universal analogy, then stanza four casts doubt on this understanding. In the first verses of this stanza, the lyrical subject now questions the existence of a cosmic order by the use of the verb "parece" (it seems): "Parece que las estrellas / compadecidas me hablan; / pero como están tan lejos, / no comprendo sus palabras" (It seems that the stars / Speak to me with pity / But are so far away / I cannot understand their words) (verses 43–46). In verses 46–51 the negation of the correspondence with the universe is continued. Even if the reader is presented with another naturalization, soul : garden ("el santo jardín del alma"(the sacred / Soul's garden) verse 48), this is a garden without flowers ("¡Qué triste es tener sin flores / el santo jardín del alma"(How sad to possess the sacred / Soul's garden, blossomless)). This is to be interpreted within the metaphysical framework constructed in the first three stanzas, where the flowers provided the element connecting earthly with heavenly. The expelling of the lyrical subject from the correspondence between heaven and earth is underscored in these verses, as they repeat the whole setting of the poem (the garden, the flowers and the spring evening), but with the central difference with respect to the appearance of these elements in stanzas 1–3, that now the lyrical subject explicitly states that the setting of the poem is the product of a dream: "¡Qué triste es [...] / soñar con [...] tardes / de primaveras fantásticas" (How sad [...] / To dream of [...] evenings / In fantastic spring seasons!) (verses 47–52).[4] In this way the main setting of the poem (the garden and the spring evening) is repeated as a metaphor expressing the subject's wish for cosmic plenitude – and the impossibility of satisfying that wish. In other words, the experience of belonging to the world that ran through the first three stanzas is no longer at work in this part of the poem. In this way, "Primavera y sentimiento" unfolds both the experience of totality of the universal analogy as well as a sceptical position towards it.

The last stanza can be regarded as a condensation of the relations between lyrical subject and nature expressed in the poem. This stanza consists of two sentences; in the first one (verses 70–73), the lyrical subject repeats the wish asserted at the beginning of the poem of dissolving into the universe. The second exclamation expresses the contrary wish, to internalize the world and to elevate it to the sky "en el cáliz de mi alma" (In the chalice of my soul, verses 77–78). The use of the word "cáliz" carries an ambiguity that is relevant for the present interpretation. On the one hand, the naturalization soul-flower is repeated now at the end of the poem through the lexicalized metaphor flower : chalice. On the other hand, it is possible to interpret the use of the term chalice in a metapoetic way if the metaphor soul : chalice is pursued seeing the lyrical subject carry out a gesture that imitates the priest's elevation of the chalice during the celebration of the Eucharist. This metaphor can be explained by focusing on the first part of the exclamation (verses 74–75), spoken in hypothetical mode: "si el mundo fuera siempre / una tarde perfumada" (if this world were but always / A perfumed evening). The perfumed evening is certainly what has been described in the poem that the reader is about to finish, whereby the elevation of the world *as* a perfumed evening could represent the writing of the poem: "yo lo elevaría al cielo / en el cáliz de mi alma" (I would lift it to the skies / In the chalice of my soul). Since Juan Ramón Jiménez belongs to a post-Romantic literary tradition it would not be incongruous to regard the writing of a poem as equivalent to the celebration of a religious act. Following this interpretation the lyrical subject is now identified with the authorial subject writing the poem. If this metapoetic interpretation is accepted, then an understanding of poet and cosmic totality arises that is closely connected to the Romantic philosophy of nature – and to the notion of *god* that Jiménez would coin in his later years.[5] On the one hand the subject is de-personalized by abandoning the voice of the ego in favour of the voice of nature, and, on the other, the subject is posited as a necessary point of convergence where the world, so to speak, lets a self-consciousness emerge. Jiménez's lyrical subject carries out an emptying of the I and at the same time the poet-subject becomes the centre of the universe, a pantheistic self-consciousness raising the world to the sky in a self-celebrating gesture.[6]

The fact, nonetheless, that the last stanza employs subjunctive and conditional verbal tenses establishes a continuity with the sceptical attitude towards the experience of unity with nature expressed in stanza four. The idiom initiating stanza five, "Quién pudiera" (Who could), unambiguously indicates the impossibility of dissolving into the universe. Consequently, the subject experiences himself as an otherness with respect to the natural world. If this interpretation is followed, then the metaphor poet : priest would still represent the lyrical subject's celebration of nature through the writing of a poetic text. However, this writing is not a strong one that creates or discloses the meaning of the world (a consonance with ontic meaning), but a weak one, where what primarily is unfolded is the contingency of both world and lyrical subject. Rather than nature, what is being revealed is the writing act itself: a person naming the experience of contingency in front of a meaningless natural world. It is possible to conclude that the poem sets up two contrary attitudes towards the poetic work: a pantheistic position letting nature speak through the authorial persona, and a sceptical position displaying a nihilistic and disillusioned I who asserts the experience of contingency. This can be understood as the working of a Kantian paradigm where art gives an intimation of the sacred realm while the divine at the same time is inaccessible to knowledge. Such a paradigm must necessarily oscillate between a vague subjective sense of the sacred and a decidedly sceptical refusal to attribute proper validity to the religious feeling.

***Eternidades*, 122 / *Eternities*, 122 (1918)**

Sé bien que soy tronco
del árbol de lo eterno.
Sé bien que las estrellas
con mi sangre alimento.
Que son pájaros míos
todos los claros sueños...
Sé bien que cuando el hacha
de la muerte me tale,
se vendrá abajo el firmamento.
(*Op*, I, 2: 417)

I know I am the trunk
of the tree of the eternal.
I know that with my blood
I nourish the stars;
that every shining dream
is a bird of my owning...
I know that when the ax
of death strikes me down,
the firmament will fall.
(*THP*: 120)

Poem 122 in *Eternidades* (*Eternities*, 1918) presents one central image: the naturalization of the lyrical subject to a tree. This "árbol de lo eterno" (tree of the eternal) (verse 2) can be understood as the mythical Tree of Life, the centre of the universe and the expression of life itself, growing and propagating endlessly (cf. García Font 1995: 9–16). This interpretation is supported by the final verse, where it is stated that when the tree is cut the firmament will sink, thereby relating the existence of the tree to the permanence of the universe. The stars nourished by the blood of the lyrical subject can be explained as the connection established by the Tree of Life between heavenly and terrestrial realms given its status as *axis mundi*.[7] In a similar way as the stars, the birds belong to the celestial sphere and are the result of another naturalization, dreams : birds.

Even if the lyrical subject could have been expected to have lost any anthropomorphic traits through his transformation into nature's generative centre, he does retain two human features, namely, the blood and the dreams. This may lead the reader to interpret the text allegorically in terms of a solipsistic notion of the I: the existence of the world depends on its perception by the subject. Nonetheless, the convergence of the death of the lyrical subject and the apocalyptic end of the world is meaningful both at a mythological and at a metapoetic level. On the one hand because the *axis mundi* is what literally sustains the universe in mythical thought; on the other because the lyrical subject's death can be interpreted as the finishing of the poem. This text can be related to the quest of modern poetry to create a pure present through art, an enclave isolated from the temporal flow.[8] No linear temporality is displayed in this poem; in fact one single image appears to the reader: the tree against the backdrop of the celestial sphere. Furthermore, the thematization of death at the end of the poem contributes to producing the effect of a single "now" because a metapoetic reading would consider the death of the tree as the ending of poetic temporality. From this viewpoint, the lyrical subject would be a textual phenomenon that vanishes at the moment the reading is finished.

In "Primavera y sentimiento", authorial self-consciousness appeared by means of the representation of the poet-subject as a priest at the end of the text. In that poem the tension in the text was to be found between the notion of the universal analogy and a sceptical position. Poem 122 in *Eternidades* is representative of Jiménez's *poesía pura*, where reference to the physical world is substituted by the creation of an autonomous textual sphere. In this poem communion with nature is replaced by an immanent textual absolute. The scepticism inherent in Modernity towards any metaphysical idea thus conditions the solution to the tension between the desire for an absolute and the doubt concerning the possibility of achieving it. The textual absolute is the last possibility of operating with the numinous without "incurring" a totalizing understanding of the world, although the consequence of this transposition of the unconditioned, the *ganz Andere*, onto the textual realm is that it becomes conditioned. The subjectively generated absolute is, evidently, the only possibility of working with a notion of the "unconditioned" if a totalizing world-understanding as that of the universal analogy must be rejected. At the same time, pantheism will be operative until the end of Jiménez's poetic career, as will be shown in the following section.

Espacio / Space (1943-1944-1954)
Octavio Paz regards the long prose poem *Espacio* as the logical consequence of the young Jiménez's poetical learning:

> La crítica se empeña en ver en el segundo y tercer Jiménez a un negador del «modernismo»: ¿cómo podría serlo si lo lleva a sus consecuencias más extremas y, añadiré, *naturales*: la expresión simbólica del mundo? Unos años antes de morir escribe *Espacio*, largo poema que es una recapitulación y una crítica de su vida poética. Está frente al paisaje tropical de Florida (y frente a todos los paisajes que ha visto o presentido): ¿habla solo o conversa con los árboles? Jiménez percibe por primera vez, y quizá por última, el silencio *in-significante* de la naturaleza. ¿O son las palabras humanas las que únicamente son aire y ruido? (Paz 1994: 111, author's emphasis)

Criticism insists on seeing in the second and third Jiménez a repudiator of "modernism": how could he be that if he carries it to its most extreme and, let me add, *natural* consequences: the symbolic expression of the world? A few years before his death he writes *Espacio*, a long poem that is a recapitulation and a criticism of his poetic life. He is in the tropical landscape of Florida (and in all the landscapes he has seen or intuited): is he talking to himself or conversing with the trees? Jiménez perceives for the first time, and perhaps for the last, the *in-significant* silence of nature. Or is it the human words that are only air and noise? (Paz 1973: 80, author's emphasis)

In these lines Paz discusses the same question that is the focus of the present chapter, namely, the relation of the lyrical subject to exterior reality. In the question "¿habla solo o conversa con los árboles?" (is he talking to himself or conversing with the trees?) the duality commented upon above is implied: is poetry a projection of human traits upon a meaningless universe or communion with nature?[9] This is the dilemma embedded in "Primavera y sentimiento". In *Espacio* the self-reflective thematics of the poet-subject in front of the natural world emerges in full. At the same time, a series of autobiographical references are scattered throughout the text, but since the question of the recovery of past experiences is not the issue discussed in this chapter, focus will remain on the tension between a poet-subject capable of communicating with the universe and a finite individual unable to read the meaning of the world.

The first part of *Espacio* appeared in the Mexican journal *Cuadernos americanos* in 1943. It appeared under the title "Espacio (una estrofa). Fragmento 1[o]" (Space (a stanza). 1st Fragment) and was set out in free verse. A final note read, "(Por la Florida, 1941-42)" (Around Florida, 1941–42). A year later the same journal published what today appears as the second fragment: "Espacio (fragmento primero de la segunda estrofa)" (Space (first fragment of the second stanza)). It was dated 1941 and, like the first instalment, composed in free verse. In 1954 the journal *Poesía española* published a long prose text divided into three "fragmentos" under the title *Espacio*.[10] This new version subverted the expectations that Jiménez had created ten years earlier. The publication of the whole text in 1954 established a cohesion by means of the denomination of the three fragments as "Sucesión 1", "Cantada", and "Sucesión: y 2" (Succession 1, Cantata, Succession 2). Furthermore, the postscript, "Por la Florida, 1941-1942-1954" (Around Florida, 1941-1942-1954), asserted a unity in terms of geographical space. Yet the homogeneity in tone and mood with respect to the two first published fragments was broken.[11] In the third one, the hymnic mood dominating the first two fragments turns into parody and self-critique, since a radical questioning of the sacralized conception of the poetic work is one of its central thematic strands.

In the following pages, the analyses will proceed from the question of whether the poet-subject is writing with the language of nature (in the sense of the universal analogy) or projecting an altogether artificial structure on the physical world. While the hymnic and declamatory mode, asserting the coincidence between poet-subject and the generative force of nature, dominates in the first fragment, in the third one the lyrical subject renounces the metaphysical notion of the universal analogy. The text ends with a defeated and disillusioned authorial subject who hands the text over to a reader subject. This authorial subject is highly conscious of his contingency and of leaving a textual testimony of his existence that he no longer possesses or controls.[12]

Fragmento 1º / 1st Fragment

Even if *Espacio* may appear as a chaotic succession of images, a number of cohesive elements appear throughout the poem. One of these is the reiteration of certain sentences – framed between quotation marks – producing a thematic rhythm as the text progresses. The opening sentence of the first fragment "«Los dioses no tuvieron más sustancia que la que tengo yo»" (*Op*, II, 4: 1269) (The gods had no other substance than the one I have) (*T&S*: 55) is repeated at the end of the third fragment with an explicit reference to the beginning of the text: "Ya te lo dije al comenzar: «Los dioses no tuvieron más sustancia que la que tengo yo»" (*Op*, II, 4: 1285) (I already told you in the beginning: "The gods had no more substance than I have") (*T&S: 73*). An ambiguous assertion of the divine status of the lyrical subject is thereby given as one of the cohesive factors of *Espacio*. In the first fragment, immediately following the cited first sentence, it is asserted that the substance of the gods is of the same transitory nature as that of man:

> Yo tengo, como ellos, la sustancia de todo lo vivido y de todo lo porvivir. No soy presente sólo, sino fuga raudal de cabo a fin. Y lo que veo, a un lado y otro, en esta fuga (rosas, restos de alas, sombra y luz) es sólo mío, recuerdo y ansia míos, presentimiento, olvido. (*Op*, II, 4: 1269)

> I have, like them, the substance of all that has been lived and all that remains to be lived. I am not only present, but a streaming flight from end to end. And what I see, on one side and the other, in this flight (roses, the remains of wings, shadow and light) belongs only to me, my remembrance and my desire, my presentiment, my forgetfulness. (*T&S: 55*)

The substance in common between the gods and the lyrical subject is a paradoxical one, since it is temporality and transience: "fuga raudal de cabo a fin" (a streaming flight from end to end). In keeping with this, in *Espacio* mutability and dynamism are emphasized to such an extent that no particular setting is depicted (with the exception of the second fragment, where a mimetic representation is actually carried out).

The perceptual impersonality of the early writings is here extended to a loss of central perspective altogether. In "Primavera y sentimiento" perception was distanced from the perceiving subject. A similar but more radically estranged perception takes place in *Espacio*, as space is temporalized, that is, the world loses its contours since it is represented in permanent transformation. This dynamic and amorphous space is an expression of the lyrical subject's transience, who appears as a passive medium of the mutability of the world:

> Pasan vientos como pájaros, pájaros igual que flores, flores soles y lunas, lunas soles como yo, como almas, como cuerpos, cuerpos como la muerte y la resurrección; como dioses. Y soy un dios sin espada, sin nada de lo que hacen los hombres con su ciencia; sólo

con lo que es producto de lo vivo, lo que se cambia todo; sí, de fuego
o de luz, luz. (*Op*, II, 4: 1269)

Winds pass like birds, birds equal to the flowers, flowers suns and
moons, moon-suns like me, like souls, like bodies, bodies like death
and resurrection; like gods. I am a god without a sword, carrying
nothing of what men produce through their science; I carry only the
product of what is alive, what may be totally changed; yes, fire or
light, light. (*T&S*: 55)

The metamorphoses of the natural world appear here by means of
a chain of similes that points to the notion of the universal analogy
as the cosmological conception underlying *Espacio*. The mention of
death and resurrection should also be understood within this paradigm, in the sense that growth and decay yield transformation and
new growth. In the present passage, furthermore, the elements
linked by the comparative particle are Jiménez's topoi of poetic ideality. The wind is a connecting element between earthly and celestial,
just as the birds and the flowers (the latter by means of their perfume, as was discussed earlier), while the moon and the sun are
celestial bodies respectively related to poetic creativity and the principle of life. This means that in the syntagma "lunas soles como yo"
(moon-suns like me) the lyrical subject conflates poetic creativity,
symbolized by the moon, and natural vital force, represented by the
sun. The equation of lyrical subjectivity and the sun becomes further
developed in the last part of the passage, where the lyrical subject
is armed with fire and light. As in "Primavera y sentimiento", it is
through the lyrical subject that a cosmic self-consciousness can
emerge. By means of this peculiar subject-centred pantheism, Jiménez's lyrical subject attains divine status, as has been noted on previous occasions.[13]

Throughout the first fragment, the lyrical subject oscillates between
faith in the universal analogy and scepticism towards it. Shortly after
the cited passage, a doubt in the idealist expectations laid upon the
poet-subject appears:

¿Por qué comemos y bebemos otra cosa que luz o fuego? Como yo
he nacido en el sol, y del sol he venido aquí a la sombra, ¿soy de sol,
como el sol alumbro?, y mi nostaljia, como la de la luna, es haber
sido sol de un sol un día y reflejarlo sólo ahora. (*Op*, II, 4: 1269)

Why do we eat or drink anything but light or fire? Since I am born from the sun and from the sun have descended here to the shade, am I made of sun, do I light up like the sun? And my nostalgia, like that of the moon, is to have been one day sun of a sun and now only its reflection. (*T&S*: 55–6, translation modified)

The metaphor of the poet as a sun is repeated here, but the superhuman properties attributed to the poet are put into question. In this passage the duality of faith and scepticism that was expressed in "Primavera y sentimiento" reappears. In the sentences following the last quotation, the divine is represented by an iridescent light that the lyrical subject suddenly sees:

Pasa el iris cantando como canto yo. Adiós iris, iris volveremos a vernos, que el amor es uno y solo y vuelve cada día. ¿Qué es este amor de todo, cómo se me ha hecho en el sol, con el sol, en mí conmigo? (*Op*, II, 4: 1269)

The rainbow passes by singing as I sing. Goodbye, iris, iris, we will see each other again, for love is one and alone, and returns each day. What is this love of everything, how has it become such for me in the sun, with the sun, within me with myself? (*T&S*: 56)

A more optimistic tone is struck concerning spiritual fulfilment through poetry in these sentences, since an equivalence is asserted between the iridescent light and the lyrical subject's singing ("[p]asa el iris cantando como canto yo" (the rainbow passes by singing as I sing)), just as universal love is experienced by the lyrical subject, "este amor de todo" (this love of everything). The confidence in the powers of poetry, equal to nature's transformative force, is stated clearly here, but before the hymnic level in this fragment is definitively reached, a despondent mood appears through a part of the text.

Poetic transformative power becomes inverted into a prosaic vision of life where the flowers – instead of depicting natural beauty and the correspondence between heaven and earth – are deprived of their figurativity, and bluntly represented as genitalia: "Las flores nos rodean de voluptuosidad, olor, color y forma sensual; nos rodeamos de ellas, que son sexos de colores, de formas, de olores diferentes" (*Op*, II, 4: 1270) (Flowers surround us with voluptuousness, scent, color and sensual shapes; we surround ourselves with them for they are sex with colors, shapes, different scents) (*T&S*: 56). A *desengaño* of language appears: "Y el idioma, ¡qué confusión!, qué cosas nos decimos sin saber lo que nos decimos" (*Op*, II, 4: 1270) (And language, what a confusion! The things we tell one another not knowing what we are saying!) (*T&S*: 56). Poetry, nature and love constitute – in keeping with the principle of the universal analogy – absolute values for Jiménez, and just as nature and poetry have been rejected, so human love is also degraded:

> Amor, amor, amor (lo cantó Yeats) «amor en el lugar del escremento». ¿Asco de nuestro ser, nuestro principio y nuestro fin; asco de aquello que más nos vive y más nos muere? (*Op*, II, 4: 1270)
>
> Love, love, love (Yeats set it to music), "love [has pitched its mansion] in the place of excrement." Disgust at our being, our own beginning and our end; disgust at what most lives in us and most dies in us? (*T&S*: 56)[14]

This is the lowest point of dejection in the *fragmento primero*, in parallel with the sceptical attitude appearing in the fourth stanza of "Primavera y sentimiento" both with regard to its nihilistic outlook as well as to the rejection of the universal analogy.

Immediately after this passage a change in mood occurs, caused by the return to the notion of the universal analogy:

> Alas, cantos, luz, palmas, olas, frutas me rodean, me envuelven en su ritmo, en su gracia, en su fuerza delicada; y yo me olvido de mí entre ello, y bailo y canto y río y lloro por los otros, embriagado. (*Op*, II, 4: 1270)
>
> Wings, songs, light, palms, waves, fruits surround me, gather me within their own rhythm, their own grace, their own delicate strength; and I forget myself within it all, and I dance and sing, laugh and cry for others, inebriated. (*T&S*: 57)

The harmony and beauty of nature is represented, and the subject's mood is of a joyful belonging to the natural world, to "este vivir de cambio y gloria" (*Op*, II, 4: 1270) (this living in change and glory) (*T&S*: 57). Throughout the rest of the first fragment, the mood is mainly joyful even if negative aspects of existence are occasionally mentioned. Towards the end of the fragment (leading up to the uninterrupted pantheistic praise that constitutes the second fragment) the tone becomes hymnic as the lyrical subject harmonizes his voice with that of nature, now represented by a bird:

> Tú y yo, pájaro, somos uno; cántame, canta tú, que yo te oigo, que mi oído es tan justo por tu canto. Ajústame tu canto más a este oído mío que espera que lo llenes de armonía. (*Op*, II, 4: 1274–5)

> You and I, bird, are one; sing to me, sing, for I hear you, my ear is fully tuned because of your song. Tune your song more precisely to this ear of mine waiting to be filled with your harmony. (*T&S*: 61)

In keeping with this ideal vision, the first fragment finally reaches its apotheosis:

> No, este perro no levanta los pájaros, los mira, los comprende, los oye, se echa al suelo, y calla y sueña ante ellos. ¡Qué grande el mundo en paz, qué azul tan bueno para el que puede no gritar, puede cantar; cantar y comprender y amar! ¡Inmensidad, en ti y ahora vivo; ni montañas, ni casi piedra, ni agua, ni cielo casi; inmensidad, y todo y sólo inmensidad; esto que abre y que separa el mar del cielo, el cielo de la tierra, y, abriéndolos y separándolos, los deja más unidos y cercanos, llenando con lo lleno lejano la totalidad! ¡Espacio y tiempo y luz en todo yo, en todos y yo y todos! ¡Yo con la inmensidad! (*Op*, II, 4: 1275)

> No, this dog does not frighten the birds, he looks at them, he understands them, he listens to them, he lies on the ground and keeps quiet and dreams in front of them. How large is the world at peace, what a beautiful blue for the one who can stop shouting, who can sing; to sing, to understand, to love! Immensity in you and now I live; neither mountains, nor quite stone, nor water, nor quite sky; immensity, all and only immensity; this is what opens and separates the sea from the sky, the sky from the earth, and opening up and separating them, it brings them closer and more united, filling the totality with the distant plenitude! Space and time and light in all of me, in everyone, and I and all! I with immensity! (*T&S*: 62)

The dog regarding and understanding the birds should be read as the poet contemplating the heavenly realm.[15] In the present text the dog-poet is observing nature's celestial envoys, the birds, as he "calla y sueña ante ellos" (keeps quiet and dreams in front of them). To perceive the world through the cosmic communication means to sense the profound unity of all things, that is, the subject is fully immersed in the fundamental onto-poetical force of the universe and in this way he both reflects and recreates cosmic harmony. In other words, the lyrical subject occupies the same position as in the first part of "Primavera y sentimiento". The subject is de-personalized, becoming the voice of nature and the point where a self-consciousness of the cosmic whole can emerge.

The hymnic mood closes the first *fragment*:

¡Yo, universo inmenso, dentro, fuera de ti, segura inmensidad! Imájenes de amor en la presencia concreta; suma gracia y gloria de la imajen, ¿vamos a hacer eternidad, vamos a hacer la eternidad, vamos a ser eternidad, vamos a ser la eternidad? ¡Vosotras, yo, podemos crear la eternidad una y mil veces, cuando queramos! ¡Todo es nuestro y no se nos acaba nunca! ¡Amor, contigo y con la luz todo se hace, y lo que haces amor, no acaba nunca! (*Op*, II, 4: 1275–6)

I, immense universe, inside, outside of you, who are safe immensity! Images of love within a concrete presence; highest grace and glory of the image, are we going to make eternity, to make the eternity, to become eternal, to become the eternal? You, I, are capable of creating eternity one and a thousand times, whenever we want to! Everything is ours and there is no end to it! Love, with you and with the light all can be made, and what you make, love, never ends! (*T&S*: 62)

In this passage poetry is conjoined with the Romantic notion of love, a conjunction that Jiménez arguably read in Shelley's essay "On Love" (1829).[16] In this way, the first fragment finishes in an ecstatic mood affirming the pantheistic worldview: the lyrical subject is immersed into a world where spirit and nature, consciousness and matter are one.

Fragmento 3° / 3rd Fragment
In contrast with the rhapsodic expression dominating the first and second fragments, the initial passages of the "Fragmento tercero" are repetitive phrases connoting orality: "«Y para recordar porqué he venido», estoy diciendo yo. «Y para recordar porqué he nacido», conté yo un poco antes, ya por La Florida" (*Op*, II, 4: 1277) ("And to remem-

ber why I came," I am saying. "And to remember why I was born," I said earlier, already in Florida) (*T&S*: 65). These sentences are variations of the beginning of the second fragment: "Y para recordar porqué he vivido" (*Op*, II, 4: 1276) (And to remember why I have lived). In the context of the second fragment this sentence refers to a reflection upon individual existence and its higher sense, but in the third fragment the variation of the phrase produces a series of puzzling statements. The cited passage could resemble the inner monologue of a forgetful person trying to recall the reason why he finds himself in a determinate place, especially by the tautological "estoy diciendo yo" (I am saying). The specificity of the place and the colloquial "un poco antes" (a little earlier) must be understood as ironic elements with respect to the pretentious claim stated within the quotation marks. The sentences framed by quotation marks entail an idea of personal destiny,[17] whereas what follows after them establishes a colloquial tone that contrasts strongly with that claim. In addition, the words "un poco antes" (a little earlier) can be regarded as a self-referential statement, that is, as the assertion of the author having written the second fragment "a little earlier" (in fact ten years earlier if the publication of the third fragment with respect to the second one corresponds to a similar interval in the writing). In this way the self-parodying mode that is introduced with the very first phrases effects a distantiation from the first two fragments.

In consequence, the notion of a divine poet-subject is represented parodically a few sentences later in the text, as in a self-ironic observation:

El mar, el sol, la luna, y ella y yo, Eva y Adán, al fin y ya otra vez sin ropa, y la obra desnuda y la muerte desnuda, que tanto me atrajeron. Desnudez es la vida y desnudez la sola eternidad... Y sin embargo, están, están, están, están llamándonos a comer, gong, gong, gong, gong, en este barco de este mar, y hay que vestirse en este mar, en esta eternidad de Adán y Eva, Adán de smoking, Eva... (*Op*, II, 4: 1277)

The sea, the sun, the moon, and she and I, Eve and Adam, at last, and again without clothes, and my naked work and naked death that pulled me so strongly. Life is nakedness, and lonely eternity is nakedness... And yet, they are, they are, they are, they are calling us to lunch, gong, gong, gong, gong, on this ship of this sea, and one needs to put on clothes, in this sea, in the eternity of Adam and Eve, Adam in a smoking jacket, Eve... (*T&S*: 65)

The beginning of this passage presents a series of topoi of the absolute in Jiménez's work, symbols of essentiality and eternity: the sea, the sun, the moon, original man and woman, and "la obra desnuda" (my naked work). Conversely, the sentence after the suspension points establishes an explicit contrast ("Y sin embargo" (And yet)) to this sublime vision that must be interrupted because dinner time has arrived. The fourfold repetition of "están" (they are) with its semantics of presentness and contingency (the verb "estar" designates the state something happens to be in, while "ser" is used to express an essential characteristic of something) underscores the specific spatiotemporal situatedness of the individual, subject to both physical needs and social conventions such as eating times and dress codes. Furthermore, Jiménez expresses a self-ironic view on his own poeto-metaphysics, since in the rest of his output the sea is connected to the notion of the *Obra* as well as to a personal and lyrical renewal.[18] Conversely, in the present passage the sea is as trivial as the social habits regulating life aboard a transatlantic liner, entailing that a change has occurred with respect to the lyrical subject's self-concept. If in *Animal de fondo* and in the first and second fragments of *Espacio* the lived experiences become one with cosmic rhythm and with the *Obra*,[19] now the subject expresses the inescapable contingency of poetry and of life itself.

Following this passage, a chaotic enumeration of autobiographical memories appears:

> ¡Qué estraño es todo esto, mar, Miami! No, no fue allí en Sitjes, Catalonia, Spain, en donde se me apareció mi mar tercero, fue aquí ya; era este mar, este mar mismo, mismo y verde, verdemismo; no fue el Mediterráneo azulazulazul, fue el verde, el gris, el negro Atlántico de aquella Atlántida. Sitjes fue, donde vivo ahora, Maricel, esta casa de Deering, española, de Miami, esta Villa Vizcaya aquí de Deering, española aquí en Miami, aquí, de aquella Barcelona. (*Op*, II, 4: 1277–8)

> How strange, all of this, sea, Miami! No, it was not in Sitjes, Catalonia, Spain, that my third sea appeared to me, it had already happened here; it was this sea, this same sea, same and green, green-same; it was not the blue, blue, blue Mediterranean, it was the green, the gray, the black Atlantic of that Atlantida. Sitjes, it was, where I am living now, Maricel, in this house of Deering, this Spanish house in Miami, this Villa Vizcaya, the house of Deering, here, in that [distant] Barcelona. (*T&S*: 65–6)

According to the principle of the universal analogy, poetic language should not aim at a deictic function but at coincidence with the hidden language of nature, which is achieved through rhythmical patterns and figurativity.[20] Nothing that could make the reader think of such a possibility appears in this passage. Rhythm is broken into pieces by the sudden appearance of two words in English and by the groping diction that once more suggests a forgetful person trying to recall a past event deeply hidden in memory. Figurativity is not unfolded either; a slide at the level of the signifier is the closest to it: "mismo y verde, verdemismo" (same and green, greensame). The latter neologism refers to the green colour of the Atlantic Ocean. Synaesthesia and metaphor are the privileged tropes of the transport between heavenly and earthly, spiritual and sensory realms, but neither of these tropes appear here. Instead of the synaesthetic fusion of the senses, a plain repetition of the colour of the sea is uttered, "azulazulazul" (blue, blue, blue), as if the poetic force of the lyrical was exhausted and the only means of expressing the colour of the sea was to repeat its signifier in order to emphasize its signification. Even more forthright is the description of the Atlantic Ocean: "el verde, el gris, el negro Atlántico" (the green, the gray, the black Atlantic). The mighty lyrical I that was able to connect celestial and earthly realms thanks to the poetic imagination, to the "naming anew" of the world ("Que mi palabra sea / la cosa misma, / creada por mi alma nuevamente" (Let my word be / the thing itself, / created anew by my soul), *Op*, I, 2: 377), is here degraded to a subject stuttering phrases that conspicuously lack lyrical elevation.

Even if the beginning of the *fragmento tercero* parodies the integration of subject and universe, a transition to a joyful celebration of the communication with nature appears at a later moment with the following passage, which is a true *tour de force* of metaphorical and synaesthetical connections:

> ¡Cómo pasa este ritmo, este ritmo, río mío, fuga de faisán de sangre ardiendo por mis ojos, naranjas voladoras de dos pechos en uno, y qué azules, qué verdes y qué oros diluídos en rojo, a qué compases infinitos! Deja este ritmo timbres de aires y de espumas en los oídos, y sabores de ala y de nube en el quemante paladar, y olores a piedra con rocío, y tocar, cuerdas de olas. (*Op*, II, 4: 1279)

> How this rhythm flows, this rhythm, my river, blood pheasants in flight burning my eyes, flying oranges from two joined breasts, and

how blue, green, golden and fused into reds, and how it moves to infinite measures! This rhythm leaves behind sounds of air and foam in the ears, and the taste of wings and clouds in the burning palate, and the smell of stone with dew, and to touch, strings of waves. (*T&S*: 67–8)

The word "ritmo" (rhythm) triggers an array of images, some of which are intelligible while others resist interpretation and recall the hermeticism of automatic writing. Semantically this excerpt is dominated by an isotopy of movement that can be related to the renewing force of both nature and poetry. The isotopy develops as follows (the words carrying the isotopy are in bold): "**pasa** este **ritmo**" : "**río** mío" : "**fuga** de faisán de sangre **ardiendo** por mis ojos" : "naranjas **voladoras** de dos pechos en uno" (this **rhythm flows** : my **river** : blood pheasants **in flight burning** my eyes : **flying** oranges from two joined breasts). These sentences, which seem to defy interpretation, should be read as a sign of the powerful linguistic creativity of the lyrical subject. At the same time, however, their hermetism or irrationality points to a loss of control of the poet-subject with respect to the mastery of his art. In comparison with the first and second fragments, where a sense of intelligibility guides the reader through the figurative and rhythmic constellations, now it is as if language runs loose, uncontrolled by the master subject.

In keeping with this verbal outbreak, a surprising double appears:

Dentro de mí hay uno que está hablando, hablando, hablando ahora. No lo puedo callar, no se puede callar. Yo quiero estar tranquilo con la tarde, esta tarde de loca creación, (no se deja callar, no lo dejo callar). Quiero el silencio en mi silencio, y no lo sé callar a éste, ni se sabe callar. ¡Calla, segundo yo, que hablas como yo y que no hablas como yo; calla, maldito! Es como el viento ese con la ola; el viento que se hunde con la ola inmensa; ola que sube inmensa con el viento; ¡y qué dolor de olor y de sonido, qué dolor de color, y qué dolor de toque, de sabor de ámbito de abismo!¡De ámbito de abismo! (*Op*, II, 4: 1279–80)

Within me there is one that is speaking, speaking, speaking now. I cannot silence it, it cannot silence itself. I wish to be at peace with this afternoon, this afternoon of mad creation (it does not allow me to silence it, I do not let it be silent). I wish for silence in my silence, and I am not about to silence it, nor does it know how to silence itself. Be silent, my second self, for you speak as I do and you do not speak as I do; be silent, I curse you! It is like that wind with the wave; the wind that sinks with the immense wave; the wave that climbs immensely with the wind; and what pain of smells and sounds, what pain of color, pain of touch, of taste of space and the abyss! Space of the abyss! (*T&S*: 68)

This passage can be understood as the text's critical self-reflection, exposing a lyrical subject split between an I emptied out in poetic creativity ("uno que está hablando, hablando, hablando ahora" (one that is speaking, speaking, speaking now) and an I desiring only contemplation ("Yo quiero estar tranquilo con la tarde, esta tarde de loca creación" (I wish to be at peace with this afternoon, this afternoon of mad creation)).[21] In a similar way as the lyrical subject has lost control over language, he has also lost his unity and is incapable of acting as he wishes: "No lo puedo callar, no se puede callar" (I cannot silence it, it cannot silence itself). A variation on this sentence appears shortly after as "no se deja callar, no lo dejo callar" (I am not about to silence it, nor does it know how to silence itself), reformulating the impossibility of acting upon the other into an ambiguous allowance to speak. The integrated and absolute subject that dominated the previous fragments becomes a split subject without control over himself or his creation. The sense of unity with cosmic totality is no longer believed, and language is perceived as beyond the subject's control. The last sentences of this passage express anguish, as if self-parody and critical self-consciousness led to such a painful state of mind. The divine poetic consciousness speaking in *Animal de fondo* and in the first two fragments of *Espacio* has now been replaced by an ironic and fragmented subject who faces nothingness and contingency.

Continuing in the same direction, this *fragmento* carries out yet another turn of textual self-consciousness, articulated in the final part of the poem. After a disheartening description of a human dwelling the celebrated crab episode starts:[22]

Un cáncer, ya un cangrejo y solo, quedó en el centro gris del arenal, más erguido que todos, más abierta la tenaza sérrea de la mayor boca de su armario; los ojos, periscopios tiesos, clavando su vibrante enemistad en mí. Bajé lento hasta él, y con el lápiz de mi poesía y de mi crítica, sacado del bolsillo, le incité a que luchara. No se iba el david, no se iba el david del literato filisteo. Abocó el lápiz amarillo con su tenaza, y yo lo levanté con él cojido y lo jiré a los horizontes con impulso mayor, mayor, mayor, una órbita mayor, y él aguantaba. Su fuerza era tan poca para mí más tan poco ¡pobre héroe! ¿Fui malo? Lo aplasté con el injusto pie calzado, sólo por ver qué era. Era cáscara vana, un nombre nada mas, cangrejo; y ni un adarme, ni un adarme de entraña; un hueco igual que cualquier hueco; un hueco en otro hueco. (*Op*, II, 4: 1283)

A cancer, only one crab now, stayed alone in the gray center of the dune, more erect than the others, the sawing claws of the widest mouth of his armor more open than the others; his eyes, stiff periscopes, nailed me with their vibrant enmity. I lowered myself slowly and taking the pencil for writing poetry and criticism out of my pocket, enticed him to fight. David would not leave, this David against the literary philistine would not leave. The pencil ended up yellow in his claws and I lifted him, caught on it, and twisted him around the horizon at greater speed, greater, greater, a larger orbit, and he hung on there. His strength seemed so small to me, so much smaller, poor hero! Was I evil? I smashed him with an unjust foot in its shoe, only to find out what he was. He was a vain shell, a name only, crab; not a speck, not even a speck of gut; a hole the same as any other hole, a hole within a hole. (*T&S*: 71–2)

In a most suggestive analysis, O'Hara (1987) interprets the crab as an *alter ego* of the poet-subject, in parallel with the talkative double just mentioned. At first the crab is killed by the lyrical subject, the "literato filisteo" (literary philistine), who reveals it as "cáscara vana, un nombre nada más, cangrejo" (a vain shell, a name only, crab). The death of the crab provokes an "innúmero silencio hueco" (innumerable hollow silence), after which the lyrical subject occupies what hitherto had been the position of the crab: "Yo sufría que el cáncer era yo, y yo un jigante que no era sólo yo y que me había a mí pisado y aplastado" (*Op*, II, 4: 1284) (I suffered thinking the Cancer was I, and that I was a giant who was not an I alone, and that I had smashed and stepped on myself) (*T&S*: 72). These sentences imply the capitulation of the lyrical subject. The "jigante que no era sólo yo" (giant who was not an I alone) can be interpreted, as O'Hara remarks, as the coming reader who will take in the text that the authorial subject no longer possesses. As a textual product, the lyrical subject is only language, dependent on a reader to be brought alive, and as such all but absolute. The reading subject is a living consciousness, whereas the textual subject belongs to the immateriality of language. This is the reason why the final part of *Espacio* is formed as a series of questions and apostrophes to consciousness, "conciencia", which represents the textual subject that is bound to leave the authorial subject and be incarnated in the future readers.[23] The idealist notion of the lyrical subject, stated in the first and second fragments, is here transformed, giving rise to a lamentation of the subject's ephemeral nature in its being bound to the empirical order. As a consequence the lyrical subject is not any longer presented as a divine consciousness but rather as a reader who passes a text on to another reader:

> Ya te lo dije al comenzar: «Los dioses no tuvieron más sustancia que la que tengo yo». ¿Y te has de ir de mí tú, tú a integrarte en un dios, en otro dios que este que somos mientras tú estás en mí, como de Dios? (*Op*, II, 4: 1285)

> I already told you in the beginning: "the gods had no more substance than I have." And must you leave me you, you to become part of a god, a different god from the one we are while you are in me, as if from God? (*T&S*: 73)

The sacralization of the poet-subject or the "finding" of the divine through poetry has thus been considerably diminished in comparison with the first and second fragments of *Espacio*. This fragment can be related to the existential attitude that Sánchez Barbudo, among others, has noted in relation to Jiménez's last years – his frequent depressions caused by the exile and Zenobia's illness, but probably also by the disillusionment with respect to the religious understanding of poetry:

> Cuando uno muere lo que queda es supremo «abono», ejemplo para otros. Y esta «cesión de la antorcha», decía, es su «concepción constante de la vida». Una concepción de la vida más bien triste, decimos nosotros; salvo para él quizás, y eso sólo en ciertos momentos de entusiasmo, cuando se sentía iluminado, como debía él sentirse cuando pronunciaba esas palabras en Buenos Aires, después de su encuentro con el «dios deseante», después de esa experiencia de total identificación de su alma con la belleza. Un estado de iluminación que, como sabemos, no le duró mucho. (Sánchez Barbudo 1981: 129–30)

When one dies what is left is the highest "manure", example for others. And this "handing over the torch", he said, is his "constant notion of life". A rather sad notion of life, we would say; except for him perhaps, and only in certain enthusiastic moments, when he felt enlightened as he must have felt when he pronounced these words in Buenos Aires, after his encounter with the "god desiring", after that experience of total identification of his soul with beauty. A state of enlightenment that, as we know, did not last long.

This abandonment of the belief in the utopian potentialities of art led Jiménez to the highest degree of self-reflection, to the deconstruction of his own idealist presuppositions. Even the final composition of *Espacio* works in this way, since the juxtaposition of the first two fragments with the third is an undermining of the principle of the universal analogy that is expressed in the first two parts. The present analysis should have shown how the first fragment – just like "Primavera y sentimiento" – oscillates between faith in art and nihilistic pathos. Conversely, the third fragment undermines this pendular movement and reveals both the idealist notion of the artist and the tragic sense of contingency as arbitrary constructions, carrying in this way the modern paradigm to its logical conclusions.

As will be discussed in the next chapter, *Espacio* may also be understood as an attempt to reconcile absolute subjectivity with the individual life course. In the third fragment the word *Destino* (Destiny) appears several times, but mostly in a parodic sense:

> Mi Destino soy yo y nada y nadie más que yo; por eso creo en Él y no me opongo a nada suyo, a nada mío, que Él es más que los dioses de siempre, el dios otro, rejidos, como yo por el Destino, repartidor de la sustancia con la esencia. En el principio fue el Destino, padre de la Acción y abuelo o bisabuelo o algo más allá, del Verbo. (*Op*, II, 4: 1278)

> Destiny is I and nothing nor anyone other than I; this is why I believe in It, and do not oppose anything that belongs to It, that belongs to me, for He is more than the customary gods, ruled as I am by Destiny, that other god, a distributor of substance with essence. In the beginning was Destiny, father of Action and grandfather or great-grandfather of something even more distant, of the Word. (*T&S*: 66)

Destiny is characterized as a "repartidor" (distributor), that is, as a milkman or a paperboy, with the difference that what it distributes is "la sustancia con la esencia" (substance with essence) – which is tautological nonsense. Similarly, destiny is inserted into a parodic reference to the beginning of the Gospel of St John. The inference is that the authorial figure that can be deduced from the third fragment is similar to the anti-author of the Avant-Gardes, as it is an author that – to an important degree – is self-parodying. The loss of control of language and the chaotic enumeration of autobiographical elements can be related to a general development of Avant-Garde literature and poststructuralist philosophy that emerges as a consequence of the breakdown of the philosophy of consciousness:

> In the wake of the disintegration of transcendental subjectivity, the analysis is directed to an anonymous occurring of language, an occurring that releases worlds from within itself and swallows worlds back up, which is superordinate to every ontic history and to every innerworldly practice, which reaches through everything, through the now porous borders of the ego, of the author and of his work. (Habermas 1992: 209)

In the third fragment of *Espacio*, Jiménez draws a completely similar consequence of the breakdown of the idealist I as the one described by Habermas. The uncontrolled and seemingly arbitrary word connections are the manifestation of a freewheeling language without the control of a rational consciousness. Also in this way is the paradigm of the modern subject carried to its final conclusions in Jiménez's production. The subject who was split between the aim for the absolute and the consciousness of being a finite I, now abandons the ambition to rise from contingency to necessity. As a consequence, a helpless lyrical subject utters a series of more or less articulate language bits. As a kind of Barthesian *écriture*, the third fragment of *Espacio* presents an authorial subject who gives up the control of the text production and lets symbols, metaphors and autobiographical pieces merge in an apparent disorder.[24] This is very similar to poststructuralist thought which gives up rationality and lets the *other* of reason be its metaphysical principle.

In this chapter, the subject of the modern paradigm has been analyzed as oscillating between pantheistic celebration and nihilistic self-emptying. In both "Primavera y sentimiento" and in *Espacio* the modern sceptical attitude towards any totalizing world-understanding leads to regarding subjectivity as an unsubstantial consciousness that artificially constructs or projects sense onto a meaningless universe. At the same time it is seen how the modern notion of self-consciousness, if its absolutization is to be preserved, can lead to a textual paradigm. In this respect, the purely textual subject of "Sé bien que soy tronco" is a coherent consequence of modern thought. In sum, the definition of a consciousness that founds itself may lead to (or is perhaps the product of) a wish for omnipotence as well as to scepticism.

CHAPTER FOUR

Poetic Time and Eternal Return

> *And so he [Heidegger] was also unable to grasp why it is that only a subjectivistically heightened and radically differentiated art, which consistently develops the meaning proper to the aesthetic dimension out of the self-experience of a decentered subjectivity, recommends itself as the inaugurator of a new mythology.*
>
> Jürgen Habermas

The break with linear time – measured by clocks and calendars – is a constant in modern literature, either as an articulation of a "now" (as in Symbolism and the Avant-Gardes) or as a fragmentation of chronological time (as in the Modernist novels). In both cases a subjective time-experience separate from the course of chronological temporality is represented. From the perspective of the present study, the treatment of time in modern literature can be considered to have its origin in the paradigm of the self-founded subject. Habermas has noted how the experience of a moment radically separated from everyday time-experience is a development of Romantic thought, carried out by both Nietzschean philosophy and modern artistic expression:

> What Nietzsche calls the "aesthetic phenomenon" is disclosed in the concentrated dealings with itself of a decentered subjectivity set free from everyday conventions of perceiving and acting. Only when the subject *loses* itself, when it sheers off from pragmatic experience in space and time, when it is stirred by the shock of the sudden, when it considers "the longing for true presence" (Octavio Paz) fulfilled and,

oblivious to itself, is transported by the moment; only when the categories of intelligent doing and thinking are upset, the norms of daily life have broken down, the illusions of habitual normality have collapsed – only then does the world of the unforeseen and the absolutely astonishing open up, the realm of aesthetic illusion, which neither hides nor reveals, is neither appearance nor essence, but nothing other than surface. Nietzsche continues the Romantic purification of the aesthetic phenomenon from all theoretical and practical associations. In the aesthetic experience, the Dionysian reality is shut off by a "chasm of forgetfulness" against the world of theoretical knowledge and moral action, against the everyday. Art opens access to the Dionysian only at the cost of ecstasy – at the cost of a painful de-differentiation, a de-delimitation of the individual, a merging with amorphous nature within and without. (Habermas 1990: 93–4)

In this passage, reference is made to the autonomy of art in Modernity ("the Romantic purification of the aesthetic phenomenon from all theoretical and practical associations"), which is a consequence of Kantian philosophy. According to Kant, aesthetics has its own sphere of validity – that of aesthetic judgement – that differentiates it from the realm of ethics (which is governed by practical reason) and from the sphere of knowledge (which is under the rule of theoretical reason). At the same time, these three domains complement each other because even if the human subject cannot attain any theoretical knowledge of God, natural beauty still transmits a feeling of the createdness of nature (cf. above p. 37f.). Therefore, even if aesthetics is not completely autonomous in Kant's philosophy, the consequence for subsequent thought is that the feeble connection between the three spheres becomes lost, and art becomes entirely separated from the domains of knowledge and ethics.[1]

This autonomy of the work of art entails that the artist is set free to create an entirely self-sufficient and self-referential realm which, in turn, may give shelter to the experience of the extraordinary, as explained by Habermas above. The domain of the extraordinary, a realm earlier belonging to religion, now becomes colonized by the aesthetic experience. This substitution of religion with aesthetics has the consequence that in the aesthetic experience the subject and subject-centred reason is transgressed and transcended. The finitude of the subject is underscored in the spheres of practical and theoretical reason, but the aesthetic experience suspends this burden.[2] For this reason, in the aesthetic experience anthropocentric thought gives way to an impersonalist and irrationalist metaphysics as the one that can be observed in Nietzsche's philosophy or in many movements of modern art. In turn, once the aesthetic expression is associated with the transgression of subject-centred reason, the dissolution of individuality becomes a logical consequence. Such a self-dissolving individual has appeared through the analyses of the previous chapter. In a parallel way, when the question of temporality is addressed, either the individual vanishes in consonance with universal rhythm in a pantheistic understanding, or the subject is detached from its empirical features in a textually created "now" sustained by a monadic rhythmical pattern of sound and meaning.

A famous passage in St Augustine's *Confessions* is relevant with respect to the understanding of how a poetic text can create an autonomous realm of time.[3] In the following lines, St Augustine defines the notion of time in a way that has decisively inspired twentieth-century philosophy on the issue of temporality, from Husserl to Ricoeur:

> Suppose I am about to recite a psalm which I know. Before I begin, my expectation is directed towards the whole. But when I have begun, the verses from it which I take into the past become the object of my memory. The life of this act of mine is stretched two ways, into my memory because of the words I have already said and into my expectation because of those which I am about to say. But my attention is on what is present: by that the future is transferred to become the past. As the action advances further and further, the shorter the expectation and the longer the memory, until all expectation is consumed, the entire action is finished, and it has passed into the memory. What occurs in the psalm as a whole occurs in its particular pieces and its individual syllables. The same is true of a longer action in which perhaps that psalm is a part. (Augustine 1998: 243 / XI, xxviii (38))

In the tradition of Western thought, two different notions of temporality can be traced. On one side appears the realistic notion of time, measured on the basis of astronomical observations. On the other side is a subjective conception that explains temporality in relation to inner time-experience.[4] The quoted passage from the *Confessions* prefigures the phenomenological notion of temporality since time is understood in relation to the unity of three different attentions: the attention towards the now, towards the earlier and towards the later.[5] These three attentions constitute a unity since the consciousness of the present moment implies an awareness of something prior and of something that will follow. As can be inferred from the example given by St Augustine, in poetry, rather than objective temporality, the time of consciousness is represented. Poetry exhibits the succession *and* co-presence of past, present and future in consciousness. The phonetic and thematic rhythm of a poetic text creates a pattern of expectations – through the retention of the repetitions and variations – prefiguring the part of the text that is to come. In this way the present of the reading or hearing of a poem is the overlap of the "no-more" and the "not-yet" of the text, and this co-presence of past and future guides the perception and understanding of the text. The temporal articulation of a poem can be said to consist on one side of a linear segment, in the sense of objective time, but also, on the other side, of a creation of an autonomous, subjective temporality. A poem is also a "monadic time"[6] that in one sense suspends limitless time-flow, because in it a temporal realm separated from unending linear temporality is preserved.

Symbolism represents a world that is devoid of a perspective endowed by either theoretical or practical rationality. A thoroughly unstable world is transmitted by an equally unstable subject. For this reason the texts produced by this aesthetic movement represent a world without firm contours and subdued by an all-consuming temporality. Only the volatile subjective experience has reality status, everything else is permanent change. In consequence, mutability and subjective temporality are features of Jiménez's entire output, as will be shown in the present chapter. The three poems that will be analyzed in the following pages all represent a sunset, that is, they display the question of subjective finitude. The implicit challenge is whether the finite subject is able to create a self-sufficient world with its own temporality separated from the empirical order of things.

Arias tristes, **3** / *Sad Airs,* **3 (1903)**

¿Está muy lejos la aldea?
–¡Oh, muy lejos!
                Una flauta
llora en la paz del sendero
su queja dormida y lánguida.
    Y entre la tarde de otoño
llena de sueño y nostalgia,
sube un humo dulce y blanco

del techo de la cabaña.
    Las cabras han vuelto, y suenan
todas las esquilas; llama
alguien lastimeramente,
tiembla una estrella temprana.
    Y la música de esquilas
y la estrella solitaria
y el humo que sube, todo
tiembla al compás de la flauta.
    El vaho de la arboleda
vela la fronda lejana,
alejando dulcemente
la ribera abandonada.
    La campiña se ha dormido,
y su paz amiga es tanta
que, mirándola, los ojos
se llenan de dulces lágrimas.
    –¿Está muy lejos la aldea?
–¡Muy lejos!
              Sobre la plácida
tristeza de la campiña
sube la luna dorada.
(*Op*, I, 1: 168–9)

Is the hamlet very far away?
– Oh, very far away!
                A flute
cries in the peaceful path
its sleeping and languid lament.
    And throughout the autumn evening
full of dream and nostalgia,
a sweet and white smoke rises
from the roof of the cottage.
    The goats have returned, and all
the sheep bells sound; somebody
calls mournfully,
an early star trembles.
    And the music of sheep bells
and the solitary star
and the rising smoke, everything

trembles at the flute's rhythm.
   The mist of the grove
veils the distant thicket,
moving away sweetly
the abandoned bank.
   The landscape has fallen asleep
and its friendly peace is such
that, looking at it, the eyes
are filled with sweet tears.
   – Is the hamlet very far away?
– Very far away!
               Over the placid
sadness of the landscape
the golden moon rises.

This poem depicts one of the many bucolic scenes that appear in Jiménez's writings between 1902 and 1912 – in this case in the form of a "romance".[7] The lyrical subject is in a natural landscape at dusk, far away from civilization. The only human dwelling referred to in the text, a hamlet, lies "muy lejos" (very far away). This text is characterized by a high degree of suggestiveness and subjective impressions, features, as has already been mentioned, of *fin de siècle* literature and art. The question initiating the poem, repeated towards the end, indicates that the lyrical subject is on a journey, and that the goal, perhaps, is the mentioned village. The lyrical subject monopolizes the text completely as neither his interlocutor nor the voice calling "lastimeramente" (mournfully) are identified. In the same way the musician is represented metonymically, as he only appears by means of the flute that sounds across the landscape. Furthermore, the representation of the scenery is dominated by the gentle sadness of the lyrical subject, who experiences the evening as "llena de sueño y nostalgia" (full of dream and nostalgia) (verse 6), whereby it is self-reflectively acknowledged that this poem is a non-objective, non-realistic representation.

Just as the subjective perspective is a central trait of this poem, transition is also omnipresent. The poem is set at dusk and in autumn, which are transitional periods that lead to one of the poles of a cyclic pattern, day/night and summer/winter. The verbs of the poem are almost exclusively uttered in the present tense (only in verses 9 and 21 is a past tense used, in verse 19 a gerund emphasizes the present of the enunciation). Furthermore, an important part of the verbs denote motion, entailing a state of continuous movement in the scenery: "sube" (rises) (verse 7), "han vuelto" (have returned) (verse 9), "tiembla" (trembles, verse 12), "sube" (rising) (verse 15), "alejando" (moving away) (verse 19), "se llena" (are filled, verse 24), "sube" (rises) (verse 28). Even if stanza six expresses, in contrast to the rest of the poem, a semantics of *stasis*, it is not a definitive immobility but rather a state of harmony that in turn causes the lyrical subject to be emotionally moved. Finally, the last stanza repeats the initial dialogue, and the poem ends with the rising of the moon above the landscape. In this way the poem finishes with a semantics of motion, at the same time that a closure is unequivocally stated. This suggests that the time represented in the poem cannot be identified as only a linear period, running continuously from an earlier moment to a later one, because the repetition of the dialogue at the end of the text – a *retornelo* – indicates the presence of both simultaneity *and* sequentiality.[8] The description between the dialogues could be regarded as a momentary view during the interaction between the interlocutors. An asymmetry, however, can be observed in the absence of the exclamation "¡Oh!" in the second appearance of the dialogue. In addition, the last verses introduce a new element: the moon appearing above the landscape. In this way the co-representation of a monadic time and of a linear temporal segment is expressed.

An analysis of the isotopies present in the text shows a pattern of repetitions creating a thematic rhythm. Two spatial isotopies can be discerned throughout the poem, a horizontal isotopy of distance within earthly limits and a vertical one of ascension towards the heavenly realm. The horizontal isotopy is constituted by a variation on the word "lejos" (far away) (verses 1, 2, 19, 20, 26, 27). In a parallel way the isotopy of ascension also appears through a single word: "sube" (rises) (verses 7, 15 and 28). The homogeneous distribution of the elements that constitute these two isotopies creates a rhythm in the text, as the lexical repetitions produce both a semantic and a phonetic pattern. A third isotopy refers to the lyrical subject's mood of mild melancholy.[9] This isotopy is in turn intertwined with the previously mentioned semantics of transition, motion and distance. In the syntagma "paz del sendero" (peaceful path), the semantics of tranquillity belonging to the noun "paz" (peace) is conjoined with the sense of distance inherent in the concept of path. In the second stanza, the verb "sube" (rises) appears between the syntagmas "llena de sueño y nostalgia" (full of dream and nostalgia) and "humo dulce y blanco" (sweet and white smoke). In stanza five, motion and mood are juxtaposed in the syntagma "alejando dulcemente" (moving away sweetly). As has been mentioned, dynamism is absent in stanza six, but a movement in the realm of feelings occurs, underscoring the presence of the lyrical subject and his emotive perception of the scenery. This is especially clear in the last verses of this stanza, where the lyrical subject asserts that by looking at the landscape "los ojos / se llenan de dulces lágrimas" (the eyes / are filled with sweet tears) (verses 23–24). Finally, stanza seven connects dynamism and mood in the last verses of the poem: "Sobre la plácida / tristeza de la campiña / sube la luna dorada" (Over the placid / sadness of the landscape / the golden moon rises). These final lines condense the melancholic mood and the calm dynamism pervading the text, thus repeating *in nuce* the poem's blending of mood and spatio-temporal dynamism.

The last isotopy to be analysed is that of musical activity. Although it is not as overtly present as the others commented upon, it is essential for the present interpretation. This isotopy is introduced in the first stanza with the sentence "una flauta / llora […] / su queja dormida y lánguida" (A flute / cries […] / its sleeping and languid lament), and reappears in stanza four with the syntagma "todo / tiembla al compás de la flauta" (everything / trembles at the flute's rhythm). These are the only manifestations of this isotopy but the assertion that the entire landscape trembles at the flute's strokes in the latter case (verses 15–16) suggests that it may be more important than the limited number of occurrences might lead one to think. Two interpretative possibilities arise. The music flowing from the flute could be understood as a metaphor for the poetic representation of the landscape, because by appropriating the landscape in a poem, it is precisely made to resonate in a rhythmical pattern. This interpretation, which would identify the musical activity with a metapoetic consciousness, points towards Jiménez's textually self-conscious attitude that has been shown in the previous analyses. At the same time, it would also be possible to interpret the poem in the direction of the pantheistic worldview that has been described above if subject, landscape and artistic activity are regarded as coalescing with cosmic rhythm: "todo / tiembla al compás de la flauta" (everything / trembles at the flute's rhythm).

An analysis of the accentual rhythm of the poem will carry the interpretation further. Being a "romance", evidently the poem is written in octosyllabic verse, including verses 2 and 27, which are *versos escalonados*, that is, each one graphically broken up into two lines that together make one octosyllabic verse.¹⁰ The seventh syllable in each verse is stressed throughout the poem as is required by metric convention. Following Navarro Tomás, the present poem consists of polyrhythmic octosyllabic verses, that is, it combines different metres.¹¹ Furthermore it can be observed that dactylic accentuation (Navarro 1965: 45) appears in verses 3, 6, 12, 16, 18 and 28, and trochaic rhythm (Navarro 1965: 44) in verses 2, 7, 13, 14 and 19–23. The most interesting coincidence between metre and semantic content is that the verse that explicitly mentions rhythm, verse 16, follows a traditionally established, dactylic, rhythmical pattern. It can also be observed that the musical instrument producing the rhythm, the flute, also appears in another verse dominated by a dactylic pattern, verse 3. Another semantic correspondence can be found in verse 12, where the solitary star is said to tremble – like the landscape did in the already mentioned verse 16. Just as these verses follow the dactylic rhythm, so does verse 28 where the moon rises. The coincidence between the accentual pattern in verses 3 and 16, where the flute appears, and the verses where the heavenly bodies appear suggests isomorphy between poetic diction and cosmic movement. In this way the principle of the universal analogy appears, the consonance of poetry with cosmic rhythm, and thereby the possibility of conflating monadic and cosmic temporality. As will be seen below, this idea is displayed in a more explicit way in the second fragment of *Espacio*.

As has been mentioned, a consciousness of linear temporality also appears in this poem. The transition from day to night – which is the actual timespan represented in the text – suggests the individual's transition from life to death, that is, the temporal and finite condition of any individual.¹² This could in turn explain the melancholy pervading an otherwise harmonic description of a beautiful landscape.¹³ This conflict between, on the one hand, a linear time in which the subject finds a limit in his finitude and, on the other, a self-enclosed poetic time is an essential part of this poem since the text develops both in a progression towards the depiction of a scenery that is completed at the end of the poem, and at the same time it enacts patterns of repetition. However, since the text closes with the appearance of the moon, the conclusion must be similar to what was arrived at through the analysis of the poem "Primavera y sentimiento" (commented on above pp. 68f.). The poem describes a series of repetitions and cyclic patterns but eventually it closes with the supremacy of the moon above the landscape, entailing that the representation belongs to the subjective reign of dreaming and poetry. Furthermore, the melancholy that pervades the text is also an indicator of the impossibility of the lyrical subject overcoming finitude, that is, the poem describes a beautiful but impossible wish: to remain in an eternal moment of perfect beauty and harmony.

This interpretation appears confirmed at the level of the macrotext, that is, with respect to the collection *Arias tristes* as a whole. The entirely subjective creation of monadic temporality is asserted in a note, signed "J.R.J.", which precedes the section "Nocturnos":

> Libro monótono, lleno de luna y de tristeza. [...] Los que os hayáis estremecido bajo las estrellas, oyendo venir en la brisa la sonata de un piano, sintiendo qué pobre es la vida entre la noche y ante la muerte; dejad caer la mirada sobre estas rimas iguales, de un mismo color, sin otros matices que los que en la noche surgen confusamente de los macizos del jardín, allá donde están las flores casi ahogadas en la negrura. (*Op*, I, 1: 201)

> Monotonous book, full of moon and sadness. [...] Those of you who have trembled under the stars, hearing a piano sonata coming on the breeze, feeling how poor life is under the night and in front of death, glance at these equal rhymes, of one colour, without other nuances than those that at night blurredly appear in the beds of the garden, where the flowers are almost drowned in blackness.

As this passage states, the poems constituting this collection are very uniform in tone, just as the sceneries described by these texts are very similar to one another. The poems will then appear as moments of subjective contemplation succeeding each other as temporal monads. Every poem creates a suspension of linear time. On the other hand, the note mentions death, both in the literal reference to human mortality ("qué pobre es la vida entre la noche y ante la muerte" (how poor life is under the night and in front of death)) as well as figuratively in the syntagma "las flores casi ahogadas en la negrura" (the flowers [...] almost drowned in blackness), thus implying a final, linear temporality in marked contrast to a poetically achieved, enclosed time. In this way, this note expresses the co-presence of monadic and objective temporality. Furthermore, through this note, the authorial subject who organizes the individual capsules of time and beauty into larger aesthetic units becomes manifest. In this way, a prefiguration of the authorial subject behind the *Obra* appears, that is, a masterful demiurgic subject who is capable of forging an autonomous aesthetic totality. As will be shown in the following, this understanding of the temporality belonging to the poetic genre is continued in subsequent phases of Jiménez's development.

Belleza, 127 / Beauty, 127 (1923)

LA OBRA

Día tras día, mi ala
–¡cavadora, minadora!,
= ¡qué duro azadón de luz!–,
me entierra en el papel blanco…
   –¡Ascensión mía, parada
en futuros del ocaso!–
   … ¡De él, ascua pura inmortal,
quemando el sol de carbón,
volaré refigurado!
(*Op*, I, 2: 793)

THE WORK

Day after day my wing
– ditch digger, cave digger! –
= what a hard mattock of light! –
buries me in the white paper…
   My ascension stopped
in futures of the sunset! –
   … From there, immortal, pure ember,
burning the charcoal sun,
I will fly refigured!

The collections *Poesía* (*Poetry*) and *Belleza* (*Beauty*) (both 1923) are two anthologies of the poetry written between 1917 and the year of their publication. During this period Jiménez worked intensively on his *Obra definitiva* or *total*, the envisaged and never finished collection of his complete works. He must have decided that these two volumes should consist of a selection of the texts that would appear in his *Obra*, since at the beginning of each book a list of titles appears indicating the collections that are represented. One of the titles mentioned is *La obra (1919-*

1920), and it is likely that this collection should have contained all the self-referential poems about the creation of his *Definitive Work*.

The subject matter of the present poem is the ongoing work with the *Obra*. Since this poem expresses a looking forward to the future fulfilment when Jiménez's task is completed, temporality plays a central role. The first stanza gives an account of the lyrical subject's present work on poetry, carried on "[d]ía tras día" (day after day). The second stanza refers in a complicated way to both present and future, while the third stanza refers to the future accomplishment. Prosodically, the poem oscillates between flowing and firm diction since the accentual rhythm of the poem shows established metrical patterns as well as extra- and anti-rhythmical accentuations. Verses 2, 6 and 9 are trochaic, and verse 1 is dactylic. Conversely, verse 4 is characterized by anti-rhythmical accent due to the accentuation of the syllable immediately before the compulsory last accent of the verse (Domínguez Caparrós 2005: 34–5). Similarly, verses 3, 5 and 7 carry extra-rhythmical accents. Corresponding with this rhythmical alternation, the poem exhibits both closure of the verses and complex enjambments. Verses 1 and 4, and 5 and 6, respectively, are connected by an enjambment but the former two are interrupted by verses 2 and 3 – framed by exclamation marks and dashes. Verses 7 and 9 are also syntactically connected but – like verses 1 and 4 – separated by verse 8 which is a parenthetical syntagma.

A semantic correlation with the tension between flowing and firm or even sharp diction can be established, since two isotopies analogous with this duality appear in the text. On the one hand an isotopy of flying appears with the words "ala", "ascensión" and "volaré" (wing, ascension, I will fly), while, on the other, an isotopy of digging is present: "cavadora, minadora", "azadón", "me entierra" (ditch digger, cave digger, mattock, buries me). These two isotopies suggest the life-death duality, but in the present poem this dichotomy is not to be regarded as a polar contradiction, since on closer scrutiny the isotopies of flying and burying are closely interwoven in what could be called an oxymoronic structure. The wing, "mi ala", is metaphorized in verses 2 and 3 as "¡cavadora, minadora!, / ¡qué duro azadón de luz!" (ditch digger, cave digger! / What a hard mattock of light!), because verse 4, continuing the sentence that started the first verse, shows that the action carried out by the lyrical subject's wing is a burying of him. Verses 5 and 6 also effect a similar oxymoronic structure. Verse 5 states that the lyrical subject's ascension is "parada" (stopped), but at the same time the reader is carried to the next verse by means of the enjambment between verses 5 and 6. In an analogous way, the syntagma "futuros del ocaso" (futures of the sunset) must also be interpreted as an oxymoron since the sunset carries a semantics of death and thereby the negation of a future. Finally, the last lines represent a motif of resurrection from death. Here the reader sees the refigured lyrical subject flying, ascending from the death symbolism of the sunset: "quemando el sol de carbon, / volaré refigurado" (burning the charcoal sun, / I will fly refigured).

Rather than regarding the last group of verses as a literal representation of the divine poet-subject triumphing over death and ascending to the heavenly realm thanks to his work on poetry, a more reader-oriented interpretation should be carried out. The text describes poetic creation as related to death because the wing, an image of poetic elevation, is said to bury the lyrical subject: "me entierra en el papel blanco" (buries me in the white paper). In this way, as in poem 122 in *Eternidades* (analyzed above pp. 72f.), the lyrical subject acknowledges his nature as a textual subject. A phenomenological "death" can be said to occur when subjectivity is transported to the surface of a paper. How, then, should the resurrection from this initial burying be explained? The third stanza (verses 7–9) begins with a reference to an element previously mentioned, "él" (there) (verse 7). Although separated from it by two verses, this pronoun refers to "el papel blanco" (the white paper) in verse 4. The suspension points initiating verse 7 can be connected to the suspension points finishing verse 4, whereby verses 5 and 6 are an intercalated clause, formally shown by the dashes opening and closing it (in the same way as verses 2 and 3, also marked by dashes, are intercalated in a full sentence). This means that the lyrical subject's flight takes off from the written page, which could be interpreted as the reader's appropriation of the poem. The resurrection of the lyrical subject refers, then, rather than to a life in the ideal sphere of poetry, to the reader's reliving of the subjectivity "buried" in a poem. Once the authorial subject has been transformed into a textual subject, it can expect a future reliving or resurrection in the readings to come because, through the reading act, the lyrical subject is refigured by the reader's consciousness and his or her personal and cultural horizon.

As has already been mentioned, this poem oscillates between flowing and fixed diction. The first and last two verses are carried by a smooth rhythm,[14] in contrast to verses 3, 4, 5 and 7, which have a much firmer and even disharmonic accentuation. Since the accentual pattern is almost identical in the first and last two verses, a repetition within variation is executed that is parallel to the repetition of the initial dialogue at the end of poem 3 in *Arias tristes*. A circularity is represented that overcomes the alternation between flow and firmness, between harmony and disharmony. Although the sound patterns of a poem possess autonomy and can never be considered merely a function of signification, it is possible to interpret this tension between harmony and disharmony as the author's work on poetry, that on one side is a burying of the individual in the paper (verses 3–4), and on the other will result in a "rebirth". In this way an ending gives way to a new beginning. This circularity or eternal return is represented metrically through the almost identical prosodic beginning and ending of the poem.

Jiménez's tireless work on an *Obra definitiva* is doubtlessly supported by such a desire to escape death through the poetic work.[15] Absolute subjectivity, the idea of a self-founded subject, correlates with the wish to create a complete and self-sufficient product, an Absolute Poetic Work to be preserved for eternity. The lyrical subject inscribed in such a work must be a divine I who has transcended all contingent aspects and all spatiotemporal bindings. Obviously, this subject is no longer an empirical being but belongs to a thoroughly textual universe. At the same time, if the understanding of poetry as a communicative chain is highlighted, then future readers will take up the *Work* and "relive" the absolute subject embedded in the writing. This is underscored by the fact that this poem actually closes the book *Belleza*. The idea of eternal return, a return with infinite variations, is in this way suggested at the same time that the finitude of the authorial subject is asserted.

Espacio, Fragmento 2° / *Space*, 2nd Fragment (1944)

In contrast to the first and third fragments of *Espacio*, in the second one a small narrative is recognizable. The lyrical subject is in New York and watches the Hudson River pass below the George Washington Bridge. He walks around Manhattan and experiences an aesthetic epiphany in the cathedral of St John the Divine. Outside the cathedral the moon has appeared above Morningside Heights (the neighbourhood where St John the Divine is located). The fragment finishes with a series of anaphoric sentences invoking the sun. As mentioned in the previous chapter, allusions and explicit references to Jiménez's life appear regularly throughout *Espacio* and this is also the case here. Mainly, these references concern autobiographical self-reflection: what has been the substance of the life-course? Is the enormous work on poetry through all these years of any value?

This fragment continues the hymnic mood that was reached at the end of the previous one and integrates, towards the end, the notion of eternal return. The title of this fragment, "Cantada", highlights the hymnic character of this part of *Espacio*, and it furthermore suggests musical qualities in a text apparently following the plain diction of prose. Throughout the entire text of *Espacio*, rhythmical patterns play an important role.[16] Lexical repetitions and transformations underscore the rhythmical sense, especially by means of three sentences that are repeated and varied as the text proceeds. These sentences initiate the fragment and are – as mentioned in the previous chapter – some of the refrain-like phrases framed between quotation marks that run through the text:

> «Y para recordar porqué he vivido», vengo a ti, río Hudson de mi mar. «Dulce como esta luz era el amor…» «Y por debajo de Washington Bridge (el puente más con más de esta New York) pasa el campo amarillo de mi infancia.» (*Op*, II, 4: 1276)

> "And to remember why I have lived," I come to you, Hudson River of my sea. "As sweet as this light was love…" "And under the [George] Washington Bridge (the incomparable bridge of this New York) the yellow field of my childhood flows." (*T&S*: 63; translation modified)

The first sentence expresses a work of memory[17] that includes an existential reflection. Such a reflection – that in turn will be parodied in the third fragment – is present in this fragment. The second sentence, "dulce como esta luz era el amor" (as sweet as this light was love), is repeated six times with small variations. As Font has noted (1972: 122) this sentence is, at an autobiographical level, a reference to Jiménez's marriage, which took place in the same city approximately twenty years before he wrote this fragment. At a speculative level, however, this sentence can be related to a Romantic pan-erotic paradigm if love is understood as a pantheistic principle – as mentioned above with reference to Paz and Shelley. At the end of the fragment the lyrical subject utters a series of apostrophes to the sun as a life-giving force, whereby love – being likened to the sun in this refrain-sentence – can be understood as the universal force driving the renewal of cosmic totality.

The last refrain-like sentence that is varied through the text, "Y por debajo de Washington Bridge [...] pasa el campo amarillo de mi infancia" (And under the Washington Bridge [...] the yellow field of my childhood flows) is repeated three times altogether. The Heraclitean flowing water can be regarded as representing the passing of time, and the vision of the "campo amarillo de mi infancia" (yellow field of my childhood), in the waters below the George Washington Bridge refers to Jiménez's remembrance of his Andalusian childhood landscape. The three sentences that have been commented upon can be regarded as complementary symbolic expressions. If a question is expressed about the lyrical subject's life-course, the answer suggested by the other two refrain-sentences relates to the loss and retrieval of things in the temporal flux through a personal remembrance that in turn involves both aesthetic and cosmic levels.

In the paradigm of the universal analogy, the work of poetry takes part in the cosmic creative principle (as was seen in the previous chapter). This understanding is expressed in the second fragment through the description of an aesthetic epiphany:

> En el jardín de St. John the Divine, los chopos verdes eran de Madrid; hablé con un perro y un gato en español; y los niños del coro, lengua eterna, igual del paraíso y de la luna, cantaban, con campanas de San Juan, en el rayo de sol derecho, vivo, donde el cielo flotaba hecho armonía violeta y oro; iris ideal que bajaba y subía, que bajaba... (*Op*, II, 4: 1276)

> In the garden of St. John the Divine, the green poplars were from Madrid; I spoke with a dog and a cat in Spanish; the choir boys' eternal language, the same as in Paradise and on the moon, sang with the bells of St. John following a straight line, a ray of sunlight, where the sky floated in a violet and golden harmony; ideal rainbow descending and climbing, descending... (*T&S*: 64)

The lyrical subject is now in the cathedral of St John the Divine and senses a sublime aesthetic experience through listening to the choir and seeing the light entering the building. In this passage, the overcoming of time and space is related to the boys' choir which sings in the "lengua eterna, igual del paraíso y de la luna" (eternal language, the same as in Paradise and on the moon). This singing is synaesthetically conflated with the light descending from the sun, "cantaban [...] en el rayo de sol derecho" (sang [...] following a straight line, a ray of sunlight), whereby it is inserted in the vertical flow between terrestrial and celestial realms. The lyrical subject is now connected to cosmic rhythm, thus transcending time and space, "los chopos verdes eran de Madrid" (the green poplars were from Madrid), and speaking nature's tongue which is at the same time his own mother tongue: "hablé con un perro y un gato en español" (I spoke with a dog and a cat in Spanish).

At the end of the fragment, the lyrical subject incorporates the consciousness of death into the hymnic mood:

> Salí por Amsterdam, estaba allí la luna (Morningside); el aire ¡era tan puro! frío no, fresco, fresco; en él venía vida de primavera nocturna, y el sol estaba dentro de la luna y de mi cuerpo, el sol presente, el sol que nunca más me dejaría los huesos solos, sol en sangre y él. Y entré cantando ausente en la arboleda de la noche y el río que se iba bajo Washington Bridge con sol aún, hacia mi España por mi oriente, a mi oriente de mayo de Madrid; un sol ya muerto, pero vivo; un sol presente, pero ausente; un sol rescoldo de vital carmín, un sol carmín vital en el verdor; un sol vital en el verdor ya negro, un sol en el negror ya luna; un sol en la gran luna de carmín; un sol de gloria nueva, nueva en otro Este; un sol de amor y de trabajo hermoso; un sol como el amor... «Dulce como este sol era el amor.» (*Op*, II, 4: 1276–7)

> I followed Amsterdam Avenue where the moon was (via Morningside) and the air was so pure! Not cold but fresh, fresh; within it came life of a nocturnal spring with the sun inside the moon and inside my body; the sun present, the sun that would never again abandon my bones, the sun in my blood and my body. And singing absent I entered the grove of the night to see the river going under the [George] Washington Bridge still with sun, always towards my Spain from this East, towards my East in May in Madrid; a sun already dead, yet alive, a sun present yet absent; a sun in embers of vital reds, a red sun vital in the green; a vital sun in the already black green; a sun in the blackness already moon; a sun in the large red moon; a sun of new glory, new in another East; a sun of love and beautiful work, a sun like love... "As sweet as this sun was love."
> (*T&S*: 64)

The representation of the setting sun implies a semantics of death, as was commented upon in Chapter 1. However, in this final passage of the second fragment of *Espacio* the dual opposition of life and death is suspended by a juxtaposition of contraries that can be related to the natural cycles of transformation and regeneration. In a pantheistic expansion of the lyrical subject, the latter incorporates the celestial bodies belonging to day and night into his body: "y el sol estaba dentro de la luna y de mi cuerpo" (the sun inside the moon and inside my body). Immediately after this sentence the lyrical subject disappears into the night, "entré cantando ausente en la arboleda de la noche" (singing absent I entered the grove of the night), which can be interpreted as the dissolution of the I into universal cosmic rhythm. In consequence, the verbs in first person disappear from the text and the reader is taken to an impersonal level of cosmic integration of life and death.

The lines of the fragment following the disappearance of the lyrical subject consist of a chain of oxymorons that aims to conflate life and death through a rhythmic variation within unity, that is, by referring to the cycles of nature. In the first publication of this fragment, the oxymoronic chain was highlighted through the versification:

> un sol ya muerto, pero vivo,
> un sol presente, pero ausente,
> un sol rescoldo de vital carmín,
> un sol carmín vital en el verdor,
> un sol vital en el verdor ya negro,
> un sol en el negror ya luna,
> un sol en la gran luna de carmín,
> un sol de gloria nueva, nueva en otro Este,
> un sol de amor y de trabajo hermoso,
> un sol como el amor...
> Dulce como este sol era el amor.
> (*Op*, II, 4: 1301)

> a sun already dead but alive,
> a sun that is present yet absent,
> a sun in embers of vital reds,
> a red sun vital in the green,
> a vital sun in the already black green,
> a sun in the blackness already moon,
> a sun in the large red moon,
> a sun of new glory, newly risen in another East,
> a sun of beautiful love and work,

a sun like a love...
As sweet as this sun was love.
(T&S: 179)

Two isotopies dominate this passage, an isotopy of life – "sol", "vivo", "presente", "vital", "verdor", "gloria nueva", "Este" (as the cardinal point where the sun rises), "amor" (sun, alive, present, vital, green, new glory, East, love) – and an isotopy of death – "muerto", "ausente", "rescoldo", "negro", "negror" (dead, absent, embers, black, blackness). The rhythmic homogeneity contributes to the dense cohesion of these verses.[18] In the first verses, the word "muerto" (dead) (fourth and fifth syllables) corresponds metrically to "presente" (present) in the second one (third to fifth syllables). Similarly, in the first verse the word "vivo" (alive) (eighth and ninth syllables) occupies the same position with respect to syllabic number and stress as "ausente" (absent) in the second verse (seventh to ninth syllables). A chiasmus thus appears, connecting "muerto" (dead) with "presente" (present) and "vivo" (alive) with "ausente" (absent). In this way Jiménez subverts a mutually exclusive understanding of the dichotomies death/life and presence/absence, as the rhythmical pattern is able to invert their order without any consequences for the pulse of the diction.

But the rhythmical pattern is given not only by accent, also by repetition within variation of syntactic and semantic structures. A series of motifs of life and death sustains the strong rhythmical sense pervading this part of the poem. This chain of transformations starts in the third verse with "vital carmín" (vital reds). In the fourth verse, this syntagma renders "carmín vital en el verdor" (red sun vital in the green), again generating "vital en el verdor ya negro" (vital sun in the already black green) in verse 5. This syntagma produces "negror ya luna" (the blackness already moon) in verse 6, which again becomes "gran luna de carmín" (the large red moon) in verse 7. Although verse 8 continues the anaphoric structure, it stops the transformative chain, as no new element is derived from the syntagma "gran luna de carmín" (the large red moon). This coincides with the disappearance of the death isotopy, no longer present after verse 6. Verse 8 indicates a result of the metamorphoses of the previous verses, since "otro Este" (another East) is invoked, thus indicating a new sunrise, a new beginning. In this way, the idea of the eternal return is expressed. The lyrical subject dissolves into the night, but cosmic rhythm will resonate for ever.

The relation between cyclic temporality and poetry was noted by Jiménez himself in the lecture "La razón heroica": "El mito del retorno, de la eterna juventud, primavera, es el de la poesía misma" (The myth of the return, of the eternal youth, spring, is that of poetry itself) (*Tg*: 119).[19] The idea of the eternal return is an ancient notion belonging to a mythical worldview that appeared in modern thought with Nietzsche's philosophy.[20] Nietzsche's relapse to mythical thought might seem puzzling but "to Nietzsche himself the doctrine of eternal recurrence was the fundamental issue of his philosophy" (Löwith 1955: 214). Through the idea of the eternal return, Nietzsche thought, the individual's contingency is redeemed in a way that avoided the Christian answer to the meaning of human existence. In *Thus Spoke Zarathustra* (1883–85), Nietzsche explains in parables and poems how the individual, through the acceptance of his fate, is reintegrated into cosmic necessity. According to Nietzsche's idea of the eternal return, the universe infinitely repeats its patterns and entities, and the superman is able to form part of cosmic totality, including the eternal recurrence of his own being, if he accepts his fate as his proper destiny. This idea conflates the modern paradigm of the self-founded subject with the archaic thought of infinite cycles. Löwith notes the specifically modern aspect of Nietzsche's version of the eternal return in comparison with that of Antiquity, because "he was unable to develop his vision as a supreme and objective order, as the Greeks did, but introduced it as a subjective ethical imperative" (Löwith 1955: 221). Behind the Nietzschean paradox, then, lies the modern ambition of autonomously elevating the subject's ontological status from contingency to necessity.

At the same time, Nietzsche's philosophy also aims at overcoming modern subject-centred reason. It does so by proposing a return to archaic times, before the history of rationalization began – which Nietzsche sees personified by Socrates and Christ. The reason why rationalization could triumph in the history of Western thought is because it in fact is an astutely masked will to power.[21] By giving art the task of awakening the mythical pasts and archaic experiences, subjectivity, rationality and morality are broken. In modern literature, the motif of eternal return should be related to the Dionysian experience described by Habermas (above pp. 93–4) in which the ordinary experience of the world is suspended. Time loses its linearity and returns upon itself as a circle or as an eternal present. Octavio Paz has remarked how this idea is a feature of modern poetry:

> Frente al tiempo sucesivo e infinito de la historia, lanzada hacia un futuro inalcanzable, la poesía moderna, desde Blake hasta nuestros días, no ha cesado de afirmar el tiempo del origen, el instante del comienzo. El tiempo del origen no es el tiempo de antes: es el de ahora. Reconciliación del principio y del fin: cada ahora es un comienzo, cada ahora es un fin. La vuelta al origen es la vuelta al presente. (Paz 1981: 220)[22]

> In opposition to historical time, successive and infinite, modern poetry since Blake has affirmed the time of origin, the moment of the beginning. The time of origin is not a before, it is a now. It is a reconciliation of the beginning and of the end; every now is a beginning and every now is an end. The return to the beginning is a return to the present. (Paz 1991a: 170)

Apparently, the second fragment of *Espacio* finishes with the pantheistic participation in the natural rhythm of creation and destruction, as it represents the suspension of linear temporality through the enactment of repetitions and variations that together create a cyclic pattern. And yet the fact that the fragment finishes with the last repetition of the refrain-sentence "Dulce como esta luz era el amor" (As sweet as this sun was love) means that it ends just as unambiguously as when a piece of music finally comes to rest on the tonic chord. Through the closure of a text that highlights cyclical repetition, both individual finitude and eternal cosmic return are expressed.

Formally as well as thematically, this fragment finishes in the same way as the third poem in *Arias tristes*, enacting patterns of repetition that suggest a sense of eternal return, and at the same time asserting the finitude of the individual through the ending of the text. Another trait shared by this fragment with "¿Está muy lejos la aldea?" is that it is part of a larger whole. For this reason, it is possible to find cohesive threads that run through the whole of *Espacio*. As has been mentioned, the first fragment leads up to the second fragment with an apostrophe to universal love:

> Imájenes de amor en la presencia concreta; suma gracia y gloria de la imajen, ¿vamos a hacer eternidad, vamos a hacer la eternidad, vamos a ser eternidad, vamos a ser la eternidad? ¡Vosotras, yo, podemos crear la eternidad una y mil veces, cuando queramos! ¡Todo

es nuestro y no se nos acaba nunca! ¡Amor, contigo y con la luz todo se hace, y lo que haces amor, no acaba nunca! (*Op*, II, 4: 1275–6)

Images of love within a concrete presence; highest grace and glory of the image, are we going to make eternity, to become eternity, become eternal, become the eternal? You, images, I, are capable of creating eternity one and a thousand times, whenever we want to! Everything is ours and there is no end to it! Love, with you and with the light all can be made, and what you make, love, never ends! (*T&S*: 62)

In this way the pantheistic principle that appears at the end of the first fragment closes this part of the text and at the same time it throws out the motif that is to be taken up in the next fragment of *Espacio*. In a completely parallel way to the poems in *Arias tristes*, each one of the three fragments can be read independently while they at the same time cohere among themselves. They are three "eternities", three large containers of "monadic time" uniform in style and tone and with themes and motifs in common. The fact that each part of *Espacio* is called a fragment expresses the ambivalence between self-enclosure and interconnection that has just been noted, suggesting the possibility that the text may continue unendingly in successive temporal monads. And yet *Espacio* closes unequivocally in the final lines of the third fragment:

Ya te lo dije al comenzar: «Los dioses no tuvieron más sustancia que la que tengo yo». ¿Y te has de ir de mí tú, tú a integrarte en un dios, en otro dios que este que somos mientras tú estás en mí, como de Dios? (*Op*, II, 4: 1285)

I already told you in the beginning: "The gods had no more substance than I have." And must you leave me, you, to become part of a god, a different god from the one we are while you are in me, as if from God? (*T&S*: 73)

Through the repetition, at the end of *Espacio*, of the sentence that opened the first fragment, Jiménez once more ends the text circularly. In this way he acknowledges that the eternity that he is able to create is that of a capsule of time, a small eternity that will, in spite of everything, pass away. In this sentence the lyrical subject expresses that he will disappear and that the part of his consciousness that is preserved in the text will be contingently apprehended by another subject.

It could be ventured that the intention underlying *Espacio* is the vindication of Jiménez's life as an aesthetically lived totality. Just as everything emerges and disappears, so too the voice that expresses the pantheistic world-feeling must be condensed in certain individuals who also are subject to the cycles of death and renewal. The lyrical subject of *Espacio* cannot be identified with the Nietzschean superman, as his disappearance into the night at the end of the second fragment is a sign of his dissolution.

The pantheistic continuity of life and work and the consequent dissolution of individuality in the writing process is expressed in a text written in 1936, "Prólogo [a un libro no realizado]" (Preface [to a not realized book]):

> Yo no soy, desde luego, un hombre que señala al marjen de su vida tales o cuales circunstancias nacidas de un choque con la realidad en determinados momentos, sino un vocativo de la belleza del mundo que se prepara tanto en la vida para la poesía como en la poesía para la vida, porque tiene la suerte o la desgracia de sentir su conciencia en cada instante. [...] El poeta es un condenado a nombrar y su gloria única, que es gloria interior, está en perder su nombre en el de las cosas, el mundo, hasta quedarse anónimo por su incorporación, incorporarse por lo creado al mundo. (Jiménez 1981: 1211)

> I am not, definitely, a man who highligts by the side of his life, such-and-such circumstances born out of an encounter with reality in certain moments, but a vocative of the beauty of the world who prepares equally in life for poetry as in poetry for life, because he has the luck or the misfortune to feel his consciousness at any moment. [...] The poet is one who is doomed to name, and his only glory, which is inner glory, is to lose his name in that of things, the world, until becoming anonymous because of his incorporation, to be incorporated by the created to the world.

In this context, poetry, subject and nature are manifestations of cosmic life-forces, and for this reason the appearance of autobiographical elements in Jiménez's texts represents the participation of the individual in this universal dynamics that in the end leads to the dissolution of the subject in pantheistic eternal recurrence.

CHAPTER FIVE

Poetic Memory

The Kantian subject has no identity in the sense of a *self*, characterized by a series of individuating traits and a personal history.[1] The course from the *cogito* to the *self* has been traversed by Paul Ricoeur in *Oneself as Another* (1990). In this work, Ricoeur defines a notion of identity that includes the notion of temporality. By understanding the subject in terms of temporality, it then neither appears as a static subjectivity across the transformations of time, nor as a non-identity characterized only by permanently changing thoughts, feelings and desires. This suggests how Ricoeur distances himself from the tradition of the philosophy of the subject, which regards subjectivity as a self-founded and autonomous I. Instead, Ricoeur considers identity as based on two main notions, *idem* and *ipse*. *Idem* is the character of a given person or, in Ricoeur's phrasing, the *what* of the *who* (Ricoeur 1994: 122). *Ipse*, on the other hand, represents the ethical part of the individual, that part which is true to the promises made. Narrative identity, in turn, is displayed between these two concepts and is what gives an account of a self possessing continuity across time. For this reason, memory plays a central role in providing an identity.

In keeping with this line of thought, this chapter will consider whether Jiménez in his poetry arrives at the description of a self, that is, of a mnemonically given identity. For this reason a different temporal dimension than that of monadic time has to be focused upon. A self must be articulated through the lived experiences, and if this is to be carried out within poetic discourse then a reference to external time is necessary. This does not imply that a poem should be regarded as a direct recording of autobiographical events, but the motif of recollection (whether fictional or autobiographical) necessarily sustains a reference (whether invented or real) to the time measured by watches and calendars. A recollection seeks to be fixed in shared historical time, and for this reason the literary elaboration of memory will establish a connection to the course of time in exterior reality.

However, in the first section of this chapter, as a result of the exploration of the theme of memory in Jiménez's poetry, a notion of memory separated from historical time will be analyzed. In Jiménez's early poems a description of recollection appears that seemingly is based upon a Platonic paradigm and its notion of *anamnesis*. As will be shown, it in fact is a consequence of the idea of the inner realm as the only absolute. By means of the analysis of this "memory of the absolute", an explication of the change of mood and style from the early to the mature works will be effected. At the end of the first section of this chapter, a comparison will furthermore be drawn between Jiménez's mature production and Derrida's critique of transcendental subjectivity as a self-presence in the "now". In order to consider the question of selfhood, the second section of this chapter will carry out an analysis of the work *Diario de un poeta recién casado* (*Diary of a Newlywed Poet*) (1917). The *Diario* is regarded as a central work in Jiménez's evolution, as it is generally considered to inaugurate the *segunda época*. The *Diario* is, from its generic outset, a work of memory and temporality, since the diary genre has the task of retaining a given person's impressions and thoughts from oblivion. Through the autobiographical and historical references found in the *Diario*, a direct immersion in the time of exterior reality appears that connects inner time-experience with historical temporality. Apparently, then, this work could seem to mark a break with the textual *poesía pura* that otherwise characterizes his mature poetry. It will be shown, nonetheless, how the *Diario* – in a number of central traits – in fact fits in with the rest of the later output.

Recollection of the Absolute and Textual Poetry: Crystallization of the *Poesía Pura*

In the early poetry, a motif resembling the Platonic *anamnesis* appears frequently. In the sonnet "El alma de la nieve" (The Soul of the Snow), from *Ninfeas*, the remembrance of the heavenly realm is expressed as the personified falling snow's nostalgia for its celestial origin:

> Tiene un Alma la Nieve, que solloza angustiada
> al recuerdo doliente del Palacio del cielo,
> donde, envuelta en los rayos de virgínico velo,
> fué una Flor embriagante, fué una Reina adorada...
> (*Plp*: 1483)

> The Snow has a Soul that sobs anguished
> at the painful remembrance of the heavenly Palace,
> where, wrapped in the rays of virgin veil,
> it was an enrapturing Flower, it was an adored Queen…

This poem shows the communication between heavenly and earthly by means of the falling snow. The snow – with its whiteness symbolizing the absolute – is said to remember its origin in the heavenly sphere. The persistence of this mnemonic motif in the early work can be inferred from the fact that it appears also at the end of the first epoch, in Jiménez's most decadent and disillusioned aspect. In the collection *Laberinto* (*Labyrinth*) (1913), where the feeling of contingency is the all-pervading mood, the theme of the remembrance of primordial being is expressed as nostalgia for a lost higher reality:

> Algo del más allá, que llega hasta la vida
>   por una senda de nostalgia,
> cual una estrella errante, que en los cielos del sueño
>   derramase un polen de plata…
> (*Op*, I, 1: 1333)
>
> Something from beyond that comes to this life
>   through a path of nostalgia,
> as an errant star that in the heavens of the dream
>   shed a silver pollen…

It is clear that, rather than a recollection of specific personal experiences, this poem expresses a remembrance or a sense of a pure, divine realm hidden beyond the temporal manifestations.[2] This is another appearance of the spatial dichotomy that was analyzed in Chapter 1, as this nostalgic recollection relates to an *above* or *beyond* from which the lyrical subject is tragically separated. Seemingly these examples refer to the Platonic *anamnesis* but, as will be shown below, the motif of remembrance of the heavenly sphere is in fact another representation of the dual empirical/absolute subject.

With the *Sonetos espirituales* (*Spiritual Sonnets*), the disillusioned and melancholic mood changes into a more reflective and self-assertive attitude. The reason for this change of feeling is in fact explained in one of the sonnets, number 16, which discloses the metapoetic consciousness that will impulse the mature poetry:

Mujer celeste

Trocada en blanco toda la hermosura
con que ensombreces la naturaleza,
te elevaré a la clara fortaleza,
torre de mi ilusión y mi locura.
 Allí, cándida rosa, estrella pura,
me dejarás jugar con tu belleza...
Con cerrar bien los ojos, mi tristeza
reirá, pasado infiel de mi ventura.
 Mi vivir duro así será el mal sueño
del breve día; en mi nocturno largo,
será el mal sueño tu cruel olvido;
 desnuda en lo ideal, seré tu dueño;
se derramará abril por mi letargo
y creeré que nunca has existido.
(*Op*, I, 1: 1537)

Celestial Woman

Changed into white all of the loveliness
With which you nature turn to somber gray,
I'll raise you to the fortress with bright ray,
Tower of my illusion and my craziness.
 And there, rose niveous, star blemishless,
With your fair beauty you will let me play...
My sadness, as my eyes fall shut to stay,
Will laugh, past faithless of my happiness.
 Thus my hard living will the bad dream see
Of day too brief; in nocturne long for me
Bad dream will then be your forgetting twisted;
 You nude ideal, I will your master be;
April will overflow my lethargy
And I'll believe you never have existed.
(*SS*: 43)

Although published in 1917, this work was written in 1914, and its origin is to be found in Jiménez's acquaintance in 1913 with the woman who would become his wife, Zenobia Camprubí Aymar (Palau de

Nemes 1974: 574–84). This means that the present sonnet can be read in a biographical key, portraying Jiménez's love for his fiancé. In this poem the lyrical subject must curb his longings for the beloved woman and elevate them to the inner domain of his thoughts and dreams.³

At the same time, this text can be read as a long apostrophe to personified poetry, prefiguring the allegorical woman of the poem "Vino, primero, pura" (She came, first, pure) (1917), which will be analyzed in the next chapter. The isotopy of purity that pervaded the representations of the memory of the absolute is here transferred to personified poetry: "Trocada en blanco" (Changed into white), "cándida rosa, estrella pura" (rose niveous, star blemishless).⁴ Through its anthropomorphosis as a "mujer celeste" (celestial woman), poetry is identified as absolute beauty. Furthermore, it belongs to "mi ilusión y mi locura" (my illusion and my craziness), that is, to the inner realm of the lyrical subject. From this perspective the present sonnet claims the consciously willed inversion of the primacy of contingency. Poetic creation becomes the construction of a pure and ideal sphere deliberately ignoring the material realm and subjective finitude. A clear logic leads from the presuppositions of the early texts to this autotelic poetics. Given that the inner realm renders the only possibility for an experience of the absolute, and given that poetry is the representation of this experience, a logical consequence is that poetic expression is separated from the contingency of everyday life. A self-enclosed domain without any relation to the world is constructed, and the only condition for its realization is to close the eyes towards physical reality: "Con cerrar bien los ojos, mi tristeza / reirá, pasado infiel de mi ventura" (My sadness, as my eyes fall shut to stay, / Will laugh, past faithless of my happiness). In this sentence the rejection of the early poetry is formulated. To allow sadness, caused by the contingency of empirical subjectivity, to dominate the mood of poetic expression is to be unfaithful to the gift of poetry when understood as a representation of absolute subjectivity. A highly conscious escapism is thus expressed. Jiménez constructs a transcendence to the realm of art that chooses to ignore the finitude of empirical subjectivity. In this way the latter is prevented from soiling the immaculate sphere of artistic creation. An inversion of the real and imaginative is expressed: existence in the real world becomes a "mal sueño" (bad dream), and when the lyrical subject thus "sleeps", he will believe that poetry is illusory ("creeré que nunca has existido" (I'll believe you never have existed)). The projection of subjective dreams and desires upon a meaningless world, a feature of the early works, coherently leads to an isolated representation of the lyrical subject's creative force. This is the meaning of the last tercet, where it is asserted that the poet-subject is the master of his creation in this artificial and ideal sphere: "desnuda en lo ideal, seré tu dueño" (You nude ideal, I will your master be).[5]

Such a consciously self-referential poetics entails a change of tone and representational procedure with respect to the early works. The mood is inverted from narcissistic melancholy to self-assertive expression of absolute subjectivity. Consequently, representation changes because poetry must now divest itself of all contingent elements, that is, it must abandon the mimetic depiction of physical reality. The already highly idealized representation of exterior reality in the early poetry becomes further abstracted in the mature texts by the absence of any "reality effect" (cf. Barthes 1994: 479–84).[6] In the sonnet "Mujer celeste" the mimetic representation has been reduced to a minimum, since the images appearing, "torre", "rosa", "estrella" (tower, rose, star), do not integrate into a spatial whole, in a recognizable setting, but are isolated symbols for the now highly abstract representation of the absolute. However, it should be noted that the mythical spatial hierarchy is not subverted. Here, as in the most abstract poems of *Animal de fondo*, the "above" as symbol of the absolute remains a constant.

The relation of this self-conscious poetic absolute with the experience of contingency and transitoriness is revealed in the sonnet "Retorno fugaz" (Fleeting Return), the poem immediately preceding "Mujer celeste" in the *Sonetos espirituales*. This sonnet thematizes the fleetingness of perception and the weakness of memory:

> ¿Cómo era, Dios mío, cómo era?
> –¡Oh, corazón falaz, mente indecisa!–
> ¿Era como el pasaje de la brisa?
> ¿Como la huida de la primavera?
> [...]
>   Todo tu cambiar trocóse en nada
> –¡memoria, ciega abeja de amargura!–
> ¡No sé cómo eras, yo que sé que fuiste!
> (*Op*, I, 1: 1536–7)

> How was it, dear my Lord, how was it there?
> Oh, heart perfidious, mind not precise!
> Was it much like the breeze gone in a trice?

> Or like the fleeing of the spring elsewhere?
> [...]
>   All of your changing turned to nothingness
> – Blind bee of bitterness, oh memory! –
> I don't know you, do know the flight you had!
> (*SS*: 41)

The subject's consciousness is here represented as a passive medium of permanently changing perceptions, incapable of letting sensory impressions cohere into a fixed form of remembrance. Rather than as a flaw in the capacity to remember, this motif should be regarded as a figurative representation of ontological nihilism. Perception as a fallacious and evasive experience, impossible to recover once it has faded, is here a metaphor for the final vacuity of existence: "Todo tu cambiar trocóse en nada" (All of your changing turned to nothingness). Similarly, memory is represented as opaque and as only a source of bitterness: "¡memoria, ciega abeja de amargura!" (Blind bee of bitterness, oh memory!). The simultaneous contrast with and complementarity to the determination of the lyrical subject in "Mujer celeste" is remarkable. In the latter text the intention of creating an abiding dwelling, even if a purely mental one, through poetic creation is clearly stated: "te elevaré a la clara fortaleza, / torre de mi ilusión y mi locura" (I'll raise you to the fortress with bright ray, / Tower of my illusion and my craziness). If "Mujer celeste" represents the creation of a purely ideal realm, "Retorno fugaz" expresses the sense of the emptiness of existence. Through the contiguity of these two poems and the order in which they are put, the inference is that the feeling of contingency is surmounted by the act of creating a self-enclosed aesthetic realm.

Within this frame, poetry is not to be regarded as an aesthetic elaboration of lived experiences but as an expression that is purified from the contingency and transience of everyday life. For this reason, Jiménez's *poesía pura* crystallizes as non-referential, abstract texts. Ramsden finds that the stylistic divergence of the *poesía pura* with respect to Jiménez's early poetry is due to the explicit wish to create a "world of self-contained and absolute beauty" (Ramsden 1981: 146). The stylistic change in Jiménez's work is, then, essentially related to the self-conscious construction of an immanent textual absolute in the mature poetry (cf. Ramsden 1981: 141–6).

In his early work Jiménez carries out a representation of the conflict between absolute and empirical subjectivity that lets the experience of contingency and finitude dominate the epiphanic experience. The lyrical subject's inner absolute pales when it faces the ultimate reality of death. As a consequence of the insight that absolute subjectivity ultimately depends on the ephemeral physical being, the feeling of contingency arises. Accordingly, the creation of spaces of beauty and independent realms of time is a futile activity because in the end poetry is just as contingent as subjectivity. Within this framework, the elegiac remembrance of primordial being is to be understood in relation to the inner absolute rather than Platonically (an *anamnesis* of the realm of Ideas), since the sense of existential and religious void that pervades the texts undermines the possibility of belief in a Platonic ideal world.[7]

An important segment of modern poetry runs through precisely the same line of evolution as the one sketched out with respect to Jiménez. In the first poems of *Les Fleurs du mal* (1857), Baudelaire displays the motif of the striving for the ideal, e.g. in the poem "L'albatros", but progressively this motif disappears from the collection. The lyrical subject abandons the quest for ideality and turns to the transformation of reality into aesthetic objects. The poetic artefacts do not refer to a supernatural realm (in either a Platonist or Neoplatonist sense[8]), but are the expression of a subject that imposes upon itself the task of creating artificial worlds. Ontological emptiness is also a central question for Mallarmé, whose lyrical subject will have no other aim than that of creating closed spheres of immanent, absolute beauty. This can be regarded as the aesthetic correlation of the philosophical Copernican turn carried out by Kantian philosophy. In Kant's anthropocentric thought the subject must raise an understanding of the world on the basis of its own cognitive forces. This means that the finite subject is assigned a task that would require omnipotent strength. Consequently, in the realm of the arts, humanity raises impressive aesthetic works but they are devoid of any positive content, either at a cognitive or at a transcendent level. In this way the work of art of Modernity becomes a monument to the both titanic and empty modern subject.

In Jiménez's mature work, the motif of nostalgia for the realm above the material world is no longer frequent. Instead, the lyrical subject asserts an arrival at a state of plenitude that at the same time is (as was shown in Chapter 2) necessarily unfulfilled. The asserted accomplishment is also an expectation, it is a presence but also a postponement. In its most conspicuous expression, as in the poem that will be analyzed below, this ungraspable absolute can be related to Derrida's philosophy of *différance*. Derridean thought represents an attempt to break with the philosophy of the subject while it, as has been shown by Habermas, at the same time remains within the paradigm it aims to overcome.[9] The parallelism that is possible to draw between Derrida's philosophy and Jiménez's poetry is based on their belonging to the same frame of thought since they can both be regarded as taking the idea of the self-founded subject to its limit. In this respect an important work by Derrida, as regards both his attempt to break with the philosophy of the subject and as regards the question of temporality, is *Speech and Phenomena* (1967).

Derrida's critique is directed against precisely the notion of inner subjectivity as a self-present, self-identical substance not dependent on any exterior determination. As a means of deconstructing the transcendental subject, he uses the notion of temporality. On the basis of Husserl's descriptions of subjective time-experience in *Logical Investigations* (1901), Derrida regards the idea of the self-present *cogito* as based on the notion of the instant. In the "now", a presence, and thus also a self-presence, is to be found. Nonetheless, Derrida argues that because consciousness is necessarily immersed in the flux of time, its non-identity appears through the retentional trace of the past:

> The living present springs forth out of its nonidentity with itself and from the possibility of a retentional trace. It is always already a trace. This trace cannot be thought out on the basis of a simple present whose life would be within itself; the self of the living present is primordially a trace. (Derrida 1973: 85)

Against the attempt to isolate transcendental subjectivity as a pure presence in the now, Derrida uses the notion of retention by assimilating it with the Structuralist idea of language as a sign-system. Apparently the line of argument is to confront Husserl with Husserl but it is clear that the Structuralist non-substantial definition of the sign, only based on a formal difference to other signs, lies at the basis of Derrida's text. Since consciousness is based on a sign-structure, transcendental subjectivity is not a transparent self-consciousness (an understanding that Derrida considers a consequence of the Western metaphysics of presence). According to Derrida, the subject is never present to itself because – in a complete analogy with the sign in the language system – it carries with it a temporal non-presence and a non-substantial content by means of difference.[10] Absence, deferral and difference are thus at the core of subjectivity.[11] In this crossbreeding of sign-system and temporality, a "protowriting" takes the place of a consciousness prior to linguistic articulation.[12] Derrida sustains that consciousness only appears with language and argues that, given that a sign only signifies through its differential relations with other signs, consciousness cannot be thought of as self-presence but, on the contrary, as immersed in a continuously deferring and differing process. This linguistic or textual character of consciousness is articulated through the celebrated notion of *différance*.[13] This notion appears by the combination of the words "difference" and "deferral", and is used to criticize phenomenology as a metaphysics of presence.[14]

Although belonging to an aesthetic context, a very similar figure of thought with respect to the relation between language and consciousness can be traced in Jiménez's poetry. A remarkable coincidence can be found between some of Jiménez's mature texts and Derrida's analysis of Husserl's description of inner time-consciousness. An example can be found in the poem "Estás viniendo siempre hasta mi imán" (You Are Always Falling Towards My Magnet) from *Animal de fondo*:

Estás viniendo siempre hasta mi imán

En mar pasas, en mar acumulado con todas las bellezas; tú, conseguido dios de la mar, de mi mar.

Tú eres el sucesivo, lo sucesivo eres; lo que siempre vendrá, el que siempre vendrá; que eres el ansia abstracta, la que nunca se acaba, porque el recuerdo tuyo también es vida como tú.

Sí, en masa de verdad reveladora, de sucesión perpetua pasas, en masa de color, de luz, de ritmo; en densidad de amor estás pasando, estás viniendo, estás presente siempre, estás futuro en mí; eres lo ilimitado de mi órbita.

Y me detengo en mi alijeración, porque, en el horizonte de mi espacio esterno, estás viniendo siempre hasta mi imán. Tu sucesión no es fuga de lo mío, es venida impetuosa de lo tuyo, del todo que eres tú, eterno vividor del todo; caminante y camino a fuerza de pasado, a fuerza de presente, a fuerza de futuro.
(*Op*, I, 2: 1192–3)

You Are Always Falling Towards My Magnet

You cross over the sea, over a sea-like accumulation
of all beauty, you, god achieved from the sea,
from my sea.

You are the becoming, you are what becomes;
what will always come, the one to come always; you
are the abstract desire, the one that never ends, for
the memory of you is as much life as you are.
   Yes, you pass in a mass of revealing truth, you
pass in perpetual succession, in a mass of color, of light,
of rhythm; you keep passing in a density of love,
you are living, always present; you are passing in me;
you are the boundlessness of my orbit.
   And I linger in my lightness, because from the horizon
of eternal space you keep falling always towards my
magnet. Your continuous passing is not a flight from what is mine,
it is the sudden arriving of what is yours,
of the whole that you are, eternal living of the whole; you
are the journey and the traveller on the strength of the
past, on the strength of the present, on the strength of
the future.
(*GDD*: 79)[15]

Despite the claim of having attained aesthetic plenitude – "mar acumulado con todas las bellezas; tú, conseguido dios de la mar, de mi mar" (sea-like accumulation of all beauty, you, god achieved from the sea, from my sea) – the never occurring unification of the split subjectivity "yo-dios" (I-god) can be regarded as the expression of the impossibility of either reaching or representing self-presence. This can be inferred from the "coming" and "becoming" that is the central isotopy of the text and which is a feature of the invoked "god": "pasas", "sucesivo", "siempre vendrá", "sucesión perpetua", "estás pasando", estás viniendo", "venida impetuosa" (you cross over the sea, becoming, you will always come, perpetual succession, you keep passing, you are passing in me, you keep falling always, sudden arriving). The emphasis on temporal succession negates the notion of an ideal "now" of absolute self-presence. In fact the text explicitly contradicts the idea of a fulfilled self-presence, as this "other" – the "dios deseado y deseante" (god desired and desiring) – is one who "siempre vendrá" (will always come) and thus never will arrive.

   Rather than as an existential experience of temporality – the sense of loss in time, the finitude of the individual, memories of things past – this text represents language-time as the medium in which poetry appears. The strong rhythmical sense of the text, created by its enumerative character, suggests temporal flow. In turn, this formal representation of temporality is highlighted thematically by the appearance of the temporal nouns closing the text: "a fuerza de pasado, a fuerza de presente, a fuerza de futuro" (on the strength of the past, on the strength of the present, on the strength of the future). In this poem, time is unrelated to events or things that happened in shared historical time, it is only linked to an anonymous force of desire and creation: "eres el ansia abstracta, la que nunca se acaba, porque el recuerdo tuyo también es vida como tú" (you are the abstract desire, the one that never ends, for the memory of you is as much life as you are). The textual absolute of the *poesía pura* thus gives way to an expression of subjectivity and time as consubstantial with language – similar to Derrida's understanding of the same question. The lyrical subject is one with the linguistic syntagmatic chain where no self-presence can ever take place.

From the perspective of the history of ideas, Derridean textuality can be regarded as a manifestation of the paradigm of the fragmented absolute. Modern thought is divided between scepticism and the necessity of operating with a notion of absolute. In a thoroughly Kantian way, Modernity is pervaded by this idea of a totality that can never be encompassed but that nevertheless is present as a vision. Derridean deconstructive thought, which claims that temporality and subjectivity are essentially linguistic, aims at overcoming the Kantian paradigm – but at the same time it confirms it. It is a central idea for Kant that it is impossible to reach any absolute form of knowledge because of the finitude of our cognitive capacities. Conversely, the notion of *différance* represents an epistemological absolute that lets cognition depend on the language system. This is a purely negative absolute,[16] a radical unintelligibility, but it still represents the absent totality inherent in the paradigm of the fragmented absolute.[17]

With respect to Jiménez, it is clear that a self in the sense of individual identity cannot be articulated on the basis of an infinitely differing and deferring subject. A subject that is primordially non-present to itself seems adequately expressed in "Estás viniendo siempre hasta mi imán". The lyrical subject appearing in this text is an anonymous and linguistically generated subject devoid of any identity. However, this is only one facet of Jiménez's work since it also conveys another expression of temporality and memory, one that belongs to an embodied subject who is situated in a specific time and space. In the following section the analysis will investigate to what extent Jiménez, in an explicitly autobiographical work, circumscribes different ideas of temporality and subject from those of the *poesía pura*.

Poetry as the Transcendence of History:
Diario de un poeta recién casado **(1917)**

On 2 March 1916, Juan Ramón Jiménez and Zenobia Camprubí Aymar were married in New York. When Jiménez left Madrid on 21 January 1916 in order to marry his fiancée, he began a poetic diary that he would keep during the entire trip, until the couple's return to the Spanish capital on 1 July 1916. In 1917 the collection *Diario de un poeta recién casado* was published, one of Jiménez's most celebrated works. The *Diario* is a day to day annotation of impressions and thoughts in the form of poems. As mentioned in Chapter 1, the work is organized into six sections corresponding with the phases of the trip, setting off and finishing in Madrid: "Hacia el mar" (Toward the Sea), "El amor en el mar" (Love at Sea), "América del Este" (Eastern United States), "Mar de retorno" (The Return Voyage's Sea), "España" (Spain), and "Recuerdos de América del Este escritos en España" (Memories of Eastern United States Written in Spain). The Jiménez criticism tends to regard the *Diario* as narrating the lyrical subject's simultaneous and complementary encounter with love and a pure poetic expression.[18] At the same time that the *Diario* effects the remembrance of the absolute that was analyzed in the previous section (e.g. in poems 14, 175, 183, 187 and 194), it also articulates a referential and autobiographical recollection that often crystallizes as entirely anecdotal texts (e.g. poems 83, 86, 111, 134, 138, 176, 199 or 224). It is probably this circumstantial nature of the *Diario* that motivated Jiménez to write the following consideration at the end of the book:

> Este *Diario*, más que ninguna otra obra mía, es un libro provisional. Es probable que, más adelante, cuando me olvide de él y lo crea nuevo, lo corrija más, es decir, algo; y es posible que le quite las leves correcciones que ahora le he hecho y lo deje casi en esencia.
>
> No sé lo que será. Sé que, hoy, me parece este libro mío un boceto de él mismo, no sé si boceto de más o de menos, que me quiero quitar de encima o de debajo, para libertarme, por este lado del alma y del cuerpo, del mí reciente, molesto y sin revisión por ahora, de hace sólo un año. (Jiménez 1994a: 273)

> This *Diary*, more than any other work of mine, is provisional. It is probable that later on, when I have forgotten it and recreate it, I may correct it more, that is, somewhat; and I may undo the minor corrections that I have made now and leave it almost in its essential form.

I don't know what it will become. I do know that today this book of mine seems like a rough draft of itself, whether of more or of less I do not know, as I want to get it off my back, to free myself from this side of my soul and body, of my recent me, troublesome and without changes for the time being, of only a year ago. (*DNP*: 492)

It seems as if Jiménez himself was puzzled by the characteristics of the *Diario* since he already at the time of its publication planned to revise it at a later date. The diversity of themes and moods is certainly in marked contrast to the discipline governing the *Sonetos espirituales*, which appeared the same year as the first publication of the *Diario*. The formal and thematic requirements of the sonnet doubtlessly convey better the abstract self-enclosure of the *poesía pura* than the episodic referentiality of the *Diario*. The diary, directly inserted into historical time, is a genre underscoring the individual's spatiotemporal existence, whereby this work apparently diverges from the textual temporality otherwise displayed in Jiménez' mature poetry.[19]

Through the annotations of date and place preceding each poem, a link is established between poetic and historical time. This juxtaposition of temporalities can be related to Ricoeur's notion of *calendar time*, which is one of the three *connectors* to which he gives the function of mediating between subjective, phenomenological time, and objective, exterior time. These connectors are *calendar time, the succession of human generations*, and *the traces of the past* (e.g. archives and monuments).[20] The importance of the connectors is to be found in their articulation of a temporality that overcomes the opposition between the two traditional understandings of time, exterior and inner temporality. They *refer* the narrative structures of human time *back* (Ricoeur 1988: 104) to the natural universe. While the calendar on the one hand relates to exterior reality through the recurrence of certain astronomic phenomena,[21] at the same time it is established by a fundamental occurrence in human time (Christ's or Buddha's birth, Muhammad's flee from Mecca, the foundation of Rome, etc.). This founding event sets year 1 in the calendar,[22] and without such an axial moment the astronomical measuring would be a limitless temporality, utterly incommensurable with human experience. The foundation of the calendar is based on the phenomenological experience of the lived present, that is, of the inner time-experience in its tension between immediate past and future:

If we did not have the phenomenological notion of the present, as the "today" in terms of which there is a "tomorrow" and a "yesterday," we would not be able to make any sense of the idea of a new event that breaks with a previous era, inaugurating a course of events wholly different from what preceded it. (Ricoeur 1988: 107)

Through such a foundation of year 1, time receives a signification and the possibility of giving events a date arises. Calendar time "cosmologizes" lived time and at the same time it humanizes cosmic time.

Evidently, the *Diario de un poeta recién casado* is inscribed into calendar time by the annotation of dates ahead of every poem. In the *Diario* epiphanic experiences just as personal anecdotes from everyday life are recorded and inscribed into calendar time. The reference to a particular day in historical time gives the *Diario* a testimonial character, just as it inserts the poems into a specific historical situation in a much more direct way than Jiménez's early and mature output otherwise does. Most of Jiménez's poetry aims at a monadic temporal representation that is either inserted into cosmic recurrence or remains enclosed as a purely verbal artefact. The following analysis will show whether Jiménez in the *Diario* – given that this work includes a direct reference to historical time – arrives at an identity built upon individual experiences and relations to others.

In the *Diario* a specific historical motif is recurrent: the critique of Modernity. New York's technical and urban environment causes the oblivion of mankind's connection to nature, as is repeatedly asserted in sections III and VI. One example of this appears in "Túnel ciudadano" (Urban Tunnel), poem 65 in the collection, which depicts the entrance of a railway tunnel and at the same time the perceptual and vital atrophy characteristic of life in the industrialized city:

> El humo y la nieve lo ennegrecen todo por igual, uno a fuerza de luto, otro a fuerza de nitidez. Nada da la sensación de que en parte alguna – dentro, encima, al borde– haya vidas con pensamientos y sentimientos de colores, con sentidos corporales. ¿Quién ha visto aquí? ¿Quién ha oído? ¿Quién ha olido, gustado ni tocado? Todo es confuso, difuso, monótono, seco, frío y sucio a un tiempo, negro y blanco, es decir, negro, sin hora ni contagio. Algo que está, pero que no se tiene ni se desea, que se sabe que no se ha anhelado nunca y que nunca se recordará sino en el indiferente e involuntario descuido del sueño difícil. (*Op*, I, 2: 104–5)

> The smoke and the snow turns everything equally black, the one by dint of mourning, the other by dint of brightness. Nothing gives the impression that anywhere – within, up above, on the edges – there is

life with thinking or a semblance of colors, with corporal senses. Who has seen things here? Who has heard something? Who has smelled, tasted or touched? Everything is confusion, diffusion, monotony, barren, cold and dirt at one and the same time, white and black, which is to say, black, timeless and incommunicable. Something that exists, but which is neither possessed nor desired, which we know has never been longed for and that never will be remembered except in the indifferent and involuntary disorder of a troubled dream. (*DNP*: 194)

In this passage of the poem, the absence of colours and the dissolution of the outlines of things in the urban environment evoke a description of a kingdom of shadows, a Hades to which the poet-subject has descended.[23] The perception of reality is compared to the numb state of mind in the borderland between wake and sleep. The inference is that life in the modern city is governed by a loss of the perceptual faculties and an oblivion of the vital powers. The industrialized city is at such a distance from nature that the vital energy of humanity has been forgotten.

Throughout section III, "América del Este" (Eastern United States), the victory of spring over the antivital aspects of Modernity is connected with the poetic gaze on the world. Poetry is a catalyst that reminds us of the human belonging to a vaster natural world than that of modern urban life. Such an understanding appears in the poem "Garcilaso en New York", where the reading of the Spanish Renaissance poet changes the vision of the metropolis:

New York,
26 de abril.

Garcilaso en New York

(A Mr. A. Huntington)

¿Cuándo vino de España aquella carabela que trajo, con esta pequeña joya de libro, seco y manchado hoy, la carga infinita de belleza? Aquí, bajo este árbol preñado de verdura, Garcilaso –que ¿desde cuándo? estaba sentado esperándome– está conmigo, es decir, en mí, mirando con mis propios ojos, en el cielo aún, la primavera nueva, que parece luz levantada con el cristal de su libro, o dilatada imagen de su mirar que vió a abril en Toledo. Sí. En ningún libro, en cuadro alguno, en ninguna insinuación de aquí hay una frescura, un verdor, una suavidad, un rumor, una trasparencia más igual a la de esta primavera que en estos once versos de Garcilaso, que yo digo en voz alta…

–…Leyéndolos yo, cada verso, doncella o doncel desnudos, con toda la hermosura tierna de abril, ha dejado, corriendo al mar por cada calle, verdes, inesperadas y alegres las once avenidas de New York…

–¡Sí! ¡Yo he sido! ¡Yo he sido! ¡Yo he sido!

Pero los policias sonríen… (*Op*, I, 2: 132–3)

New York,
April 26.

Garcilaso in New York

(To Mr. A. Huntington)

When did that caravel come from Spain bringing, along with this little jewel of a book weathered and spotted today, the infinite cargo of beauty? Here beneath this tree pregnant with greenery, Garcilaso – how long has he been sitting here waiting for me? – is here with me, which is to say, inside of me, observing with my own eyes, even in the sky, the new springtime that has the appearance of light risen with the crystal of his book, or the dilated image of his observation that saw April in Toledo. Yes. In no other book, in no painting, in no insinuation here is there any freshness, any greenery, any softness, any sound, any transparency more like that of this spring than in those eleven verses of Garcilaso, that I repeat aloud…

– …As I read them, each verse, maiden or chaste youth disrobed, with all the tender loveliness of April, has left, flowing down to the sea along every street, green, unexpected and joyous, the eleven avenues of New York…

– Yes! It was me! It was me! It was me!

But the policemen smile… (*DNP*: 258; translation modified)

Garcilaso's poetry causes a profound identification of reader (the lyrical subject) and author (Garcilaso), expressed as Garcilaso having waited for the lyrical subject under that particular tree where the reading takes place. The subject experiences a loss of I through the reading, since it is the old poet who is said to look through the young poet's eyes: "Garcilaso […] está conmigo, es decir, en mí, mirando con mis propios ojos" (Garcilaso […] is here with me, which is to say, inside of me, observing with my own eyes). The poetic gaze is in direct connection with the renewal of spring because through the reading, the lyrical subject sees "la primavera nueva, que parece luz levantada con el cristal de su libro" (the new springtime that has the appearance of light risen with the crystal of his book). Finally, the reading of poetry causes a transformation of reality because the transfigurative and vital powers of poetry leave "verdes, inesperadas y alegres las once avenidas de New York…" (green, unexpected and joyous, the eleven avenues of New York). Poetic epiphany and renewal of life converge despite the great city's inorganic environment. However, the end of the poem suggests a certain self-conscious irony towards the actual efficacy of poetry since the smile of the police officers is preceded by the conjunction "pero" (but): "Pero los policías sonríen…" (But the policemen smile). This smile could reflect a condescending and sceptical attitude towards the lyrical subject who exclaims "–¡Sí! ¡Yo he sido! ¡Yo he sido! ¡Yo he sido!" (Yes! It was me! It was me! It was me!).

It must be asked, however, whether this I who speaks coincides with the empirical individual Juan Ramón Jiménez, or is it perhaps his absolute alter ego who utters this poem? As has been shown in the previous chapters, in Jiménez's lyrical output a Romantic notion of the poet prevails: the poet-subject is able to enter into contact with the vital force of nature. In this sense the poet is a figure with a mnemonic function, which is to bring forth the natural and vital forces that are repressed or forgotten in modern society. This poem is about a reading, it is a text thematizing the experience of another text. The new poem – "Garcilaso en New York" – describes the revitalization of the old poem through the reading experience, whereby the poetic gaze upon the world is repeated, a gaze that renders the world new. In a certain sense, the poem "Garcilaso en New York" is the re-actualization of the old poet's writing. This also means that instead of representing the individual experience of Jiménez's reading, this text describes the impersonal poetic vision that every true poet is capable of. In turn, this means that despite the inscription of historical time in the *Diario*, the ultimate aim is to transcend the historically given contingencies and to effect a connection to nature's cyclic time and eternal return.

Towards the end of section V, "España", a different mode of recollective writing appears with respect to the day to day annotations of events and thoughts. The representation of the trip finishes at the end of section V with the return to Madrid. Similarly, reference to calendar time has disappeared in section VI, "Recuerdos de América del Este escritos en España" (Memories of Eastern United States Written in Spain). Poem 217 is the last one in section V, but already poem 213, dated 1 July, is the last one that refers to a recently experienced episode. Until text 214 the poems refer to an immediate past, since the dates written ahead of the poems imply, in accordance with the generic conventions of the diary, that experience and annotation are only separated by a brief lapse of time. Conversely, the last poems of section V and the whole of section VI represent a recollection of a more distant past (with the exception of the penultimate poem in this section, number 216, to which reference will be made below). In this way, a different recollective writing appears with respect to the first sections of the work, but it will be seen how the aim of this mnemonic work is consistent with the pantheistic recollection that has just been analyzed.

This continuity can be inferred from the last four poems in section V. The annotations at the top of the texts situate them in Madrid, thus referring to the time after the end of the trip. All four poems except the last one thematize the sea, that is, the memory of the sea, since it now is beyond the immediate perceptual reach of the lyrical subject.

Madrid,
3 de octubre.

Elegía

Ahora parecerás ¡oh mar lejano!
a los que por ti vayan,
viendo tus encendidas hojas secas,
al norte, al sur, al este o al oeste;
ahora parecerás ¡oh mar distante!
mar; ahora que yo te estoy creando
con mi recuerdo vasto y vehemente.
(*Op*, I, 2: 205)

Madrid,
October 3.

Elegy

Now, oh distant sea, you will appear

> to those who sail across you,
> looking at your fiery desiccated leaves,
> to the north, to the south, to the east or to the west;
> now you will appear oh distant sea!
> as sea; now that I am creating you
> with my vast and vehement reminiscences.
> (*DNP*: 444)

In the last two verses of this poem, number 216 in the collection, the memory of the sea becomes related to poetic creation. Separated from the sea, now the poet-subject remembers it in the writing. The initial assertion in verses 1–4 apparently refers to the persons to whom the sea will be present at this moment, that is, those actually at sea while the lyrical subject is in Madrid. However, the metaphor "viendo tus encendidas hojas secas" (looking at your fiery desiccated leaves) points rather to the readers of the *Diario* – in the pages of which the sea is in fact recreated.[24] The poetic gaze upon the world, that in the *Diario* has forged a specific vision of the sea, will be taken over by the readers, which is why they are not said to be reading but *looking at*, "viendo", both the pages of the book and the sea.[25]

The reading of poetry passes the poetic gaze over to the reader, a theme that was analyzed with respect to "Garcilaso en New York". The consciousness of this can be inferred from the verbal tenses of the poem, since it can relate both to the present time of the writing, "ahora que yo te estoy creando" (now that I am creating you), and of the reading, "Ahora parecerás […] a los que por ti vayan, / viendo" (Now […] you will appear to those who sail across you, / looking at), as if the poem was still in the process of being written and simultaneously finished and received by the readers. This ambivalent presentness is yet another escape from historical time since it refers to the monadic present detached from historicity that will return infinitely through the readers actualizing it. As a subtle indication of this escape from historical time, the date at the top of this poem, "3 de octubre", is posterior to the date written in the introductory note to the *Diario*, "3 de setiembre de 1916", supposedly the date when the work was finished by the author. Rather than an incongruence, the product of a distraction during the editing of the final version of the text, this temporal displacement should be understood as a sign of the consciousness of the author having handed his expression over to the infinitely recurring future readings.

This means that the part of the *Diario* which is specifically a diary (sections I–V) ends with the consciousness of being a work conceived of and written within a specific timespan but open towards ahistorical temporality. This understanding points towards the final section of the work, where a central theme is the "life" of the work of art in contrast with individual finitude. In the poem just analyzed the contrast between subjective transience and poetic permanence is present through the title, "Elegía". Despite the preservation of the subjective experience in the poetic writing, the sense of loss is expressed in the title of the text. Individual experience is destined to disappear in unending time but the poetic vision preserved in the written page will remain.

"Elegía" is the last poem in the *Diario* that includes a temporal reference since the one following it, which at the same time is the last text in section V, only carries the indication "Madrid, domingo" (Madrid, Sunday). This poem, titled "Sencillez" (Simplicity), has no thematic connection with the voyage. It does not describe any event or any observation that took place during the trip, but asserts that the aesthetics of purity emerges with the same necessity as the sun that rises every morning:

Madrid,
domingo.

Sencillez

¡Sencillez, hija fácil
de la felicidad!
              Sales, lo mismo,
por las vidas, que el sol de un día más,
por el oriente. Todo
lo encuentras bueno, bello y útil,
como tú, como el sol.
              ¡Sencillez pura,
fuente del prado tierno de mi alma,
olor del jardín grato de mi alma,
canción del mar tranquilo de mi alma,
luz del día sereno de mi alma!
(*Op*, I, 2: 205–6)

Madrid,
Sunday.

SIMPLICITY

Simplicity, guileless daughter
of happiness!
                Out you come, into lives,
just like the sun of one more day
into the eastern sky. Everything you
find good, beautiful and useful,
as are you, as is the sun.
                      Pure simplicity,
fountain of the tender meadow of my soul,
aroma of the pleasant garden of my soul,
song of the tranquil ocean of my soul,
light of the serene daytime of my soul!
(*DNP*: 444; translation modified)

The notion of "sencillez" can be identified with the aesthetics of *poesía pura*. This is confirmed by the epiphoric structure of the last four verses, all ending with the syntagma "de mi alma" (of my soul). The contemplation of interiority brings forth the simple and pure poetic expression. The abandonment of the temporal and geographical reference proper to the diary genre entails a return to the abstract, self-enclosed poetic expression that was initiated with *Sonetos espirituales* and *Estío*. In this way, by leaving the spatiotemporal reference behind, this poem marks the end of the diary. This also means that the notion of the self-enclosed poetic text cannot be regarded as the outcome of a process taking place through the voyage – as is sometimes claimed – but as a return to the poetry that had already crystallized before the *Diario*. This mode of writing was suspended by the generic presuppositions of the diary, but once these are left behind, the momentum of the *poesía pura* returns. From this perspective, then, the *Diario* fits consistently into Jiménez's poetic development.[26]

Nonetheless, the book as a whole does not end with the mode of *poesía pura* as its outcome, since the last section of the *Diario* is a reprise, as it were, of the impressions of New York that appeared in section III. In this way, the question of memory and temporality is re-enacted in section VI, "Recuerdos de América del Este escritos en España" (Memories of Eastern United States Written in Spain). An important theme in the last section of the *Diario* is – as in section III – the oblivion of the poetic gaze in the modern world. This motif was analyzed above in relation to the poem "Garcilaso en New York" and it reappears in poems as "Walt Whitman" and "La casa de Poe" (Poe's House). In the latter poem it is represented as the oblivion of the nation's poets. The young people only shrug their shoulders in answer to an inquiry about the location of Edgar Allan Poe's house. The old woman who, as the only person, has heard of it has a "memoria arruinada" (shattered memory) and has forgotten where it is. Even if nobody remembers where it is, the lyrical subject is the privileged individual able to *see* Poe's house:

> Y, sin embargo, yo la veo, yo la he visto en una calle, la luna en la fachadita de madera blanca, una enredadera de nieve en la puertecilla cerrada ante la que yacen muertos, con una nieve sin pisadas, igual que tres almohadas puras, tres escalones que un día subieron a ella. (*Op*, I, 2: 223)

> Nevertheless, I see it, I have seen it in a street, the moon reflecting on the modest facade of white wood, a strand of snow on the little closed doorway in front of which lie inert, covered with untouched snow like three pure-white pillows, three steps that once went up to it. (*DNP*: 486)

This is a non-referential, poetic vision, as can be inferred from the verbal tenses used in this the final paragraph of the poem. Although the house at first is mentioned in the present tense ("yacen" (lie)), at the end of the text the description is written in the past tense, "tres escalones que un día subieron a ella" (three steps that once went up to it), implying that it does not exist any longer. The house seen by the lyrical subject is to be interpreted as a metaphor for the permanence of Poe's writings in his consciousness. Poe has a house to dwell in even if the physical "Poe's house" has been consumed by time. It is clear that the historical reference – the Ricoeurean *trace of the past* – is absent in this poem, it is the poetic gaze itself which finally is the reference. The recollection that is effected in this poem is, once more, one that transcends the contingency of the historical entities. The *yo* able to see Poe's house, then, is the elevated poet-subject, a medium for the atemporal poetic regard.

In this way a double subject appears in the poems of the *Diario*. If, on the one hand, these poems refer to the physical reality encountered in New England and thus also to a specific author at a given historical time and place, on the other hand, through the theme of the poetic gaze, an impersonal and ahistorical poet-subject utters these texts. If the individual Juan Ramón Jiménez is referred to at one level, at another level he disappears. In this latter sense, what is described in the *Diario* is not primarily a travel narrative but, precisely as Jiménez himself asserts in the introductory note, a voyage to the elevated realm:

> No el ansia de color exótico, ni el afán de «necesarias» novedades. La que viaja, siempre que viajo, es mi alma entre almas.
> Ni más nuevo, al ir, ni más lejos; más hondo. Nunca más diferente, más alto siempre. (*Op*, I, 2: 55)

> Neither the longing for exotic color nor the desire for something "necessarily" new. What travels, whenever I travel, is my soul, among souls.
> Neither newer, on going, nor farther; deeper. Never more different, always higher. (*DNP*: 84)

In turn this means that the *Diario* circumscribes, rather than a *self* based on central events through which the individual achieves an identity, a subjectivity whose individual features are dissolved. Even if the generic conventions of the diary should pull towards a description of the autobiographical circumstances of the self, the impulse of absolute subjectivity is stronger, resulting in the prevalence of an anonymous subject searching for the unconditioned.[27] In an entirely parallel way to what was shown in the previous chapter, this absolute subject expresses the idea of the eternal recurrence where the same – impersonal poetic gaze, essential connection with nature – is constantly returning although with infinite variations.

In the *Diario* historicity is, then, a secondary temporality, only inscribed into the work due to the generic requirements, while the primordial time remains that of the cosmic cyclic return. As has been mentioned, historical time is vital for the constitution of a self. Conversely, if this measure of time is lost then the subject dissolves, either through an implosion into cosmic totality – in a pantheistic understanding – or through a simple disappearance into nothingness – in an ontological nihilism. In both cases the subject is lost, in a similar way to the Indian kings mentioned by Kierkegaard in a famous passage in *The Concept of Dread*:

> When time is correctly defined as infinite succession, it seems plausible to define it also as the present, the past and the future. However this distinction is incorrect, if one means by it that this is implied in time itself; for it first emerges with the relation of time to eternity and the reflection of eternity in it. If in the infinite succession of time one could in fact find a foothold, i.e. a present, which would serve as a dividing point, then this division would be quite correct. But precisely because every moment, like the sum of the moments, is a process (a going-by) no moment is a present, and in the same sense there is neither past, present, nor future. If one thinks it possible to maintain this division, it is because we *spatialize* a moment, but thereby the infinite succession is brought to a standstill, and that is beause one introduces a visual representation, visualizing time instead of thinking it. But even so it is not correctly thought, for even in this visual representation the infinite succession of time is a present infinitely void of content. (This is the parody of the eternal.) The Hindus speak of a line of kings which has reigned for 70,000 years. About the kings nothing is known, not even their names (as I assume). Taking this as an illustration of time, these 70,000 years are for thought an infinite vanishing; for visual representation they widen out spatially into an illusive view of a nothing infinitely void. (Kierkegaard 1967: 76–7, author's emphasis)

The first part of this passage explains temporality in terms of past, present and future as a successive process. Just as St Augustine defined time as *distentio animi*, that is, as the distension of the soul between past and future in the present, Kierkegaard argues that there is no such thing as a present separated from the past and the future because there is no dividing point between them, any instant is always part of a process that includes the past and the future. The incorrect spatialization of time occurs if an instant is understood as a point in space because the image as such (the row of points) is spatial, not temporal. According to the spatial extension of a point, the instant becomes a void, a nothingness. But the visualization of time as points in space is also misleading with respect to a longer timespan because then temporality as a whole appears as nothingness: "infinite vanishing". Conversely, if time is anchored in eternity, in a divine realm beyond temporality, then a human sense of time can appear. From a purely naturalistic perspective, time is either infinite vanishing or eternal return, whereas from a religious viewpoint time is neither, as both its origin and end lie beyond successiveness. Evidently, Kierkegaard's religious substrate is to be found here since he sees the divine subject as governing both temporality and eternity. For this reason he also regards the instant as "an atom of eternity" (Kierkegaard 1967: 79) because time and subject are related to the Creator, who encompasses both time and eternity and who has put eternity in the human soul.[28] It is remarkable that Ricoeur puts forward a similar argument when he defines calendar time as the intersection of cosmological time and existential time. The founding of year 1 is the axial moment thanks to which time becomes humanized instead of appearing as an infinite temporality without boundaries.

CHAPTER SIX

The Obra as Subjective Memory

Jiménez's tireless work on his *Obra* is a famous anecdote of twentieth-century Spanish literary history. He envisaged and worked on a perfectly closed and finished *Work* – the *Obra definitiva* or *total* – that would include his entire output, completely organized and revised. The altogether more than 100,000 manuscripts[1] kept in the archives of Puerto Rico, Moguer and Madrid testify to his perseverance in this project. The difference between this material and the posthumous legacy of other authors can perhaps be found in Jiménez's refusal to consider his texts finished. Again and again he would return to already written and published poems in order to, in his own expression, relive them – "revivirlos". This meant the introduction of changes, ranging from small replacements to the rewriting of an entire text. Jiménez's process of rewriting has entailed that today, depending on the approach to the production, two different Jiménez *Obras* exist. The first one is given diachronically, and appears if Jiménez's evolution is followed from the first texts to the last. This *Obra* crystallizes as the series of publications that appeared during the poet's lifetime and it should be complemented with the vast volume of manuscript materials gathered in the archives. An edition of each poem published during Jiménez's life can be made with reference to the existing variants (even if this is a large and complicated task because of Jiménez's many rewritings and republications). In this way it is possible to arrive at a coherent structuring of his work. When it comes to the publication of the *Obra definitiva*, the task becomes more complicated since Jiménez's plans regarding its organization would change over time, entailing that a considerable number of drafts of the articulation of his complete works exist. The editors are then forced to choose one configuration, leaving the other possibilities aside. Due to this the second possible way of approaching

Jiménez's output, appears what could be called the synchronic work. This textual body includes an indefinite series of manuscripts and variants of poems and prose texts (a large number of the manuscripts are variants of published poems, while many other texts do not have a definitive version but exist only as a series of drafts with crossing outs and corrections), as well as Jiménez's lectures, essays, aphorisms, letters, his designs for the covers of his books, the sketches of the organization of his *Obra*, etc. Considered as a synchronic whole, Jiménez's legacy can be regarded as a system of infinite permutations, as Octavio Paz characterizes Mallarmé's *Un coup de dés* (Paz 1994).[2]

A graphic description of the *Juanramonian* text legacy was given by the critic Ricardo Gullón when he depicted the poet's archive as it appeared at the end of his life. The annotation is dated 12 November 1952:

> Y a punto de marchar me pasa a la habitación donde guardan el archivo, ordenado por Zenobia, de sus cartas y papeles. Es una estancia reducida, abarrotada de carpetas, sobres, cajas, llenas de original publicado e inédito; uno y otro con numerosas tachaduras y correcciones, casi siempre hechas a lápiz sobre el texto mecanografiado o impreso. Veo una masa inmensa de poemas, borradores en prosa y verso, apuntes, notas, aforismos, etcétera, en papeles de diferentes clases y tamaño –incluso en el revés de un sobre, en pequeños trozos–; escritos a mano, sin señales de haber sido corregidos ni revisados. Sí; haría falta toda una vida para descifrar y ordenar este laberinto. (Gullón 1958: 84–5)

> When I am about to leave he leads me to the room where they keep the archive, ordered by Zenobia, of his letters and papers. It is a small room, bursting with folders, envelopes, boxes, filled with published and unpublished originals; all with numerous crossing outs and corrections, almost always with pencil over the machine typed or printed text. I see an immense mass of poems, prose and verse drafts, notes, aphorisms, etc., in papers of different types and sizes – even on the back side of an envelope, in small pieces – handwritten, without any sign of having been corrected or revised. Yes; an entire life would be needed to decipher and put this labyrinth in order.

It can be inferred from this annotation how the vision of an *Obra total* was entangled in the process of rewriting. In a Foucaultian perspective this development would expose the proliferation of meaning inherent in literary discourse, something that the author-function has the task of regulating, just as it would demonstrate the inadequacy of the notion of author in this respect (Foucault 1984). In Barthesian terms it would show how the *Work* was pursued while the outcome was a fragmented and open-ended *Text*.³ In the following, however, focus will be put on the relation between Jiménez's work on the *Obra* and the extent to which this task can amount to the constitution of a personal identity. Can the creation of the *Obra* converge with – or perhaps even articulate – a self?

The *Obra* as an Atemporal Absolute

Jiménez conceived at an early stage the idea of publishing his works as a complete whole. In the note referring to his first visit to the poet, on 27 May 1913, Juan Guerrero Ruiz⁴ tells of Jiménez's intention to publish his collected works:

> Va a publicar todas sus obras; tres libros cada año por lo menos, dos nuevos y uno de los agotados. En breve quiere dar *Libros de Amor*.
> –"*Almas de Violeta* y *Ninfeas* quisiera hacerlos desaparecer; son libros de la adolescencia. Voy a publicar desde *Arias Tristes*. Tengo una labor muy copiosa, dispuestos para su impresión hasta veintitantos volúmenes." (*Vv* I: 28)

> He is going to publish all his works; three books every year at least, two new ones and one of those out of print. In short he wants to publish *Love Books*.
> – "*Violet Souls* and *Water Lilies* I would like to make disappear. They are books of puberty. I am going to publish from *Sad Airs* on. I have a very copious work, up to twenty-something volumes ready to print."

Here appear *in nuce* the anticipations that would be repeated throughout Jiménez's life concerning the publication of his *Obra*: the imminence of the publication of the *Work* or – what sometimes amounts to the same – the intention of publishing it within a very demanding time schedule; the inclusion of the already existing collections as well as the future ones in a coherent unity; the mention of new titles (implied by the reference to the "twenty-something volumes ready for print"); finally, the expurgation of already published works.⁵

Guerrero Ruiz's next note of his conversations with Jiménez, two years after the first one, on 15 May 1915, also mentions Jiménez's intention to publish his complete works:

> Hemos hablado primero de sus libros. Tiene en pruebas, según me ha dicho, el primer volumen de la edición de sus *Obras Completas*, que han de constar de siete volúmenes de 500 páginas, en cada uno de los cuales irán cinco o seis de los libros primeros, publicando de esta forma los 36 tomos que en la actualidad forman su obra. Desde 1912, ésta se ha aumentado con un libro titulado *Sonetos Espirituales*; otro, de elogio a Giner de los Ríos: *Elegía a la Memoria de un Hombre Puro*; otro, *La Colina de los Chopos*, del pabellón de la Residencia, que él ha denominado así, etc., que son notas de poesía, paisaje, los niños, etc. (*Vv* I: 31)

> At first we spoke of his books. He has in proofs, he tells me, the first volume of the edition of his *Complete Works*, which will count seven volumes of 500 pages. Each of these will include five or six of the first books, publishing in this way the 36 volumes that make up his work at the moment. Since 1912 it has grown with a book titled *Spiritual Sonnets*; another a eulogy of Giner de los Ríos: *Elegy in Memory of a Pure Man*; another *The Poplars' Hill*, about the buildings of the Residencia de Estudiantes, that he has named thus, etc., which are notes about poetry, landscapes, the children, etc.

Even if this plan of the *Obras Completas* is considerably more precise than the one in the previous note, it follows the same pattern, envisaging the production as a finished and unified whole: seven volumes of 500 pages, each containing five or six of the 36 books his total output would comprise.

Through the *Obra* Jiménez doubtlessly strived to make a creation that would be the highest expression of the work of art, a perfect and self-sufficient universe in itself. This is expressed in the poem closing the collection *Piedra y cielo* (*Rock and Sky*) (1919):

> Quisiera que mi libro
> fuese, como es el cielo por la noche,
> todo verdad presente, sin historia.
>   Que, como él se diera en cada instante,
> todo, con todas sus estrellas; sin

que niñez, juventud, vejez quitaran
ni pusieran encanto a su hermosura inmensa.
 ¡Temblor, relumbre, música
presentes y totales!
¡Temblor, relumbre, música en la frente
–cielo del corazón– del libro puro!
(*Op*, I, 2: 537–8)

I wish my book might be
as is the sky at night,
all present truth, without history.
 That, as the sky, it might give itself
entirely at every moment, with all its stars; nor
should childhood, youth, old age detract
or add in charm to its great beauty.
 Tremor, flash of light, music
present and total!
Tremor, flash of light, music in the mind
– heaven of the heart – of the pure book!
(*THP*: 136; translation modified)

As can be inferred from this text, the *book* – which can be interpreted as a metonym for the *Obra* – should be a pure presence, as unquestionable as the firmament. Furthermore, the *Work* should suspend linear time, it should be "todo verdad presente, sin historia" (all present truth, without history). This vision of the *Obra* implies that temporality and contingency are overcome in a plenitude of form and meaning, in an absolute work of art. As two sides of the same coin, to absolute subjectivity corresponds the absolute work. This means that the voice uttering the *Obra definitiva* would not belong to an embodied subject, immersed in the physical and corruptible world, but to a divine atemporal I.

In a note dated 7 March 1922, Guerrero Ruiz recorded yet another plan for the *Obra*:

Estuvimos mucho tiempo hablando de su obra. Si quisiera podría dar un volumen por mes, hasta unos cien que hoy forman su obra. Muchos libros están acabados, depurados; otros, en borradores todavía. Juan Ramón ve su obra como un todo armónico, perfecto. Dice que si él tuviera tiempo de depurarla como sueña, no quedaría

una página que diera sombra a la obra; no quedaría nada de paja, sino sólo y todo obra de plenitud, madura y perfecta.
[…]
Yo le he animado mucho a que publique los libros de prosa a que corresponden las elegías andaluzas, que él titula "La muy noble villa de Moguer", "Urium", "Las flores de Moguer", etc. Juan Ramón me contesta que no quiere dar más libros provisionales como los que lleva publicados, ya que no le gustan. Él ve su obra con una perfección tal, que sólo así quiere darla, y como es capaz de mejorarla cada día, no se decide a dejarla… Claro que en esta pugna a que está sometido entre la creación y la labor de depuración se le van pasando los años sin publicar y puede que muera sin ver su obra editada. (*Vv* I: 52–3)

We spent a long time talking about his work. If he wanted to, he could deliver one volume every month, up to about one hundred that today make up his work. Many books are finished, purified; others still in drafts. Juan Ramón sees his work as a harmonious, perfect whole. He says that if he had the time to purify it as he dreams, no page would be left to cast shadows over the work; nothing superfluous would be left but only and entirely work of plenitude, mature and perfect.
[…]
I have encouraged him to publish the prose books to which the Andalusian elegies belong, that he titles "The Very Noble Town of Moguer", "Urium", "The Flowers of Moguer", etc. Juan Ramón answers me that he does not want to deliver more provisional books as the ones he has already published since he does not like them. He sees his work with such a perfection that he only wants to deliver it in this way, and as he is able to improve it every day, he does not take the decision to end it… But in this fight he is subject to between creation and purification the years pass by without publishing and he might die without seeing his work in print.

As this note shows, Jiménez was conscious of the infinite perfectibility of the *Obra definitiva*. In this extract from Guerrero Ruiz's diary, the fear of never finishing the *Work* is clearly expressed. The atemporal perfection that Jiménez aimed at in the *Obra*, "sólo y todo obra de plenitud, madura y perfecta" (only and entirely work of plenitude, mature and perfect), appears here confronted by the temporal condition to which the empirical individual is tied. A clear acknowledgment is in this way expressed of the utopian aspect of his project. Nonetheless, Jiménez must have worked intensely on the *Obra* from 1917 onwards, and especially from around 1922,[6] as is suggested by the absence of book publications between 1923, when *Poesía* and *Belleza* appeared, and 1936, when *Canción* (*Song*), the only published volume actually pertaining to an edition of the *Obra*, saw the light of day.[7]

It is also possible to observe Jiménez's consciousness of the utopian character of his project in other sources than Guerrero Ruiz's testimony.[8] During the 1920s and 1930s Jiménez published – possibly inspired by the Avant-Garde movements – a journal series, the *Cuadernos* (*Booklets*), where the literary public could follow the development of his writing. The journal is a publication form that emphasizes temporality, sometimes even provisionality, that is, it points in the opposite direction of the atemporality that Jiménez's writings pursued. To let the *Obra* appear through a series of booklets means exposing the temporal circumstance that underlies and conditions it. Jiménez's *cuadernos* point to the specific historical and existential context surrounding the production of a work of art, to how the creative process is unavoidably related to external circumstances.[9] Not only the outbreak of the Spanish Civil War the same year as Jiménez finally undertook the publication of the *Work*, but also the many drafts of the organization of his *Obra* kept in the archives of Puerto Rico, Moguer, and Madrid are proof of the conflict between envisaged absolute and empirical conditions.

Jiménez's work on the *Obra* can be related to the fragmented absolute of modern thought: the vision of an absolute or a totality that is bound to remain out of reach. The impossibility of achieving the end goal of the *Obra*, then, is not due to a lack of consistency in Jiménez's efforts but, on the contrary, to a consequence of the speculative paradigm he belonged to. Jiménez's initial quest for the *Obra* can be regarded as determined by the idea of an absolute subjectivity to be expressed and preserved in poetry, finally revealed as conditioned by a finite, that is, by an empirical subject. In this way Jiménez embodied the idea of the fragmented absolute by envisaging and pursuing an absolute without ever reaching it.

Even if Jiménez usually referred to his *Work* in a rather grave tone, his self-consciousness with respect to the utopian aspect of his enterprise is clear, since it is possible to find self-ironic texts regarding the project of finishing the *Obra definitiva*. An example of such a text is the prose poem "El poeta" (The Poet):

EL POETA

> *(Une belle vie, c'est une pensée de la*
> *jeunesse réalisée dans l'âge mûr.*
> *Alfred de Vigny.)*

Harto ya de tanta duda y tal martirio, se dijo, firme, un día: "No más llevarme los pensamientos al sofá ocioso, a acariciarlos infinitamente; no más soñar y contemplar lo hecho, lo haciéndose y lo por hacer."

"Supondré que he muerto y que otro yo libre de mí nace para aislar mi obra en quintos borradores. Al fin y al cabo, ya he pensado, contemplado y soñado bastante, y la aristocracia última está en no contemplar, no soñar, no pensar dos veces lo mismo."

Una gran alegría de eterna primavera interior lo llenó todo. Y, loco con su idea definitiva, cantando en las ventanas al sol de la mañana azul, decidió ponerla en práctica al instante. Y… se la llevó al sofá ocioso, a acariciarla infinitamente.

(1922-24.)

(Jiménez 1960: 105)

THE POET

> *(Une belle vie, c'est une pensée de la*
> *jeunesse réalisée dans l'âge mûr.*
> *Alfred de Vigny.)*

Fed up with so much doubt and such a torment, he told himself, firm, one day: "No more taking thoughts to the idle couch to caress them infinitely; no more dreaming and contemplating what is done, what is being done and what remains to be done."

"I will imagine that I have died and that another I free of me is born to isolate my work in fifth drafts. After all, I have thought, contemplated and dreamt enough, and the ultimate aristocracy consists in not contemplating, not dreaming, not thinking twice the same."

A great joy of eternal inner spring filled everything. And, crazy with his definitive idea, singing in the windows to the sun of the blue morning, he decided to put it into work at once. And… he took it to the idle couch to caress it infinitely.

(1922-24.)

This poem exhibits an evident autobiographical reference that shows the tension between the vision of the *Obra total* and the empirical nature of the author, who can only envisage the perfection of his work in a daydream. The finite condition of the author appears explicitly in this text, since the person who is supposed to finish the *Obra*, presumably a literary critic, is somebody "libre de mí" (free of me). Only somebody separated from the empirical circumstances of the authorial subject – in turn destined to fantasize about his idea in the "sofá ocioso" (idle couch) – would be able to close, "aislar" (isolate), the *Work*. This poem appeared in one of the *Cuadernos* (no. 2 of *Unidad* in 1925) and it shows that already at the moment when Jiménez was working most intensely in his *Obra definitiva* he was conscious of its utopian nature. The vision of the *Work* reproduces, then, the modern split subject and the consequent oscillation between the ambition for an absolute and a fragmentation impossible to overcome.

The *Obra* as an Evolving Fulfilment

A conception of subjective plenitude other than that of the atemporal absolute subject can be observed in connection with the *Obra*, this one based on a poetic evolution. Jiménez's probably first self-interpretation of this kind was given with the publication of the anthology *Poesías escojidas (1899-1917)* (Selected Poems). On 11 July 1917, shortly before the release of the book, Guerrero Ruiz records Jiménez's comments about it:

> Pasada una hora, Zenobia, cuya simpatía deja maravillado, se marcha a visitar a su madre, y Juan Ramón me ruega le acompañe a la imprenta Fortanet, donde ha de corregir las pruebas de su libro de *Poesías Escojidas*. Por el camino me va explicando que se trata de un libro donde se contiene como una historia muda de toda su obra poética. (*Vv* I: 46)

> After one hour, Zenobia, whose charm leaves one enchanted, goes to visit her mother, and Juan Ramón asks me to go with him to Fortanet printing house, where he has to correct the proofs of his book *Selected Poems*. On the way he explains to me that this is a book in which a sort of silent history of his entire poetic work is contained.

Despite Jiménez's claim that this volume represents his diachronic development, the revised character of the volume is obvious already in the table of contents. The first two collections of poems are omitted and replaced by the title of a book that never appeared, *Anunciación* (*Annunciation*). The title of this non-existent book suggests the latent presence of the complete *Obra* at the very beginning of Jiménez's poetic career. Out of the five poems included under this heading only one was actually published in one of Jiménez's first two books, "Mayas", from *Ninfeas*. Nonetheless, the version of "Mayas" appearing in *Poesías escojidas* is considerably changed in style and content with respect to its first publication. The declamatory tone and the alexandrine verses of the original sonnet have been transformed into a serene expression and to hepta- and hendecasyllabic verses. Similarly, the other poems supposedly composed during the years 1899–1901 are written in the style that Jiménez had arrived at in 1917, the *poesía pura*. With *Poesías escojidas*, Jiménez aimed at giving a vision of his poetic production as fully developed in form and content from the outset, when in fact this book expresses the aesthetic ideal he had developed by 1917.

The celebrated poem "Vino, primero, pura" ("She came, first, pure") appeared for the first time in this volume. This text has been interpreted by some critics to be a poetic autobiography describing Jiménez's evolution as an author.[10]

Vino, primero, pura,
vestida de inocencia.
Y la amé como un niño.
    Luego se fue vistiendo
de no sé qué ropajes.
Y la fui odiando, sin saberlo.
    Llegó a ser una reina,
fastuosa de tesoros…
¡Qué iracundia de yel y sin sentido!
    …Mas se fue desnudando.
Y yo le sonreía.
    Se quedó con la túnica
de su inocencia antigua.
Creí de nuevo en ella.
    Y se quitó la túnica,
y apareció desnuda toda…
¡Oh pasión de mi vida, poesía
desnuda, mía para siempre!
(*Op*, I, 2: 378)

> She came, first, pure,
> dressed in innocence.
> And I loved her as a child loves.
> > Then she began dressing up
> in all manner of lavish clothes.
> And I began hating her without realizing it.
> > She came to be a queen,
> ostentatious with treasures…
> What senseless wrath of gall!
> > …But she began undressing.
> And I smiled at her.
> > She stood at last with the tunic
> of her innocence of old.
> I believed in her again.
> > And she took off the tunic
> and appeared completely naked…
> Oh passion of my life, poetry
> naked, mine forever![11]

This poem describes a woman – personified poetry – appearing to the lyrical subject in an alternation between nakedness (i.e. purity) and sumptuous clothes. At first the woman appears "vestida de inocencia" (dressed in innocence), and the lyrical subject, in turn, loved her "como un niño" (like a child loves). Gradually the two persons become estranged from each other, and this process culminates in the description of poetry as a kind of opulent but sterile Snow Queen. From this point on, the development is reversed into a gradual re-encounter with poetry that leads to the eternal passionate union between the two lovers that closes the text. The poem describes a circular development, as it begins and ends with the union of lyrical subject and personified poetry. In this way it is implied that the lyrical subject has evolved almost like the protagonist of a *Bildungsroman*, returning home with an insight into the true nature of the world. It is noteworthy that this narrative does not include any breaks in the evolution of the lyrical subject but sees it as gradually changing. The seamless unity of the development cannot be more conspicuously expressed than through the anthropomorphic representation of poetry: it is one and the same throughout, only the external "ropajes" (lavish clothes) change. With the culmination of the narrative a definitive plenitude, a totality, is reached. The lyrical subject arrives at, accomplishes, his vital goal. The lifelong devotion to poetry bears as its fruit the consummation of the work and the man in an eternal oneness. However, the protagonist of this narrative is still a textual subject since the development does not relate to anything external to the poet and his work on poetry – no reference to autobiographical or historical events is given at all. The lyrical subject of "Vino, primero, pura" is thus a textual twin of the individual Juan Ramón Jiménez but devoid of the latter's lived experiences.

The same pattern appears in another famous representation of Jiménez's diachronic development, the notes at the end of *Animal de fondo*. In that text he describes his poetic evolution as having passed through three phases:

> Es decir, que la evolución, la sucesión, el devenir de lo poético mío ha sido y es una sucesión de encuentro con una idea de dios. Al final de mi primera época, hacia mis 28 años, dios se me apareció como en mutua entrega sensitiva; al final de la segunda, cuando yo tenía unos 40 años, pasó dios por mí como un fenómeno intelectual, con acento de conquista mutua; ahora que entro en lo penúltimo de mi destinada época tercera, que supone las otras dos, se me ha atesorado dios como un hallazgo, como una realidad de lo verdadero suficiente y justo. Si en la primera época fue éstasis de amor, y en la segunda avidez de eternidad, en esta tercera es necesidad de conciencia interior y ambiente en lo limitado de nuestra morada de hombre. Hoy, concreto yo lo divino como una conciencia única, justa universal de la belleza que está dentro de nosotros y fuera también y al mismo tiempo. (*Op*, I, 2: 1197–8)

> That is to say, the evolution, the succession, the development of my poetry has been and is the development of an encounter with an idea about god. At the end of my first period, when I was about twenty-eight years old, god appeared to me as a mutual sensitive surrender; towards the end of the second, when I was about forty years old, god passed through me as an intellectual phenomenon, with an accent on mutual conquest; now, when I am entering the penultimate stage of my appointed third period, which includes the other two, god has treasured himself within me as a finding, as a reality of what is exact and sufficiently true. If during the first period it was an ecstasy of love, and in the second an intense desire for eternity, in this third one it is rather the need for inner consciousness and the limited horizon of our moderate name. Today I define the

divine as a unique consciousness, an exact consciousness, a universal consciousness of beauty which is inside ourselves and also outside simultaneously. (*GDD*: 127–9)[12]

The organic unity of the development appears in this citation as the threefold repetition of the encounter with god, a god that – as has been noted above in Chapter 2 – is identical with poetic consciousness. The relation between the I and the god is thus similar to the one between subject and personified poetry in "Vino, primero, pura" (She came, first, pure). Even if the latter poem presents a phase of estrangement that is absent in the notes to *Animal de fondo*, both texts finish with the unification of subject and poetry. In both cases Jiménez already carried the germ of his encounter with poetry/god from the outset of his poetic career. His poetic consciousness advances in cycles while remaining essentially the same.

The model for this pattern of development is the Hegelian thesis-antithesis-synthesis dialectic, that is, the logic of the self-revealing Reason that through history arrives at itself in its absolute form. The lyrical subject possesses a full potential for achieving plenitude and reaches it by surmounting each vital stage. The search culminates in an absolute self-conquest. Consistently following the idea of the *Obra* as the manifestation of absolute subjectivity, Jiménez's descriptions of his evolution are completely immanent, that is, no reference at all is made to exterior, let alone existential influences. Jiménez's development is to be likened to the revolutions of a celestial body driven by an immanent force. The Goethe quotation that Jiménez used as an epigraph in his mature works expresses precisely this idea: "Wie das Gestirn, ohne Hast, aber ohne Rast / Como el astro, sin aceleración y sin descanso" (Like the stars, without haste, but without rest). The momentum of the evolution comes only from the inner world of the subject, which is why he understands his work as a homogeneously developing body of texts with a profound unity. The culmination occurs in the last phase of the production through a sort of Hegelian *Aufhebung* (sublation) of the previous stages: "mi destinada época tercera, que supone las otras dos" (my appointed third period, which includes the other two).[13] A similar figure of thought appears as in the one Habermas notes is a constant in Modernity, that the I can only gain itself by posing a non-I that then is progressively conquered by the I (Habermas 1990: 262–4). In contrast to the notion of an absolute subject that is mirrored by an atemporal *Work*, now self-sufficient subjectivity is conquered through time when the subject becomes consubstantial with poetry – an ending that was prefigured from the outset.

Whether in the form of an atemporal whole or as a diachronic fulfilment, Jiménez was haunted throughout his mature years by the vision of the *Obra definitiva*, and he put enormous efforts into it until the end of his life. However, as has been mentioned, his awareness of its utopian character is clear. In a letter to the Mexican writer and activist José Revueltas, dated 12 July 1943, Jiménez states the impossibility of achieving the perfection of the *Obra*:

> Yo no creo en la perfección; creería en la "perfección sucesiva imposible", como en la "posible sucesiva imperfección". En este momento tengo más labor escrita que nunca. Si yo me considerara perfecto, es decir, estéril por acabamiento perfecto, para mí o para los otros, cortaría mi vida de su libertad. [...] Ordenar no es terminar, es empezar. (Jiménez 1977: 52)

> I don't believe in perfection; I would believe in the "impossible successive perfection", as in the "possible successive imperfection". At this moment I have more written work than ever. If I considered myself perfect, that is, sterile because of perfect closure, for me or for the others, I would cut my life from its freedom. [...] To order is not to finish, it is to begin.

The explicit acknowledgment of the infinitely perfective character of the *Obra* is here related to the question of finitude, since creativity and unending correction are linked to life, whereas the end of the work on the *Obra* is equivalent to sterility and mistaken destiny. In this text the expectation of self-conquest through the achieved perfection of the *Work* is abandoned and instead an unending transformative process is expressed. The good infinity (the plenitude of a totality) that was envisaged in "Vino, primero, pura" and in the notes to *Animal de fondo* is finally replaced by a bad infinity (unending succession).[14]

Finitude and Individual Identity

The unfulfilment of what self-founded subjectivity promises – the absolute *Work* – engenders the self-ironical and demonstratively fragmented subject that has been analyzed in Chapter 3 above. Jiménez himself proposed, nonetheless, a third understanding that connects lived experience and poetic evolution in another way, by relating to the pantheistic attitude that has been discussed above. This is expressed in the essay "El modernismo poético en España y en Hispanoamérica" (Poetic Modernism in Spain and Latin America), where Jiménez relates his poetic evolution to a series of biographical experiences centred around the *Diario de un poeta recién casado*:

> El *Diario* fue saludado como un segundo primer libro mío y el primero de una segunda época. Era el libro en que yo soñaba cuando escribía *Ninfeas*; era yo mismo en lo mismo que yo quería. [...] La crítica mayor y mejor está de acuerdo en que con él comenzó una nueva vida en la poesía española (un "gran incendio poético", dijo uno). En realidad, el *Diario* es mi mejor libro. Me lo trajeron unidos el amor, el alta mar, el alto cielo, el verso libre, las Américas distintas y mi largo recorrido anterior. Es un punto de *partidas*. (*Tg*: 231–2, author's emphasis)

> The *Diario* was saluted as a second first book of mine and the first of a second epoch. It was the book that I dreamed of when I was writing *Water Lilies*; it was myself in what I wanted. [...] The greater and better criticism agrees that with it a new life in Spanish poetry began (a "great poetic fire", one said). In fact, the *Diario* is my best book. Love, the open sea, the high sky, the free verse, the different Americas, and my long previous trajectory, together brought it to me. It is a point of *departures*.

The motif of a cyclic and organic evolution is still present (as can be inferred from the chiasmus "un segundo primer libro mío y el primero de una segunda época" (a second first book of mine and the first of a second epoch) and from the claim that it was the book Jiménez dreamed of when he wrote his first collection of poems), but the main cause for the inauguration of his *segunda época* is the encounter with love and the natural elements.[15]

In a note dated 17 December 1953, Ricardo Gullón recorded a similar self-interpretation by Jiménez:

> Voy a dar, por orden cronológico, la obra total. El fin de la primera época son los *Sonetos espirituales*. Mi renovación empieza cuando el viaje a América y se manifiesta con el *Diario*. El mar me hace revivir, porque es el contacto con lo natural, con los elementos, [...] y mu-

chos años después, gracias también al mar, con ocasión del viaje a la Argentina, surge *Dios deseado y deseante*. (Gullón 1958: 120)

> I am going to publish, in chronological order, the total work. The end of the first epoch is *Spiritual Sonnets*. My renewal begins with the journey to America and becomes manifest with the *Diario*. The sea revives me because it is the contact with the natural, with the elements, […] and many years later, also thanks to the sea, on the occasion of the trip to Argentina, *God Desired and Desiring* appears.

Here a tripartite organization of the *Obra* is presented, again suggesting the cyclic evolution that appeared in the notes at the end of *Animal de fondo*. Apparently, as in the previous quotation, the reference to Jiménez's life entails that the subject speaking in the last passage is an embodied individual influenced by lived, personal, experiences. However, the fact that on both occasions it is the sea that revives and renews him is a pointer to identifying nature as the motive power behind the renewal. In this way pantheism is, actually, the notion that underlies the absolutization of subjectivity. In an entirely parallel way as was shown in the above chapters, the subject connects with nature and thus achieves a substantial content. Rather than related to the constitution of a self, the poetic evolution is described as reaching an absolute expression thanks to the profound connection of subjectivity with nature.

In one manuscript Jiménez imagined, in a highly original way, how autobiographical reference could coalesce with the *Obra* on the basis of the individually lived experiences. He envisaged an *Obra* that would at the same time incorporate his lived experiences and exhibit a total synchrony. In a note, cited by Antonio Sánchez Romeralo in the preface to *Leyenda* (Legend), Jiménez states the following:

> …mi ilusión sería poder correjir todos mis escritos el último día de mi vida, para que cada uno participase de toda ella, para que cada poema mío fuera todo yo. Como esto no puede ser, empiezo a mis 71 años [i.e. in 1952/53], ¿por última vez?, esta corrección. (Jiménez 1978: XI)

> … my dream would be to be able to correct all my writings on the last day of my life, for all of them to participate in all of it, for every poem of mine to be all I. Since this is impossible, I begin at my 71 years [i.e. in 1952/53] – for the last time? – this correction.

The wish to correct his entire output on the last day of his life condenses perfectly the unsolvable conflict between the vision of an absolute *Obra total* and the processing conditions necessarily underlying it. In this last quotation, however, the author of the *Obra* is the individual in his biographical determination: "todo yo" (all I). In this way the paradigm of the fragmented absolute would have been overcome, and precisely through the finitude of the subject, since it is exactly this finite condition that would put an end to the infinite corrections. If it had been possible for Jiménez to rewrite his immense output on the last day of his life ("day" is, strictly speaking, a metonym for instant) then all his works would have been relived – *revividos* – in accordance with his lived experience. The *Obra* that emerges from this perspective is not an atemporal work but one that would express the life of the person Juan Ramón Jiménez. His *Work* would then be a unity integrated by his irrevocably final perspective upon his life course. The envisaged totality is in this case Juan Ramón Jiménez's life and work as a whole.

Jiménez's rewriting of poems originally composed thirty or forty years previously can from this perspective be understood as a work of memory actually *reliving* the past through the rereading and rewriting. By means of the reliving of his poems, Jiménez would infuse new life into the memories necessarily subjacent to his texts. From a biographical perspective, this could be the reason why Jiménez became absorbed in the process of rereading and rewriting since he became, in the words that Ricoeur recovers from Proust, a reader of himself.[16] If the notion of the *Obra* is on one side equivalent to an ideal of finished form and atemporal beauty, on the other side it may represent a strictly personal work of remembering and self-interpretation. The work on the *Obra*, then, was for the most part determined by the notion of subject given by the philosophical tradition from Descartes through Kant to Husserl, but at the same time Jiménez also imagined the idea of an autobiographically determined selfhood as the horizon of the *Obra* – looking in this way beyond the limits of modern subjectivity.[17]

CONCLUSION

> *Exalted subject, humiliated subject: it seems that it is always through a complete reversal of this sort that one approaches the subject; one could thus conclude that the "I" of the philosophies of the subject is* atopos, *without any assured place in discourse.*
>
> Paul Ricoeur

Ortega y Gasset describes in the essay "Las dos grandes metáforas" (The Two Great Metaphors) (1924) the two predominant images of consciousness in the history of Western thought. Antiquity and the Middle Ages regarded consciousness as a wax tablet upon which exterior reality was impressed. This realistic thinking stresses the independent reality of the world and, correspondingly, it regards perception as the impression of the object upon the subject. Modern thought – which Ortega regards as initiated by the Renaissance and Descartes – inverts this idea and considers only the independent reality of consciousness by means of the metaphor of the container and its contents. Things are ideas contained in consciousness. This idealist paradigm highlights the imaginative faculty, that is, the creative forging of reality by consciousness:

> Con la imaginación creamos y aniquilamos los objetos, los componemos y descuartizamos. Pues bien: los contenidos de la conciencia, no pudiendo venirnos de fuera –¿cómo la montaña puede entrar en mí?–, tendrán que emerger del fondo subjetivo. Conciencia es creación.
> (Ortega y Gasset 1963: 400)

With the imagination we create and annihilate the objects, we compose them and tear them apart. Well, then, since the contents of consciousness cannot come to us from outside – how can the mountain enter inside me? – they must emerge from the subjective depth. Consciousness is creation.

At the same time, the subject acquires immense proportions in contrast to previous periods where it was a thing among things, a perceptual entity:

> Como en las consejas de Oriente, el que era mendigo se despierta príncipe. Leibniz se atreve a llamar al hombre *un petit Dieu*. Kant hace del yo sumo legislador de la naturaleza. Y Fichte, desmesurado como siempre, no se contentará con menos que con decir: el Yo es todo. (Ortega y Gasset 1963: 400)

> As in the oriental tales, he who was a beggar wakes up as a prince. Leibniz dares to call man *un petit Dieu*. Kant makes of the I the supreme legislator of nature. And Fichte, excessive as always, will not be satisfied with less than saying: the I is all.

However, as the previous analyses have shown, this is only a partial view of the modern subject. The subjectivity that has been circumscribed in the preceding chapters oscillates between being a sovereign, world-generating consciousness and a fragmented, contingent and even self-parodying subject. The emphatic expression of the omnipotent poetic *fiat* is permanently in conflict with the lyrical subject's finite condition. Modern subjectivity aims for an absolute, but its finitude appears as an invincible hindrance for accomplishing this striving. Jiménez's poetry can, with the preceding analyses in mind, be regarded as a scene where these two facets of the modern subject are, so to say, acted out. On the one hand a divine I appears, creating a world with his divine imagination. On the other, a corporeal, transitory and contingent subject arises as the *alter ego* of the former. The present book can be regarded as a hermeneutical exercise, not only with respect to the literary texts that have been analyzed but also with respect to the tradition of the philosophy of the subject. In the previous chapters the aim has been to set the subject of that paradigm before the reader's eyes: an I that acknowledges (against its own will, so to speak) its self-elevation to a metaphysical principle as untenable.

To summarize: in the above pages it is shown how Jiménez's lyrical subject generates a mythical spatial representation consisting of a tension between a heavenly, sacred sphere – that at the same time is identified with the inner world of the subject – and an earthly, profane realm marked by transience and death. This spatial dichotomy appears in Jiménez's output from the earliest until the last works. It is also seen how the consciousness of the subject's finite and contingent condition eventually undermines the sense of plenitude given by absolute subjectivity. As if in reaction to this fragmentation, the mature poetry displays a purely textual writing that is uncontaminated by the contingency of the physical world. For this reason, the works written after 1913 mostly express a triumphant mood. At the same time, the analysis of the motif of desire shows that Jiménez's poetry is pervaded by desire and lack even in the texts that most intensely claim to have reached fulfilment. The modern paradigm operates with a merely virtual notion of the absolute, and this conviction receives a clear illustration in the texts of *Animal de fondo*, quintessentially formulating the desire for the absolute that pervades Jiménez's entire output and modern thought as a whole. A kind of compensation for the finitude of subjectivity can be observed in the transformation of the lyrical subject into the voice of the natural world. This pantheism appears through the principle of the universal analogy (Octavio Paz) and is present from the early poems onwards. The scepticism inherent in modern thought towards any totalizing world-understanding appears in the third fragment of *Espacio* as a parody (which is also a self-parody) of the sacralized notions of art and the artist. In addition, the third fragment of *Espacio* displays the lyrical subject's consciousness of being merely a linguistic entity at the mercy of a reader actualizing it. In this way the whole tradition of modern poetry is drawn, from Romanticism to the Avant-Gardes, since both the tragic expression of individual contingency and the notion of the sacralized poet-subject appear in earnest and ridiculed in the same text.

The analysis of temporality opened the way for a discussion of whether a *self* is attained in Jiménez's poetic work, that is, a personal identity achieved by means of lived experiences and their mnemonic elaboration. Nonetheless, the lyrical subjectivity that this analysis brought to light is also fundamentally conditioned by the notion of the absolute subject. A temporal representation appeared which is related to the aesthetic experience and corresponds with the notion of time as a product of consciousness. Consequently a poem becomes identified as monadic time detached from historical temporality. In turn, the duration of a poem correlates with subjective finitude since a poem in the end is finite just as an individual is. The finite condition of poet-subject and text can, however, be regarded as "overcome" through the recovery of the poetic time in the reading, as the temporality of a poem is unendingly recurrent thanks to the future readers. The reading of *Diario de un poeta recién casado* disclosed that, despite this book having the character of a poetic diary, Jiménez's aim is to escape historical temporality. History appears as contingent as subjectivity, and for this reason, instead of developing a self, Jiménez strives to escape contingency by means of the typically modern connection between inner and outer nature. The subject becomes a medium for the cosmic cycles and is dissolved in eternal recurrence. Finally, the analysis of Jiménez's work on his *Obra* revealed that among the ideas of the *Work* as a product of absolute subjectivity, an intention to reach a self could perhaps be unearthed.

If the latter manifestation of an idea of selfhood is put aside – given that it eventually is a variation of the idealist self-conquest – then three different solutions to modern split subjectivity are proposed in Jiménez's work. The first solution is to regard lyrical subjectivity as a purely linguistic entity, that is, as an impersonal textual subject that creates an immaterial poetic kingdom and in this way overcomes the corruptibility and frailty of empiricity. The second solution appears when Jiménez's lyrical subject becomes a medium of the natural universe in a pantheistic worldview. This connection between subject and cosmic totality has some traits in common with Nietzschean thought. Both above-mentioned solutions proposed in Jiménez's poetry entail, however, the dissolution of the individual: an empty or impersonal self-concept arises. For this reason, the third solution to the split subjectivity is entirely consistent with the presuppositions of modern subjectivity, since it preserves the empirical I at the cost of the absolute subject and leads to an ironical and disillusioned self-regard. The lyrical subject regards himself as a contingent entity that can give birth to the poetic expression of this contingency, an expression, however, that ultimately is also arbitrary. This is the self-mocking I speaking in the last fragment of *Espacio*, a sceptical consciousness that – from a global perspective of Jiménez's lyrical output – finally overshadows the former two solutions to the modern split subject. The promise implicit in a self-founded subjectivity – the elevation from contingency to necessity on the basis of the subject's own forces – is abandoned and the I faces his own arbitrariness with despise. The drama of the titans who tried to conquer the dominion of the gods is, so to speak, repeated in a modern version.

The above analyses show, among other things, the extent to which the modern subject is devoid of identity. Even when Jiménez composes an autobiographical work, *Diario de un poeta recién casado*, the lyrical subject speaking in that collection is a consciousness desiring atemporality and the absolute rather than an autobiographically given self. Conversely, it must be noted that prose works such as *Españoles de tres mundos* (*Spaniards from Three Worlds*) (1942), *Olvidos de Granada* (*Oblivions from Granada*), *Recuerdos* (*Remembrances*) and *La isla de la simpatía* (*The Island of Sympathy*) are all written from the perspective of an I immersed in a social and emotional order, clearly in contrast with the solipsism of Jiménez's lyrical subject.[1] In his poetry, Jiménez operates with a lyrical subject vitally determined by the modern notion of subjectivity. This lyrical subject *does* utter part of Jiménez's output in prose, e.g. many prose poems in the *Diario* or the whole of *Espacio*. However, in the more contextually related prose texts Jiménez would leave this subject behind and engage in empirical questions such as literary rivalries, the moral behaviour of others or cultural idiosyncrasies in the Americas.[2] Among the few exceptions to this generic pattern separating poetry and prose, mention can be made of *Vida y muerte de Mamá Pura* (*Life and Death of Mummy Pure*), which describes Jiménez's memory of his mother and which includes both poetic and prose texts. Another exception to this rule is a series of only recently published poems on traditional Christian themes, written before the crystallization of the *poesía pura* (Jiménez 2000; cf. Palau de Nemes 1974: 477–88). Significantly, these works remained at the level of an experiment. It must be acknowledged that collections of poems such as these would not have been integrated easily into an *Obra* written under the sign of Modernity.[3]

In this way the limitations of the philosophy of the subject arise. It could be ventured – with Ricoeur and Habermas among others – that the individual actually finds itself through the giving of the I that intersubjective relationships demand.[4] The I of modern subjectivity is an autonomously acting and world-generating subject, whereas identity is only reached if the challenges of alterity are accepted and dealt with. Alterity appears in the form of the many different others surrounding the individual, but it is also present *in* the I, in its being flesh or by means of its moral conscience (Ricoeur 1994). From this perspective, Modernity represents an excluding anthropocentrism that – contrary to its explicit intentions – ends up incorporating archaic and mythical elements in order to maintain its subject-centredness.[5] If the illusion of a self-sustained subject is abandoned, then a wider notion of individuality can be ambitioned, perhaps an understanding of the person as a living corporeity that can aspire for an authentic self-conquest through self-giving. In the above pages, the modern notion of the subject has been exposed to an interpretative process in which its weakness is revealed as the self-deification and self-enclosure of a defectively embodied consciousness. Such a conception prevents the encounter with alterity: the alterity within oneself, the alterity of the neighbour and – for those willing to engage with it – the primordial alterity of God.

NOTES

INTRODUCTION

1. A proposal on how to distinguish between philosophical and literary discourses appears in the last chapter of Paul Ricoeur's *The Rule of Metaphor* (1975). Even if Ricoeur regards literature and philosophy as two different discourses, they can interact and intersect: "My inclination is to see the universe of discourse as a universe kept in motion by an interplay of attractions and repulsions that ceaselessly promote the interaction and intersection of domains whose organizing nuclei are off-centred in relation to one another; and still this interplay never comes to rest in an absolute knowledge that would subsume the tensions" (Ricoeur 1978: 302).

2. Jiménez's production is vast, and especially the prose writings display an enormous diversity (poetry in prose, literary criticism, literary portraits and caricatures, aphorisms, etc.). This study operates with the presupposition that Jiménez's *poetry* can actually be dealt with separately because the historically given generic framework of poetic discourse, which in this case includes the notion of the sacralized poet-subject, determines his lyrical production. Even if this subjectivity is not homogeneously dominant in his entire output, it is assumed that the privileged poet-seer is a central element of Jiménez's poetry. A few prose poems are included just as an analysis of the long prose text *Espacio*. As will be shown in the analyses of these texts, they are undoubtedly uttered by the above-mentioned poet-subject. As regards the generic question of Jiménez's prose: Blasco and Gómez Trueba (1994 and 2000), Young (2005), Wilcox (2005) and León Felipe (2005).

3. In *Oneself as Another*, Ricoeur compares the imaginative variations of subjective identity in literature and Derek Parfit's thought experiments about personal identity. Even if they belong to different discourses, both literary and philosophical fictions elaborate on the consequences of a given philosophical paradigm for the notion of subjectivity: "In this sense, literature proves to consist in a vast laboratory for thought

experiments" (Ricoeur 1994: 148). Ricoeur expresses the same idea in the conclusions to *Time and Narrative*, asserting that the function of fiction is "to serve as a laboratory for an unlimited number of thought experiments" (Ricoeur 1988: 271). This also means that the notion of exemplarity used in the following is not to be regarded as a parable made with the intention of illustrating a certain theory, but in the sense that Jiménez's work develops the implications of the modern paradigm.

4. "The step out of the Middle Ages was not to be taken until the next generation – by William of Ockham" (Pieper 1960: 147).

5. "Nominalist thinking demoted the *formae rerum* to *signa rerum*, which are merely associated with things by the knowing subject – to names that we tack on to things. Hume further dissolved the desubstantialized individuals left over from nominalism into the sense impressions out of which the perceiving subject initially constructs its representation of objects. In a counter maneuver, idealist philosophy renewed both identity thinking and the doctrine of Ideas on the new foundation that was exposed by the shift in paradigms from ontology to mentalism: subjectivity" (Habermas 1992: 31).

6. Kant uses the notion of *synthetic a priori knowledge* to refer to judgements that are necessary and universal, and that can be applied to attain knowledge of reality. Examples of synthetic a priori knowledge can be found in mathematics. Nonetheless, thought after Kant has tended to adopt his Copernican turn as a subjectivist axiom. Meillassoux has noted that "ever since the Kantian revolution, it has been incumbent upon 'serious' philosophers to think that *the condition for the conceivability of the Copernican decentring wrought by modern science is actually provided by a Ptolemaic re-centring of thought*. While modern science discovered for the first time thought's capacity to accede to *knowledge* of a world indifferent to thought's relation to the world, philosophy reacted to this discovery by discovering the naïvety of its own previous 'dogmatism', seeing in the 'realism' of the pre-Critical metaphysics the paradigm of a decidedly outmoded conceptual naïvety" (Meillassoux 2008: 118, author's emphasis).

7. Habermas notes that "[t]he I can only take possession of itself and 'posit' itself by positing, as it were unconsciously, a not-I and trying gradually to retrieve this thing posited by the I. This act of mediated self-positing can be understood under three different aspects: as a process of self-knowledge, as a process of growing reflective awareness, and as a process of self-formation. In each of these dimensions, European thought of the nineteenth and twentieth centuries sways between theoretical approaches that mutually exclude each other – and in each case the attempt to evade unhappy alternatives ends in the snares of a self-deifying subject consuming itself in acts of vain self-transcendence" (Habermas 1990: 262).

8. "Self-consciousness, the relationship of the knowing subject to itself, has since Descartes offered the key to the inner and absolutely certain sphere of the

representations we have of objects. Thus, in German Idealism metaphysical thinking could take the form of theories of subjectivity. Either self-consciousness is put into a foundational position as the spontaneous source of transcendental accomplishments, or as spirit it is itself elevated to the position of the absolute. The ideal essences are transformed into the categorial determinations of a productive reason, so that in a peculiarly reflexive turn everything is now related to the one of a generative subjectivity" (Habermas 1992: 31–2).

9. "The [Romantic] artist creates in his work, as it were, a miniature universe, a whole which has its goal in itself, and does not refer beyond to anything else" (Taylor 1985: 230).

10. In Kantian philosophy, the idea of the world as a finished totality, the idea of God, and the notion of the soul are *ideas of reason* that cannot be verified theoretically but they are nonetheless *regulative principles* that we should use in order to formulate correct hypotheses about the world. Hegelian thought – and its subsequent ramifications and developments – can be regarded as the necessary presence, within Modernity, of the notion of the absolute: "Hegel now makes reflection itself absolute – reflection as the self-reference of a spirit that works its way up out of its substantiality to self-consciousness and which bears within itself the unity as well as the difference of the finite and the infinite. What still had been true for Schelling is inverted: the absolute subject is precisely not supposed to *precede* the world process. Rather, it exists only in the relationship of the finite and the infinite to each other, in the consuming activity of reflection itself. The absolute is the mediating process of a self-reference that produces itself unconditionally" (Habermas 1992: 129, author's emphasis).

11. This is evidently a simplification since self-referentiality is a feature of modern literature. Apel (1988: 68-91) thus shows the continuity of the self-enclosure and self-thematization of poetry in the works of Eichendorff, Heine, Mörike, Baudelaire, Mallarmé, Tennyson, Swinburne, Hofmannsthal and George.

12. I will use the masculine personal pronoun to refer to the lyrical subject of Jiménez's poetry due to the strong autobiographical substrate in his writings. As will be explained below, one of Jiménez's aims is the unification of life and work. Even if this conflation is to be carried out by a divine poet-subject, that is, by a constructed subjectivity, this I nonetheless exhibits enough features to allow a reference to the biographical Juan Ramón Jiménez. The identity of Jiménez's lyrical subject is ambivalent, as it oscillates between demiurgic subjectivity and autobiographical reference.

13. If the tradition from Descartes to Husserl regards self-consciousness as transparent and immediate, this study adheres to Ricoeur's hermeneutic phenomenology according to which the subject is constituted also through the worlds of language and tradition. In consequence, this means that temporality and spatiality

are not only forms of intuition preceding any experience of the world, but are also formed through language, culture and beliefs. For this reason, the literary representation of time and space will to a certain extent be constituted in conformity with the paradigm a given author belongs to.

14. A series of studies have argued for Jiménez's belonging to a Romantic tradition: Valente (1971), Cardwell (1977), Coke-Enguidanos (1982), Pujante Sánchez (1990), Paraíso (1991), López Castro (1995), Jensen (1997), Silver (2001), Cardwell (2005), and Martínez Torrón (2006) to mention only some.

15. This is not to be understood in the sense that a literary text is open to any interpretation. Even if the hermeneutical process is open-ended, it is possible to refute misreadings, since "the entire theory of hermeneutics consists in mediating this interpretation-appropriation by the series of interpretants which belong to the work of the text upon itself. Appropriation loses its arbitrariness insofar as it is the recovery of that which is at work, in labour, within the text" (Ricoeur 1981: 164).

1. EARTHLY AND HEAVENLY: MYTHICAL SPATIALITY

1. "Kant's moral philosophy can be understood in general terms as an attempt to reconstruct the categorical ought of divine imperatives in discursive terms. The transcendental philosophy, taken as a whole, has the practical meaning of transposing the transcendent divine standpoint into a functionally equivalent *inner-worldly* perspective and to preserve it in the form of the moral standpoint" (Habermas 2008: 228, author's emphasis).

2. Paz refers mainly to William Blake when unfolding this trait of the history of literature (Paz 1981: 80–7), but the same thought is a constant in Romantic thought, as has been shown by Behler (1993: 154–64 and 195–201). Novalis expresses it in fragment 71 in *Blüthenstaub*: "In the beginning, poets and priests were one; it was only in later times that they became separated. The true poet, however, has always remained a priest, just as the true priest has remained a poet. And will not the future restore this former state of affairs?" (quoted by Behler 1993: 198). The religious substrate of modern poetry will be further unfolded in the following chapters.

3. Taylor describes the epiphanic quality of the work of art in Modernity in the following way: "A work of this kind is not to be understood simply as mimesis, even though it may involve a descriptive component. In fact there are two different ways in which a work can bring about what I'm calling an epiphany, and the balance over the last century has shifted from one to the other. In the first, which dominated with the Romantics, the work does portray something – unspoilt nature, human emotion – but in such a way as to show some greater spiritual

reality or significance shining through it. [...] In the second, which is dominant in the twentieth century, it may no longer be clear what the work portrays or whether it portrays anything at all; the locus of epiphany has shifted to within the work itself. Much modernist poetry and non-representational visual art is of this kind" (Taylor 1989: 419). Chapter X in Abrams (1953) describes the analogy author-God in the modern period.

4. A series of studies in the Jiménez criticism has addressed the religiosity of Jiménez's poetry, the most important being Saz-Orozco (1966), Cole (1967), Río (1973) Santos-Escudero (1975), Xirau (1980), Azam (1983), López Castro (1995) and Garfias (2002). The contribution of the present chapter in relation to these studies is to be found in regarding the mythical spatial articulation in Jiménez's poetry as a factor of continuity, as the same hierarchy of realms appears throughout his work.

5. Also Eliade regards the sky as the primordial precinct of the divine: "Simple contemplation of the celestial vault already provokes a religious experience. The sky shows itself to be infinite, transcendent. It is pre-eminently the 'wholly other' than the little represented by man and his environment" (Eliade 1959: 118).

6. The colour blue as a token of pure, ideal beauty is one of the most pervasive *topoi* of Spanish and Latin-American *modernismo*. Rubén Darío called his epoch-making collection of poems *Azul* (1888), and in Juan Ramón Jiménez this colour recurrently symbolizes pure beauty. It could be ventured that this topos has its origin in its metonymic reference to the blueness of the sky, by a transference of the divine qualities associated with the region of the sacred to its colour. From a literary historical perspective, the topos can be traced back to Novalis's *Heinrich von Ofterdingen*, where the protagonist's dream of a blue flower in a landscape in blue tones is the origin of his vocation as a poet. This topos also appears in French Symbolism, for example in Mallarmé's poem "Les fenêtres". In this text a dying man looks at the sky through a window, longing for the ideality he imagines in the celestial blueness and in the sunlight.

7. In the following, isotopy is understood as a thematic field, that is, as the presence, through repetition, of a specific semantic content in a text. The notion has been used in a variety of ways, cf. Greimas and Courtés (1982: 163–5). Segre unfolds the notion with respect to the analysis of poetic texts (1985: 40–2).

8. "The acute sensitivity to the hidden mysteries sets the poet apart from his fellows. But the longing for the infinite, the desire to comprehend the enigma of life and the hope of felicity and transcendence through art all too often disappoint the artist. He puts his trust in art only to find that at the end Beauty, too, is Nothingness and that he has been cheated of transcendence, meaning and consolation" (Cardwell 1977: 207).

9. "The artist who is a philosophical ironist must always play a dual role. He must create, or represent, like God, a finite, ordered world to which he can enthusi-

astically commit himself; and *at the same time* he must acknowledge his own limitations as a finite human being and the inevitable resultant limitations of his merely fictional creations. The artistic process, then, must be one of simultaneous creation and de-creation: a fictional world must be both sincerely presented and sincerely undermined, either by showing its falsities or limitations or, at the very least, by suggesting ways of responding to it other than whole-hearted assent" (Mellor 1982: 14, author's emphasis).

10. The interpretation of the inner world as both the origin and reference of Jiménez's poetry is also maintained by Coke-Enguidanos (1982: 116–22).

11. Specialists such as Sánchez Barbudo (1962), Predmore (1973), Cardwell (in Jiménez 1994b), Blasco (in *Op*, I, 2) and Lanz (2007).

12. Zenobia Camprubí Aymar (1887–1956) was of mixed Spanish, Puerto Rican and North American origin. Jiménez met her in Madrid in 1913, and after a difficult engagement period they married in 1916.

13. The *Diario* establishes an "autobiographical pact" in the sense defined by Philippe Lejeune: "The protagonist does not have a name in the narrative, but the author has declared explicitly in an initial pact that he is identical to the narrator (and thus to the protagonist, since the narrative is autodiegetic). Example: *Histoire de mes idées* (*Story of My Ideas*), by Edgar Quinet; the pact, included in the title, is clarified in a long preface, signed Edgar Quinet. The name does not appear one single time in the narrative, but, because of the pact, 'I' always refers to Quinet" (Lejeune 1989: 17). The situation is entirely similar in the *Diario*: Even if the lyrical subject is not identified with his name in the texts, the title of the work refers to the identification of the lyrical subject with the author, an identification unambiguously established in the introductory note, signed "J.R.J."

14. The idea of an essential personal identity that runs uninterruptedly from the earliest poetry to the last texts will be discussed in Chapter 6.

15. Jiménez published *Animal de fondo* in 1949, but intended it at a later moment to become part of a larger work with the title *Dios deseado y deseante* (*God Desired and Desiring*), a book which did not appear during his lifetime. In the newly published *Obra poética*, the original poems of *Animal de fondo* have been supplemented with material found in the Jiménez archives. The English translation of this work appears as part of the book *God Desired and Desiring* (*GDD*).

16. Jiménez was received as a celebrity in Argentina and Uruguay. For this reason the stay greatly encouraged him both personally and professionally. Jiménez's first biographer, Graciela Palau de Nemes, remarks the following when summing up what this trip meant to him: "A su regreso de la Argentina y el Uruguay, Juan Ramón se sentía rejuvenecido. Había vuelto a predicar su evangelio de poesía y belleza y había encontrado muchos seguidores. Durante el viaje de regreso, en alta mar, escribió la obra más reciente y trascendental del pensamiento

juanramomiano, *Animal de Fondo*, cuyo comentario precisa en relación con otros sucesos de la vida del poeta" (Palau de Nemes 1957: 330) (When he returned from Argentina and Uruguay, Juan Ramón felt rejuvenated. He had once more preached his gospel of poetry and beauty, and he had found many followers. During the return trip, on high sea, he wrote the most recent and momentous work produced by his thought, *Animal of Depth,* the commentary of which requires relation to other events in the poet's life).

17. Most critics (Sánchez Romeralo (1961), Gullón (1960: 139–50), Olson (1967: 220), Río (1973: 155–61)) agree in identifying Jiménez's "dios" with his poetic creativity. Gilbert Azam explains the idea of the divinity of *Animal de fondo* in the following terms: "En *Animal de fondo*, el poeta instaura un concepto de interioridad y de profundidad que conducirá finalmente a una «teología» de la ausencia y de la muerte de Dios. Pues de eso se trata en definitiva; y en adelante, el dios nombrado por Juan Ramón, por más que suceda el vago sentimiento de lo divino difundido en las cosas y ocupe el vacío dejado en su metafísica, se identifica plenamente con la conciencia del poeta" (Azam 1983: 590) (In *Animal of Depth* the poet establishes a notion of interiority and depth that eventually will lead to a "theology" of the absence and death of God. For that is the issue all in all; from now on, the god named by Juan Ramón, however much it succeeds the vague feeling of the divine dissolved in things and occupies the void left in his metaphysics, is fully identified with the consciousness of the poet).

18. A very similar image is presented in *Almas de violeta* (1900): "y triste, mi pensamiento / batía sus grandes alas" (*Plp*: 1534).

19. Emilio del Río relates Jiménez's poetry to idealist philosophy on the basis that in the latter "el sujeto se reconoce a sí mismo como fuente primera de la renovación del cosmos, como teniendo en sí un principio absoluto de universalidad […], y de ahí que el sujeto tienda a ser concebido como […] conciencia, universalidad formal que lo abarca todo y en que sólo el objeto tiene su objetividad […]. De esa misma manera Juan Ramón establece su yo como centro consciente de sí mismo y de su mundo, creador de sí y de su «dios», conciencia suma de lo hermoso conseguido y nombre único" (Río 1973: 172) (the subject recognizes itself as the first source of cosmic renewal, as having in itself an absolute principle of universality […], and for this reason the subject tends to be understood as […] consciousness, formal universality that embraces everything and in which only the object has its objectivity […]. In that same way Juan Ramón establishes his I as conscious centre of himself and of his world, creator of himself and of his "god", highest consciousness of the achieved beauty and unique name).

20. As will be seen below with reference to the poem "Luna del hombre" from *La estación total*, the sun can also be related to sexuality in the mature poetry.

21. The autonomous temporality of poetry will be analyzed below in Chapter 4.

22. The gold symbolism can – in a similar way as the blue and its connection with the sky – be identified with the symbolism of the sun by metonymical relation.

23. The metaphor of the painting as a window on reality dates from the Renaissance. Leon Battista Alberti described in *Della pittura* the painting as a window on the visible world, and Leonardo da Vinci described the perspective as "nothing else than seeing a place behind a pane of glass, quite transparent, on the surface of which the objects behind the glass are to be drawn" (quoted by Gombrich 1960: 299).

24. The influence of Ortega's thought on Jiménez has been discussed by Blasco (1981: 153–8). Given that Ortega is strongly influenced by phenomenology, an apparent discordance may appear between the phenomenological attitude of going *to the things themselves,* and the creation of a sphere of autonomous perfection. However, it must be underscored that in *The Dehumanization of Art*, Ortega displays a notion of art very close to Jiménez's idea of pure poetry, as a representation radically separated from our everyday experience of reality.

25. In classical mythology the moon is represented by the goddess Artemis and the sun by Apollo; apparently the moon is universally associated with the feminine principle of the universe and the sun with the masculine principle (Cirlot 1988: 283–4).

26. "Vino, primero, pura" will be analyzed in Chapter 6 below.

2. INFINITE LONGING AS A DYNAMIC SPATIAL FORCE

1. Graciela Palau de Nemes (1971) observes the same fundamental "sed de ilusiones infinitas" from *Ninfeas* to *Animal de fondo*. In the mentioned study, Palau de Nemes observes that the conjunction of sensuality and spirituality of the early works is repeated in *Animal de fondo* with its imagery of erotic desire. Cardwell has discussed the presence of motifs related to Lacan's psychoanalytic theories in the poetry of Gustavo Adolfo Bécquer (Cardwell 1992), Antonio Machado (Cardwell 1990), and Juan Ramón Jiménez (Cardwell 1997). In these articles he finds a correspondence between Symbolism and Psychoanalysis. In the following I draw inspiration from the work Cardwell has carried out in the mentioned studies but instead of referring to a psychoanalytical framework, I will relate to the Romantic motif of infinite longing.

2. "The *Critique of Pure Reason* thus reaches the point from which, in its own way, it connects with that metaphysical figure of thought, universal unity. That is, the transcendental unity of the knowing subject who relates itself to itself requires, on the side of what is known, a symmetrical concept of everything that stands over

and against the subject, a transcendental concept of the world as the totality of all appearances. Kant calls this world-concept a cosmological idea, i.e., a concept of reason by means of which we make the totality of conditions in the world into an object. A new type of synthesis thereby comes into play. Cosmological ideas generate the "unconditioned synthetic unity of all conditions in general"; by aiming at the whole of possible experiences and at the unconditioned, they follow principles of completeness and perfection that transcend all experience. This idealizing surplus distinguishes the *world-constituting* synthesis of reason from the synthetic accomplishments of the understanding, which allow us to know something *in the world*. Because the ideas are concepts that project a world, nothing that looks in any way like an object of experience could correspond to them. In relation to the world of appearances, they are suitable only as principles that regulate the use of the understanding and obligate it to the goal of systematic knowledge, that is, to theory formation that is as unitary and complete as possible. They have heuristic value for the progress of knowledge" (Habermas 1992: 125, author's emphasis).

3. "Condorcet appears to be the first to have applied without reserve the idea of an infinite perfectibility to the arts when he sketched his *Esquisse d'un tableau historique des progrès de l'esprit humain* in 1793-94" (Behler 1986: 296). Cf. also Behler (1989) and Behler (1993: 66–71).

4. The notion of an aesthetic idea has within Kant's philosophy a special meaning as it is the counterpart of an idea of reason, which is a concept to which no representation of the imagination can be adequate, such as God, the soul, freedom, etc. The genius is able to represent the supersensible domain without giving it a fixed form that would close it for the understanding. Also the moral law inspires in Kant a sense of a higher Being, cf. the final conclusion of the *Critique of Practical Reason* (1788).

5. This poem belongs to those related to Jiménez's stay at Doctor Lalanne's sanatorium in Castel d'Andorte in 1901. According to Ignacio Prat, who has studied this period in Jiménez's life, Jiménez was in Arcachon, a town of thermal baths on the French Atlantic coast, during the summer of 1901. Prat notes that it is doubtful that he spent the autumn of the same year there, as he claims in his autobiography published in *Renacimiento* in 1907. Based on unpublished notes and manuscripts, Prat argues that the woman appearing in the poem has a factual existence, and that the mention of the month of April in the title is due to the youth of the woman, and not to the month when Jiménez visited the town (Prat 1982: 33–6).

6. An isotopy of rest can be found in this part of the poem in the following syntagmas: "reposó la arboleda" (the grove rested), verse 16; "empezaron las flores a dormirse" (the flowers started to sleep), verse 17; "la rítmica y quieta placidez / de los campos" (the rhythmic and still / peacefulness of the fields), verses 20–21.

7. Sørensen (1997) describes how this topos appears in the *Roman de la rose* as well as in Renaissance literature. The motif had been discredited during the Enlightenment but was reinstated by the Romantic poets, among others Tieck, Eichendorff, Brentano, Hauch, Shelley, and Hugo. In his analysis of Eichendorff's tale "Das Marmorbild", Sørensen remarks upon the cosmic eroticism implied in the topos.

8. In the already mentioned poem by Baudelaire, "Correspondences", the last verse of the sonnet explicitly marks out the perfume as the element that establishes the correspondence between the spiritual and the sensory, as it "sings / the transports of the senses and the soul" (Baudelaire 1952: 8).

9. *Sonetos espirituales* were writen in 1914–15 and appeared in 1917, whereas *Estío* was composed in 1915 and published in 1916. Both works express Jiménez's love for Zenobia Camprubí Aymar.

10. The lines "Nada más. / –¿Acaso eres" are a "verso escalonado", as the two lines together make up one octosyllabic verse.

11. By Teresa Gómez Trueba in *Op*, I,1: 1490.

12. The following is indebted to Hernández-Pacheco (1995: 112ff.).

13. As is expressed in the following fragment of Novalis: "One finds what one loves everywhere, and sees similarities everywhere. The greater the love the more extensive and manifold is this similar world. My beloved is the abbreviation of the universe, the universe is the extension of my beloved" (Novalis 1997: 85).

14. As mentioned above *Animal de fondo* (1949) and *Espacio* (1943–54) are regarded as the summit of Jiménez's mature output.

15. "Estoy con eso y con los aforismos y terminando *Dios deseado y deseante* que, completo, tendrá ochenta poemas en lugar de los treinta publicados en *Animal de fondo*" (Gullón 1958: 119) (I am working on that and on the aphorisms and finishing *God Desired and Desiring* that, complete, will have eighty poems instead of the thirty published in *Animal of Depth*).

16. Even the impressive and beautiful edition of *Dios deseado y deseante* published by Bejarano and Llansó (Jiménez 2008) does not escape this condition. In an article in the Spanish newspaper *ABC* of 28 June 2009, "El Dios poético de Juan Ramón Jiménez" (p. 3), these two critics tell how they found, shortly after having finished the mentioned edition (which contains 58 poems), what they consider to be two additional poems belonging to the collection. However, even if these critics should publish a new edition of *Dios deseado y deseante* with 60 poems, it will still remain a (re)construction of a projected book and not the book itself as it would have appeared if Jiménez had finished it during his lifetime.

17. Arturo del Villar (2002) interprets *Animal de fondo* as a Satanic book in the tradition from Byron and Baudelaire. This interpretation is not in contradiction

with the one that will be proposed here, only a different facet of the work will be highlighted.

18. This text, in turn, makes reference to a local religious tradition in Moguer, "El Domingo de la Cruz", cf. *Op*, I, 1: 717. In this way traditional religion is included in "Conciencia hoy azul" and, as it were, sublated through self-reference and rewriting. This is one facet of Jiménez's unending rewriting, cf. Chapter 6 below.

19. St John of the Cross exposes in his *declaración* of the *Cántico espiritual* how the unification of the soul with God is a spiritual marriage where the soul becomes *deiforme* but retains its individuality (San Juan de la Cruz 2002: 194). Similarly, in the philosophical metaphysical tradition the unification of the illuminated individual with the One is not to be understood as a dissolution of the former: "According to Plotinus, in the medium of thought the soul forms itself into a self, which becomes conscious of itself as a self in the recollective, reflexive intuition of the one. *Henosis*, the uniting of the philosopher with the one, for which discursive thinking prepares the way, is at once ecstatic self-transcendence and reflexive self-reassurance" (Habermas 1992: 119).

20. Acillona considers the duality I-god as a self-mirroring: "Yo/tú es lo mismo que dios/Dios. La "tuidad" es la mismidad, como el Yo es el dios. Y parece imposible salir de este laberinto de espejos enfrentados" (Acillona 2007: 53) (I/you is the same as god/God. The "youity" is the selfhood, as the I is the god. And it seems impossible to escape from this labyrinth of mirrors facing each other).

21. Olson has explained this aspect of Jiménez's poetry in the following way: "In order to understand that 'truth of being' which is the *esencia* spoken of in the central section of the poem ["Tal como estabas" from *Animal de fondo* – JJ], one must recognize the 'butterfly of the form' as an allusion to the famous poem from *Piedra y cielo* [number 70 – JJ], in which beauty is a 'butterfly of light' that always eludes the poet's grasp, leaving him only with the 'form of its flight.' The evocation of this last concept makes it evident that here, too, the word 'form' and the 'essence' with which it is equated must be understood as meaning the 'form of flight.' At the end, therefore, of Jiménez's lifelong search for the inner reality of things, of himself, and of God, he perceives it, not as inert substance or as purely static being, but as dynamic form, a structure of movement" (Olson 1967: 222).

22. An example is the *nouveau roman* (Robbe-Grillet, Claude Simon) which, in sharp contrast to Aristotelian precepts requiring a clear plot and an unambiguous ending, indulges in repetitions, bifurcations and contradictions in order to avoid any possibility of a plot and thereby a closure.

23. Another version of this wish is the work on the *Obra definitiva*, which will be analyzed in Chapter 6.

3. PANTHEISTIC AND TEXTUAL SPACE

1. The source of Jiménez's pantheism – which strictly speaking is panentheism – can be traced back to the influence that the *Institución Libre de Enseñanza* exerted upon him. This teaching institution represented to a great extent the ferment that nourished the artistic and intellectual renaissance of Spanish culture in the first decades of the twentieth century. The *ILE* was based on a specifically Spanish intellectual current termed *krausismo*, referring to the German Idealist philosopher Karl Christian Friedrich Krause (1781–1832). Krause's philosophy operates with the notion of *panentheism* (the world is *in* God, encompassed by God). With respect to this notion in Jiménez's poetry, see note 6 below.

2. Verses 1–10 are from Olson (1967: 119).

3. The notion of reversibility is essential in the last stage of Merleau-Ponty's philosophy. Thus, in the unfinished essay "L'entrelacs – le chiasme", this thinker formulates the thesis that the experience of the world takes place through an interweaving of subject and object prior to the expressions of language and thought. Evidently, Paul de Man's writings do not advance in this direction.

4. The use of the adjective "fantásticas" in Spanish could not, around 1900, mean "extraordinary" but simply, in its literal sense, "a product of the fantasy". In the 1869, 1899 and 1914 editions of the *Diccionario de la Real Academia Española de la Lengua* the definition of "fantástico" reads: "adj. Quimérico, fingido, que no tiene realidad, y consiste sólo en la imaginación. // Perteneciente a la fantasía. // fig. Presuntuoso y entonado." Only in the 1992 edition of the *DRAE* was the following definition added to the ones quoted: "fig. y fam. Magnífico, excelente." It seems therefore unlikely that this latter meaning of the word could have been intended by Jiménez.

5. Saz-Orozco explains the self-reflexive nature of Jiménez's god in the following way: "Canta el poeta con la voz de su dios, que le enseña el camino de esa unión anhelada: vivir en oro todo el día. Es como un resumen de toda su carrera: abrirse totalmente a la belleza e integrarla –en conciencia– a su vida. Allí quiere encontrar el poeta a su dios. Es un hallazgo en lo más íntimo de su alma después de haber elevado el mundo exterior" (Saz-Orozco 1966: 192) (The poet sings with the voice of his god that shows him the road to that desired union: to live in gold the whole day. It is like a summary of his entire career: to open oneself totally to beauty and to integrate it – in consciousness – into one's life. There the poet wants to find his god. It is a find in the most intimate of his soul after having elevated the exterior world).

6. This could seem an expression of a peculiar form of panentheism where the lyrical subject becomes the godhead who contains the world. In the light of Jiménez's later writings, however, it is more accurate to regard this incorporation

of the world as an appropriation of it through poetry – an appropriation that eventually does not escape the sense of ontological contingency. A thorough and clarifying analysis of this question can be found in Saz-Orozco (1966: 105–41). For a description of the post-Kantian philosophical debate about pantheism and panentheism (especially with respect to Novalis), cf. Crowe (2008).

7. With respect to mythical world views, Eliade notes that "around this cosmic axis lies the world […], hence the axis is located 'in the middle', at the 'navel of the earth'; it is the Center of the World" (Eliade 1959: 37).

8. This aspect will be further developed in the next chapter.

9. Besides *Espacio*, Paz alludes to the poem "Árboles hombres", which first appeared in the Mexican journal *Taller, poesía y crítica* in 1940. In *Op* I it is included in the collection *Romances de Coral Gables* (poem no. 14).

10. The first two fragments of *Espacio* were, as the subtitle indicates, written in Florida, where Juan Ramón Jiménez and Zenobia Camprubí lived during the years 1939–42. Zenobia Camprubí's diaries have recently been published and give a vivid account of the couple's life in exile in the Americas. The third fragment must have been written in Puerto Rico, where the poet and his wife lived from March 1951 until their deaths, cf. Young (1968).

11. Young notes the difference between fragments one and two, on the one side, and the third one, on the other: "Los dos primeros fragmentos parecen una introducción al éxtasis de Animal de fondo; el tercero parece una retirada de él, especialmente el episodio del cangrejo comentado por Sánchez Barbudo" (Young 1968: 463) (The first two fragments seem an introduction to the ecstasy of *Animal of Depth*; the third seems a retreat from it, especially the crab episode commented upon by Sánchez Barbudo). The change from free verse to prose does not entail any significant alteration with respect to rhythm or content, as will be argued in the next chapter.

12. Given that the contrast in the lyrical subject's self-concept is to be found between the first two fragments and the third, only the first and the third fragments will be analyzed in the present chapter. The second fragment will be discussed in the next chapter with focus on the notions of time and poetic rhythm.

13. The relation between pantheism and idealism in Jiménez is explained by Saz-Orozco in the following way: "Su trayectoria que comienza con el panteísmo idealista se desarrolla en esa conciencia universal creadora de la belleza, de la poesía, que cada individuo lleva como en germen, excluyendo todo materialismo positivista. Según el poeta, se trata de hallar lo superior que existe dentro del hombre "como un diamante en una mina". Declara amar lo material, pero lo encuentra totalmente limitado, incapaz de satisfacer las ansias infinitas del hombre; de ahí nace su ansia por lo divino que vaya modelando al hombre en su misma sencillez, en su "inocencia primitiva". El hombre, pues, por

sus propias fuerzas, en el concepto juanramoniano, se alza a la altura de lo divino, se constituye en dios" (Saz-Orozco 1966: 132) (His career, beginning with idealist pantheism, develops into that universal consciousness that creates beauty, poetry, and that every individual carries as in seeds, excluding any positivistic materialism. According to the poet the goal is to find the superior that exists within man "as a diamond in a mine". He declares to love the material but he finds it completely limited, incapable of satisfying man's infinite longings; here is born his yearning for the divine that molds man in his own simplicity, in his "primitive innocence". Thus man, within the Juanramonian paradigm, rises, by his own forces, to divine heights, constitutes himself as god). With respect to pantheism in Jiménez, cf. Martínez Torrón (2006) and Acillona (2007).

14. Young cites the verses by Yeats that Jiménez alludes to: "But love has pitched its mansion in / The seat of excrement" (Young 1980: 89).

15. For other appearances of the dog in the mature poetry, see Saz-Orozco (1966: 121–2).

16. In this text love is defined as follows: "It is that powerful attraction towards all that we conceive, or fear, or hope beyond ourselves, when we find within our own thoughts the chasm of an insufficient void, and seek to awaken in all things that are, a community with what we experience within ourselves" (quoted by Young 1980: 75). This particular influence is only the superficial occasion for the coincidence between Shelley and Jiménez, since the belonging to a common paradigm of thought is the cause in a strict sense.

17. In fact these sentences seem a variation of John 18,37.

18. Cf. note 25 in Chapter 5.

19. This will be shown in the analysis of the second fragment in the next chapter. Maria Teresa Font (1972: 213) and Mercedes Juliá (1988: 16) both coincide in this role of the autobiographical references in *Espacio*.

20. "La analogía es el reino de la palabra *como*, ese puente verbal que, sin suprimirlas, reconcilia las diferencias y las oposiciones" (Paz 1981: 102, author's emphasis) (Analogy is the kingdom of the word *as*, that verbal bridge that, without abolishing them, reconciles the differences and oppositions); "El ritmo poético no es sino la manifestación del ritmo universal" (Paz 1981: 135) (Poetic rhythm is none other than a manifestation of the universal rhythm (Paz 1991a: 94)).

21. This opposition between a subject wishing for contemplation and another subject who is endlessly talking can be contrasted with a passage in the second fragment where the lyrical subject experiences an aesthetic epiphany and speaks with a dog and a cat in Spanish. In the passage from the second fragment, language and contemplation are one, whereas in the current excerpt they are experienced as conflicting. Cf. p. 108 below.

22. This passage of *Espacio* was first published under the title "Leyenda de un héroe hueco" in the Argentinian newspaper *La Nación* on 11 January 1953. Martínez Torrón (2006: 40) considers the possibility that, since the crab is called a *cáncer*, this passage alludes to Zenobia Camprubí's cancer that was diagnosed and treated in the years 1951–53, that is, the period when Jiménez must have worked on the third fragment. Zenobia Camprubí died from this illness in 1956, a few days after the announcement that Jiménez had been awarded the Nobel Prize.

23. Jiménez's notion of *conciencia* has been analyzed by, among others, Saz-Orozco (1966: 125ff. and 197ff.), Cardwell (1977: 37–44) and Blasco (1981: 239–43). In the present context, *conciencia* is understood as the incorporation of the perceived world by means of poetry, including also the collective consciousness that will assimilate the knowledge and the seeing of the poet. When understood and internalized by others, the writings of the poet will cease to be private and will be part of a wider consciousness.

24. Despite this defeated subject, the ending of the third fragment clearly represents a closure of the text. This will be commented upon in the next chapter.

4. POETIC TIME AND ETERNAL RETURN

1. With reference to Kant, Taylor states: "What the object of beauty gives us is something quite distinct either from utilitarian satisfactions or from the fulfilment of moral demands. The basis is there for a declaration of independence of the beautiful relative to the good" (Taylor 1989: 423). Cf. also Bürger (1974: 57–75).

2. Taylor notes how Schopenhauer regards art as having such an emancipatory potential: "Schopenhauer takes from Kant the key doctrine that aesthetic contemplation is disinterested, and translates that as a disengagement from the pressure of the will" (Taylor 1989: 443–4).

3. Since it is illustrated with the act of reciting a psalm, St Augustine's description of time will evidently apply to any poem, but with respect to the analysis of the absolute subject's construction of an autonomous temporality, it is especially useful in the present context, as will be shown in the following analyses.

4. In his monumental work *Time and Narrative* (1983–85), Ricoeur's contribution to the understanding of temporality is the notion of *narrative time*, combining characteristics and functions belonging to both objective and subjective time. Reference to it and to a corollary developed from this concept – *narrative identity* – will be carried out in the next chapter.

5. Husserl's understanding of the triple intentionality in time-experience is divided into *primal impression*, intending what is now, *retention*, intending what has just passed, and *protention*, intending what is to come.

6. The expression belongs to Walter Benjamin's *Theses on the Philosophy of History* (1939).

7. Jiménez's importance for the use of the "romance" genre in twentieth-century Spanish poetry is consensually accepted by the criticism. The first to observe Jiménez's renewed use of this traditional form was probably Rafael Alberti in the lecture "La poesía popular en la lírica española contemporánea" (1932). Here he stated that "Juan R. Jiménez es, sin duda, el verdadero creador del romance moderno" (Alberti 1973: 126) (Juan R. Jiménez is, beyond doubt, the true creator of the modern *romance*). The authority of Tomás Navarro Tomás in questions of metric corroborates this claim: "Su [Jiménez's] invariable adhesión al romance a lo largo de su labor es una de las manifestaciones de su actitud respecto a la lírica tradicional. Su ejemplo elevó la estimación de esta forma métrica en los círculos de la poesía culta y contribuyó a ganarle partidarios entre poetas más jóvenes" (Navarro Tomás 1973: 274) (Jiménez's constant adherence to the *romance* throughout his work is one manifestation of his attitude towards traditional lyric. His example heightened the esteem of this metrical form in the circles of learned poetry and contributed to gain followers for it among the youngest poets).

8. Tomás Navarro Tomás observes that the *retornelo* is often used by Jiménez in his incorporation of traditional metric patterns: "Entre esta serie de recursos, el que aparece practicado por Juan Ramón con juego más variado en cuanto a su forma y disposición en el poema es el retornelo, que consiste, como es sabido, en la repetición de una estrofa, ordinariamente la primera, o de parte de ella, al final o en el curso de la composición" (Navarro Tomás 1973: 272) (Among this series of means, the one that is most used by Juan Ramón with the most varied play, with respect to its form and disposition in the poem, is the *retornelo*, which consists, as is known, in the repetition of a stanza, usually the first one, or part of it, at the end of or along the composition). Also Olson has noted that this is a recurrent procedure in Jiménez's poetry, "suggesting a temporal circularity which closes off and limits the segment of time within which the poem unfolds, providing the illusion of a return to the starting point, of a successful setting apart of a circle of temporal succession tangential to time's linear advance" (Olson 1967: 111).

9. The following elements constitute this isotopy: "llora en la paz" (cries in the peaceful) (verse 4), "su queja dormida y lánguida" (its sleeping and languid lament (verse 5), "llena de sueño y nostalgia" (full of dream and nostalgia) (verse 7), "dulce" (sweet) (verse 8), "lastimeramente" (mournfully) (verse 12), "dulcemente" (sweetly) (verse 20), "su paz amiga es tanta" (its friendly peace is such) (verse 23), "dulces lágrimas" (sweet tears) (verse 25), "la plácida / tristeza" (placid / sadness) (verses 28–29).

10. Cf. note 10 in Chapter 2.

11. "Combina las variedades anteriores [octosílabo trocaico, dactílico, mixto (a) y (b)]. Utiliza el efecto de cada una de ellas según la conveniencia de la expresión. Constituye la forma histórica y ordinaria del metro octosílabo" (Navarro 1965: 46) (It combines the previous variations. It uses the effect each one of them has depending on the convenience for the expression. It constitutes the historical and usual form of the octosyllabic metre).

12. In the *Poetics*, 1457 b, one of Aristotle's examples of a metaphor on grounds of analogy is precisely that of life's evening: "as old age is to life, so is evening to day" (Aristotle 1951: 39).

13. Several other poems from the same collection express the distressing knowledge of a world continuing after the subject's death, e.g. *Op*, I, 1: 174–6 and 203.

14. According to Domínguez Caparrós, the trochaic octosyllabic verse "tiene un carácter lento, lírico y suave" (Domínguez Caparrós 1999: 251) (has a slow, lyrical and gentle character).

15. This idea is present in a number of poems in the same collection. A very clear example of the overcoming of death by means of the *Obra* is poem number 17 in *Belleza* (*Op*, I, 2: 738).

16. Young remarks that in the first edition of the second fragment, 58 out of the 73 verses were hendecasyllables (Young 1968: 470). Márquez (2003) notes that 54% of the verses in *Espacio* are hendecasyllables. Furthermore, this critic observes that Jiménez's prose contains a high degree of prosodic features. For Jiménez, this critic shows, free verse and poetic prose are not rhythmically different. Herrera Espinosa (2006) has shown how rhythmical patterns, from the phonetic to the thematic level, pervade the first fragment of *Espacio*. A useful synthesis of the critical reflections upon Jiménez's idea from his later years to turn his poems in free verse into prose can be found in León Felipe (2005).

17. The sentence "Y para recordar porqué he vivido" (and to remember why I have lived) is not repeated in this fragment, but a variation of it appears in the "fragmento primero" and two other variations open the third one (which were commented upon in the previous chapter).

18. The cited verses present the following accentual pattern. The dashes represent the unstressed syllables and the numbers refer to the stressed ones, indicating their number in the verse:

-2-4---8-
–2–4---8
-2-4---8-10
-2-4-6---10
-2-4---8-10-
-2---6-8-

            -2---6---10
            -2-4-6-8-10-12-
            -2-4---8-10-
            -2---6
            1----6.7--10

19. The idea of the eternal return also appears in Jiménez's narratives about his evolution as a poet. In "Vino, primero, pura" (the celebrated poem 5 in *Eternidades*), in the notes at the end of *Animal de fondo* or in the Goethe citation he used as epigraph in his mature years – "Wie das Gestirn / Ohne Hast, / Aber ohne Rast" (Like the stars, / without haste / but without rest) – his evolution is regarded as cyclical. Jiménez passes through different stages but each phase is the repeated return to the point of departure at a new level. Perhaps the clearest expression appears in the text "Invitación a un juicio sobre la poesía actual" ("Invitation to an assessment of contemporary poetry"): "Si un poeta auténtico viviera siempre, su poesía sería siempre la misma y distinta siempre, en cada época; y eso es lo que es la poesía de los poetas mejores de cada época, poesía de todas las épocas; pues un poeta debe significar todo el pasado y todo el porvenir" (*Ci*: 221) (If a true poet lived for ever, his poetry would always be the same and different always in each epoch; and that is what the poetry of the best poets of each epoch is, poetry of all epochs; because a poet must signify the entire past and the entire future). The notion of cyclic return in relation to Jiménez's self-concept will be developed in Chapter 6.

20. See Löwith (1955: 214–22): "Nietzsche's Revival of the Doctrine of Eternal Recurrence". The following presentation of Nietzsche's idea of eternal return is indebted to Löwith's text.

21. "The theory of a will to power operating in every event provides the framework within which Nietzsche explains how the fictions of a world comprised of entities and of goods arise, as well as the illusory identities of knowing and morally acting subjects; how, with the soul and self-consciousness, a sphere of inwardness is constituted; how metaphysics, science, and the ascetic ideal achieved dominance – and, finally, how subject-centred reason owes this entire inventory to the occurrence of an unsalutary, masochistic inversion of the very core of the will to power" (Habermas 1990: 95).

22. Also Jiménez adheres to this idea: "Transición es presente completo, que une el pasado y el futuro nada menos; es el movimiento del pasado, el presente y el futuro en un éstasis momentáneo sucesivo, en una sucesiva eternidad, eternidad verdadera de eternidades, momentos eternos" (*Tg*: 136) (Transition is the complete present that unifies the past and the future, nothing less; it is the movement of the past, of the present and of the future in a successive momentary ecstasy/stasis, in a successive eternity, true eternity of eternities, eternal instants).

5. POETIC MEMORY

1. "Since Kant, the transcendentally revaluated ego has been conceived simultaneously as a *world-generating* and *autonomously acting subject*. For the concept of individuality, however, this combination initially provides only the notion of a spontaneously acting subjectivity. In Kantian philosophy the individuated ego falls through the cracks, as it were, between the transcendental ego, which stands over and against the world as a whole, and the empirical ego, which finds itself already in the world as one among many" (Habermas 1992: 158, author's emphasis).

2. In the two examples purity is symbolized by celestial, white or luminous elements. The whiteness of the snow and its radiant veil in the first text, the star and its silver pollen in the second.

3. In her biography of Jiménez, Graciela Palau de Nemes remarks that Zenobia Camprubí's mother was strongly opposed to Jiménez's advances. For this reason, their engagement period was complicated, entailing among other things that if they wanted to see each other it had to be occasionally and often in secret (Palau de Nemes 1974: chapters XVII–XIX). Jiménez had to be cautious with letting anybody know about his feelings, and this is the reason why Zenobia is not mentioned in the *Sonetos espirituales* even if the book was written as an expression of the author's love for the woman who would become his wife (Palau de Nemes 1974: 576). The present poem belongs to this emotionally turbulent period. Without the intention to contradict the biographical interpretation, in the following a supplementary understanding will be presented, as in all the poems from this period the beloved woman can also be interpreted as personified poetry.

4. It is important to note that within a biographical framework the idea of purity refers to the elevation of the sexual drive to a spiritual unification of body and soul. The analysis of *Sonetos espirituales* and *Estío* by Graciela Palau de Nemes is highly illuminative in this respect (Palau de Nemes 1974: 569–97). Palau de Nemes unfolds the analogy between woman and poetry in Jiménez's texts and regards it as referring to a psychobiographical development. When love becomes elevated from the primary sexual drive and becomes a feeling integrated into body and soul, then the intellect will enter a neomystical process beyond the merely sensual aspects. The *poesía desnuda* corresponds to this achievement (Palau de Nemes 1974: 634–41). It is not my intention to contradict this interpretation, only to supplement it with a strand of meaning belonging to the history of ideas.

5. An interpretation of the purifying process in Jiménez's mature poetry as a bracketing of everyday world-experience has been suggested by Jofré (1981: 211). The similarity with the phenomenological *epoché* should, however, be taken cautiously, as Jiménez's aim is not to investigate the way in which cognition of the

world takes place and how it is possible at all, but to create a realm where the idea of absolute subjectivity is unfolded without reference to the empirical world. However, the understanding of consciousness as the primary world-generating principle is common to both phenomenology and Jiménez's aestheticism.

6. Barthes's analysis refers to the mimetic mode of Realism, which evidently is a very different mode than Jiménez's.

7. Ramón Xirau has noted the divergence between Platonism and Jiménez's writings (1980: 47–9). Silver corroborates this claim arguing that "while this 'divinity' and 'immortality' [of the poet's soul] may often suggest a Platonic anamnesis, they in fact signal a very romantic (very Protestant) interiorization of Being" (Silver 2001: 372). Amigo analyzes the extent to which Jiménez can be regarded a Platonist and concludes that even if it is possible to see a series of Platonic traits in his texts, Jiménez eventually goes beyond Platonism (Amigo 2007).

8. According to Hans Robert Jauss, "Baudelaire specifically thematized the modern rejection of the Platonism of the older tradition" (Jauss 1982: 254).

9. Habermas characterizes Derrida's philosophy as continuing along the path shown by the philosophy of consciousness: "Derrida does not take as his point of departure that nodal point at which the philosophy of language and of consciousness branch off, that is, the point where the paradigm of linguistic philosophy separates from that of philosophy of consciousness and renders the identity of meaning dependent upon the intersubjective practice of employing rules of meaning. Instead, Derrida follows Husserl along the path of separating off (in terms of transcendental philosophy) every innerworldly thing from the performances of the subject that are constitutive of the world, in order to take up the battle against the sovereignty of ideally intuited essences within its innermost precincts" (Habermas 1990: 172).

10. The paradigmatic manifestation of language is for Derrida not the spoken expression (since it conveys the illusion of presence and self-presence) but writing. A written text is separated from its author and represents better the non-presence inherent in expression and subjectivity: "The anonymity of the written *I*, the impropriety of the *I am writing*, is, contrary to what Husserl says, the "normal situation." The autonomy of meaning with regard to intuitive cognition, what Husserl established and we earlier called the freedom or "candor" of language, has its norm in writing and in the relationship with death" (Derrida 1973: 97, author's emphasis).

11. "Derrida pursues Husserl's idealizations right to the most inward point of transcendental subjectivity in order to make plain here, at the source of the spontaneity of experience that is present to itself, the ineradicable difference which, if it is presented on the model of the referential structure of a written text,

as an operation dissociated from the performing subject, can thus be conceived precisely as an *event without any subject*" (Habermas 1990: 178, author's emphasis).

12. "This protowriting is at work at the origin of sense. Sense, being temporal in nature, as Husserl recognized, is never simply present; it is always already engaged in the 'movement' of the trace, that is, in the order of 'signification'" (Derrida 1973: 85).

13. Derrida defines *différance* as "the operation of differing what at one and the same time both fissures and retards presence, submitting it simultaneously to primordial division and delay. *Différance* is to be conceived prior to the separation between deferring as delay and differing as the active work of difference" (Derrida 1973: 88, author's emphasis).

14. In a long footnote in *Time and Narrative*, Ricoeur acknowledges part of Derrida's argument but at the same time he observes that Husserl in *The Phenomenology of Internal Time-Consciousness* does not operate with a pure "now" as the time of consciousness. In that text, the time-experience of consciousness precisely takes place in a present that is in tension between protention and retention. Ricoeur adheres to a notion of *trace* similar to Derrida's but adds that his notion "can only counter a phenomenology that confuses the living present with the point-like instant. By contributing to the defeat of this confusion, Husserl sharpens the Augustinian notion of the threefold present and, more precisely, of the 'present of the past'" (Ricoeur 1988: 283).

15. The versification is different in the English translation because the translator has used the edition by Sánchez Barbudo from 1964, which is partially different from the one appearing in the *Obra poética*. Nonetheless, the wording is almost identical in the two versions.

16. Habermas has called this position a negative metaphysics since it "after all continues to offer an equivalent for the extramundane perspective of a God's-eye view: a perspective radically different from the lines of sight belonging to innerworldly participants and observers" (Habermas 1992: 144–5).

17. "It is important to note that in the course of pursuing this line of thought Derrida by no means breaks with the foundationalist tenacity of the philosophy of the subject; he only makes what it had regarded as fundamental dependent on the still profounder – though now vacillating or oscillating – basis of an originative power set temporally aflow" (Habermas 1990: 178–9).

18. Similarly as in the *Sonetos espirituales* and *Estío*, love and poetry are conflated in this work. As has been mentioned above, the woman appearing in the texts is to be understood as both the beloved woman, Zenobia Camprubí Aymar, and the personification of poetry (Palau de Nemes 1974: 619).

19. The *Diario* as a work of historical temporality would not fit into Jiménez's idea of an *Obra total*, as can be inferred from one of the planned configurations of

the *Work*. On 7 April 1931, Jiménez told Juan Guerrero Ruiz of his intention to divide the *Diario* into two sections, thus dissolving the chronological organization of the work: "En cuanto al *Diario de un Poeta Recién Casado* [sic] quedará dividido en dos libros, porque en su forma actual ya no le gusta; quizá poca gente lo habrá leído completo, y como lo componen dos partes, una lírica en verso y otra descriptiva e irónica en prosa, será mejor separar estas dos partes. Dejará el *Diario* con lo lírico y formará otro libro en prosa con las impresiones de América, que se titulará *Norteamérica* u otra cosa así" (*Vv* I: 202) (With respect to the *Diary of a Newlywed Poet*, it will be divided into two books because he does not like it any more in its current form; perhaps only a few people have read it entirely, and since it is made up of two parts, one lyrical in verse and another one descriptive and ironical in prose, it is better to separate these two parts. He will leave the *Diario* with the lyrical and he will make another book in prose with the impressions of America that will be titled *North America* or something like that).

20. The concept of *connector* is developed in the third volume of *Time and Narrative* (Ricoeur 1988: 104–26).

21. The day as based on measuring the interval between the rising and setting of the sun; the month, defined as the interval between the same conjunction of the sun and the moon; the year as the interval defined by one complete return of the seasons and by the position of the sun.

22. It is remarkable that a similar axial moment was established by Jiménez himself with respect to his production, as he considered that year 1 of his *segunda época* was founded with the writing of the *Diario*.

23. As is proposed by Blasco in *Ap*: 262–3.

24. In Spanish *leaves* and *pages* are homonymous since both are designated by the word "hojas".

25. The symbolism of the sea in the *Diario* has been interpreted in a variety of ways. One of them is to see it as a representation of the lyrical subject's consciousness: "El mar –con su fluencia permanente, con su eterno cambio, etc.– será, a lo largo de todo el libro, la imagen en la que la conciencia vendrá a reconocerse, generando una rica y variada gama de metáforas" (Blasco in *Op*, I, 2: 16) (The sea – with its permanent flow, with its eternal change, etc. – will be, throughout the book, the image in which the consciousness recognizes itself, generating a rich and varied range of metaphors). If this proposal is followed, then the sea plays a metapoetic role in this poem because if the sea is a symbol of poetic consciousness, then the *Diario* is that metaphorical sea which is handed over to the readers.

26. At the same time it must be emphasized that the *Diario*, as a work highlighting spatiotemporal reference, must be considered an exception within the series of books that Jiménez published during the period 1916–23. This is probably the reason why Jiménez included the above quoted note (p. 129) at the end of the

Diario. This book must be considered an experiment that, in contrast with other projects that remained drafts, finally was sent to the printing house.

27. It is remarkable that no explicit reference to Jiménez's wedding is to be found in the *Diario*. Only veiled references to it can be found, as in the poems "Oro" and "Anillo". The mention of love in the book has more a cosmic-pantheistic sense than a personal one, as for example in the poems "Sol en el camarote" or "Menos". In this sense, the title that Jiménez chose for the republication of this book in 1948 – *Diario de poeta y mar* (Diary of Poet and Sea) – is much more fitting than the original one.

28. In the first of his *Edifying Discourses in a Different Vein* (1847) Kierkegaard quotes Ecclesiastes 3:11: "He has made everything beautiful in its time. He has also set eternity in the hearts of men". This is in perfect accordance with his idea that the human being is a synthesis of time and eternity, and it is precisely this synthesis that prompts the subject to become a self. In *The Sickness Unto Death* (1849), Kierkegaard defines the human being as a "a synthesis of the infinite and the finite, of the temporal and the eternal, of freedom and necessity" (Kierkegaard 1954: 146). A Judaeo-Christian anthropology can be recognized in this definition: man is created in God's image but is at the same time a fallen being.

6. THE OBRA AS SUBJECTIVE MEMORY

1. According to Expósito Hernández (2005: 26).

2. For a discussion of the problems regarding the edition of Jiménez's works, see Gómez Trueba (2005), Expósito Hernández (2005), Blasco and Silvera (2007) and León Liquete (2010).

3. This is at least what would follow from a Foucaultian or Barthesian approach where the *writing* (*écriture*) exceeds the subject to the extent that the dissolution of the latter is the final consequence of any authorship. See e.g. Barthes's essay "From Work to Text".

4. Juan Guerrero Ruiz was an admirer and close collaborator of Jiménez. Guerrero kept a diary where he recorded his conversations with Jiménez during the years when the poet lived in Madrid.

5. The rewriting of already published poems can be observed as early as in Jiménez's third book. In *Rimas* (1902) there appear revised poems that had been published in his two first collections, *Almas de violeta* and *Ninfeas* (both 1900). This means that the rewriting and reediting of already published texts takes off with the initial phase of his work. In the same way, the mention of projected titles that subsequently would not appear is also present at this early stage, since in *Ninfeas* Jiménez announced three works that were supposed to appear in a

near future (*Besos de oro, El poema de las canciones* and *Rosa de sangre*), and three books in preparation (*Siempreviva, Laureles Rosas* and *Rubíes*). None of these books were published. It could be ventured that Jiménez envisaged his work as a unity from the outset of his career, since the intention of correcting and rewriting already written and published poems implies the consciousness of a work in progress guided by an idea of totality – an idea that in turn would change across time.

6. In *Piedra y cielo*, from 1919, as well as in *Poesía* and *Belleza*, both published in 1923, appear series of poems under the thematic thread *La Obra*.

7. Jiménez started the publication of his *Obra* in 1936 with *Canción*, the first out of twenty-one volumes organized according to genres; seven books were to contain his poetic texts, seven his prose works and the last seven would consist of appendixes. The Spanish Civil War sent the poet and his wife into exile and cut short this project. It must be asked, however, with Antonio Sánchez Romeralo, "¿se habría realizado aquel gran proyecto de no interponerse la guerra civil española?" (Sánchez Romeralo in Jiménez 1982: 14).

8. In a letter dated 27 september 1924 Jiménez expressed his project to the famous German Romanist Ernst Robert Curtius: "Debo decir a usted, sin embargo, que casi nada de lo que le mando, ni de lo que he publicado hasta el día, lo considero sino como «material poético» para la *Obra* definitiva que voy –¿este otoño?– a empezar a publicar en hojas sueltas diarias. A mis 42 años –y después de 25 de incesante trabajo con la Belleza–, siento, pienso, veo claramente que ahora es cuando comienzo; y si vivo 15 ó 20 años más, creo que podré ver realizada mi *Obra* –que, de modo informe, existe ya toda–" (Jiménez 1960: 217) (I must tell you, nonetheless, that almost nothing of what I send you, nor of what I have published until today, I consider but "poetic material" for the definitive *Work* that – this autumn? – I am going to publish in daily loose pages. At my 42 years – and after 25 years of incessant work with Beauty – I feel, I think, I clearly see that it is now that I begin; and if I live 15 or 20 years more, I think that I will see my *Work* accomplished – which, in a formless way, already exists entirely).

9. Jiménez's awareness of the utopian character of the *Obra definitiva*, can also be observed in a change of its name, as he began to call it *la Obra en marcha* (the Work in progress). *Obra en marcha* is the title of one of the *Cuadernos*. It appeared in only one issue in 1928.

10. "En [esta] poesía que va trazando su trayectoria poética [Juan Ramón] nos ha dado la más cabal autobiografía poética que concretó jamás poeta alguno" (Díez-Canedo 1944: 58) (In this poem that sketches out his poetic career, Jiménez has given us the most exact poetic autobiography that any poet ever produced). "Juan Ramón repasa, en esquemas magistrales, su evolución poética" (Díaz-Plaja 1958: 230) (Juan Ramón revises, in masterful outlines, his poetic evolution). Palau

de Nemes's valuable interpretation of this poem has already been alluded to in the previous chapter (note 4).

11. Translation by Ramsden (1981: 146–7).

12. The wording of the English translation is not exactly the same as the one in Spanish in the *Obra poética* because they follow different versions of the same text. The differences are, however, irrelevant for the present purpose.

13. Silver relates this figure of thought to M.H. Abrams's notion of "Romantic Plot" in *Natural Supernaturalism* (1971): "Abrams [...] explained that to structure his poetic conversion narrative, Wordsworth reactivated the self-reflexive structure of Augustinian religious psychobiography, except that now the guiding "grace" issued from Nature instead of God. Moreover, while ostensibly attending solely to Wordsworth's poetry, Abrams suggested the contours of what he termed the "Romantic Plot", a spiral pattern of return-upon-itself, reminiscent of Hölderlin's *vaterlandische Umkehr*, but particularly notable because it was also a partial reworking of the Biblical paradigm of an initial union with Nature, corresponding to childhood and to Genesis; then a Fall; and finally, through suffering and reeducation by Nature, a redemption or spiritual marriage" (Silver 2001: 375).

14. The duality good-bad infinity belongs to Hegel's philosophy (Frank 1979: 163–200; Behler 1988).

15. The same claim is stated in the letter to Luis Cernuda: "Se escribió que el *Diario* era un segundo primer libro mío. La coincidencia de amor y mar grande, y América, obró el prodijio" (*Ci*: 174) (Somebody wrote that the *Diario* was a second first book of mine. The coincidence of love and great sea, and America, produced the wonder).

16. "The subject then appears both as a reader and the writer of its own life, as Proust would have it. As the literary analysis of autobiography confirms, the story of a life continues to be refigured by all the truthful or fictive stories a subject tells about himself or herself. This refiguration makes this life itself a cloth woven of stories told" (Ricoeur 1988: 246).

17. Habermas regards Kierkegaard as one of the first thinkers who breaks with the self-enclosure of the philosophy of consciousness. Referring to what in fact is a central element of Christian thought, Habermas notes that "[s]ince Kierkegaard we have been in a position to know that individuality can only be read from the traces of an authentic life that has been existentially drawn together into some sort of an appropriated totality. The significance of individuality discloses itself from the autobiographical perspective, as it were, of the first-person – I alone can performatively lay claim to being recognized as an individual in my uniqueness" (Habermas 1992: 143–4).

CONCLUSION

1. It is remarkable that only one of the mentioned works, *Españoles de tres mundos*, was published in Jiménez's lifetime.

2. There are exceptions to this pattern but, as a general rule, Jiménez operates with a central differentiation between poetry and prose in the sense that the former treats themes beyond the circumstantial while the latter is oriented towards the specific: "Los poemas en verso del *Diario* los considera de lo mejor de su poesía metafísica y su intención era recogerlos, en un tomo titulado *Lo permanente*, junto con otras poesías "metafísicas de este tipo"; éstas eran las de *Eternidades* "muy corregido" y *Piedra y cielo*, "también muy corregido". Estas poesías eran, con otras (las destinadas al volumen inédito *La flor más alta*, formado a su vez por "La Obra", "La Muerte" y "La mujer desnuda"), las que Juan Ramón pensaba agrupar en uno de los tomos que en 1934 formaban su *Obra Completa: Verso desnudo*. Antes de salir de España trabajó mucho en la formación de este volumen, el cual agrupaba la poesía que Juan Ramón consideraba más metafísica, y del que quedaron totalmente excluidas todas sus prosas" (Gómez Trueba 1995: 22–3) (The poems in verse from the *Diario* he considers as among the best of his metaphysical poetry. His intention was to collect them in a volume titled *The Permanent*, together with other poems "metaphysical of this kind"; those from *Eternidades* "corrected very much" and *Piedra y cielo* "also corrected very much". These poems were, together with others (intended for the unpublished volume *La flor más* alta, in turn comprising "La Obra", "La Muerte" and "La mujer desnuda"), those that Juan Ramón wanted to group in one of the volumes that in 1934 made up his *Obra completa: Verso desnudo*. Before leaving Spain he worked very much on the shaping of this volume, which comprised the poetry that Juan Ramón considered most metaphysical and from which all his prose texts became totally excluded).

3. At least if Modernity is understood as a strictly anthropocentric paradigm. It is possible, however, to observe a current of modern thought that does operate with a Christian divine subject. Among the names that belong to such a paradigm are: Erasmus, Pascal, Leibniz, Bousset, Schleiermacher, Kierkegaard, Maritain or Ricoeur – to mention only a few.

4. Ricoeur's hermeneutic phenomenology of the self represents a break with the philosophy of the subject, since it regards selfhood as dependent on the many *alterities* that the individual encounters throughout the life course (Ricoeur 1994). Habermas's philosophy of communicative rationality displays a similar aim to depart from the philosophy of consciousness without falling into the negative metaphysics of poststructuralist thought: "The ego, which seems to me to be given in my self-consciousness as what is purely my own, cannot be maintained by me solely through my own power, as it were for me alone – it does not "belong" to

me. Rather, this ego always retains an intersubjective core because the process of individuation from which it emerges runs through the network of linguistically mediated interactions" (Habermas 1992: 170). In a recent context, Habermas has noted that – perhaps in a parallel way as the subject – reason itself is not self-founded: "The starting point for the philosophical discourse about reason and revelation is a recurrent idea: namely, that when reason reflects on its deepest foundations, it discovers that it owes its origin to something else. And it must acknowledge the fateful power of this origin, for otherwise it will lose its orientation to reason in the blind alley of a hybrid grasp of control over its own self" (Habermas 2006: 40).

5. A similar sort of *dialectic of Enlightenment* can be observed in the relapse to mythical forms of power in political Modernity. This is disclosed in the sacralization of politics that was a vital part of totalitarian forms of government from Nazism to Communism, cf. Gentile (2001).

ABBREVIATIONS

Works by Juan Ramón Jiménez

Ap   (1989) *Antología poética*. Edited by Javier Blasco (Madrid: Cátedra).

Ci   (1961) *La corriente infinita*. Edited by Francisco Garfias (Madrid: Aguilar).

DNP   (2004) *Diary of a Newlywed Poet*. Translated by Hugh A. Harter (Selinsgrove: Susquehanna University Press).

GDD   (1987) *God Desired and Desiring*. Translated by Antonio T. de Nicolás (New York: Paragon House).

Op   (2005) *Obra poética I (1-2) – II (3-4)*. Edited by Javier Blasco and Teresa Gómez Trueba (Madrid: Espasa-Calpe).

Plp   (1959) *Primeros libros de poesía*. Edited by Francisco Garfias (Madrid: Aguilar).

SS   (1996) *Spiritual Sonnets / Sonetos espirituales*. Translated by Carl W. Cobb (Lewiston, Queenston and Lampeter: Edwin Mellen Press).

SW   (1957) *Selected Writings of Juan Ramón Jiménez*. Translated by H.R. Hays (New York: Farrar, Straus and Cudahy).

Tg   (1961) *El trabajo gustoso (Conferencias)* Edited by Francisco Garfias (México: Aguilar).

THP   (1962) *Three Hundred Poems, 1903–1953.* Translated by Eloïse Roach (Austin: University of Texas Press).

T&S   (1988) *Time and Space: A Poetic Autobiography.* Translated by Antonio T. de Nicolás (New York: Paragon House).

Other works

Vv   (1998) Juan Guerrero Ruiz, *Juan Ramón de viva voz 1-2* (Valencia: Pre-Textos).

BIBLIOGRAPHY

Juan Ramón Jiménez: Works Cited
(1943) "Espacio (una estrofa)", in *Cuadernos Americanos* 11, no. 5: 191–205.
(1944) "Espacio (fragmento 1° de la segunda estrofa)", in *Cuadernos Americanos* 17, no. 5: 181–3.
(1960) *Cuadernos*. Edited by Francisco Garfias (Madrid: Taurus).
(1977) *Cartas literarias*. Edited by Francisco Garfias (Barcelona: Bruguera).
(1978) *Leyenda (1896-1956)*. Edited by Antonio Sánchez Romeralo (Madrid: Cupsa).
(1981) *Antolojía jeneral en prosa (1898-1954)*. Edited by Ángel Crespo (Madrid: Biblioteca nueva).
(1982) *Poesías últimas escojidas (1918-1958)*. Edited by Antonio Sánchez Romeralo (Madrid: Espasa-Calpe).
(1994a) *Diario de un poeta reciencasado*. Edited by de Antonio Sánchez Barbudo (Madrid: Visor).
(1994b) *Poemas escogidos*. Edited by Richard A. Cardwell (Barcelona: Vicens Vives).
(2000) *Bonanza*. Edited by Ana Recio Mir (Moguer: Fundación Juan Ramón Jiménez).
(2008) *Dios deseado y deseante (Animal de fondo)*. Edited by Rocío Bejarano and Joaquín Llansó (Madrid: Akal).

General Bibliography
Abrams, Meyer Howard (1953). *The Mirror and the Lamp: Romantic Theory and the Critical Tradition* (New York: Oxford University Press).
Acillona, Mercedes (2007). "Dios en la conciencia y la poesía última de Juan Ramón y Unamuno", *Letras de Deusto* 37, no. 114: 37–58.
Alberti, Rafael (1973). *Prosas encontradas* (Madrid: Ayuso).

Amigo, Mª Luisa (2007). "Experiencia de la belleza en Juan Ramón: rasgos platónicos y superación del platonismo", *Letras de Deusto* 37, no. 114: 59–90.
Apel, Friedmar (1988). "Wandlungen des Romantischen. Zur Geschichte des poetischen Subjekts im 19. Jahrhundert", in *Propyläen Geschichte der Literatur* vol. V (Berlin: Propyläen), 68–91.
Aristotle (1951). *Aristotle's Theory of Poetry and Fine Art. With a Critical Text and Translation of the Poetics*. Translated by S.H. Butcher (New York: Dover Publication).
Augustine (1998). *Confessions* (Oxford: Oxford University Press).
Azam, Gilbert (1983). *La obra de Juan Ramón Jiménez: Continuidad y renovación de la poesía lírica española* (Madrid: Editora Nacional).
Barthes, Roland (1988). "The Death of the Author", in *Modern Criticism and Theory: A Reader*. Edited by David Lodge (New York: Longman), 167–72.
Barthes, Roland (1994). *Oeuvres complètes* 2 (Paris: Gallimard).
Baudelaire, Charles (1952). *Poems of Baudelaire: A Translation of Les Fleurs du mal by Roy Campbell* (New York: Pantheon Books).
Behler, Ernst (1986). "The Idea of Infinite Perfectibility and its Impact upon the Concept of Literature in European Romanticism", in *Sensus communis, Festschrift für Henry Remak, Contemporary Trends in Comparative Literature, Panorama de la situation actuelle en littérature comparée*. Edited by H.H. Remak, J. Riesz, P. Boerner and B. Scholz (Tübingen: Gunter Narr), 295–304.
Behler, Ernst (1988). "Zum Verhältnis von Hegel und Friedrich Schlegel in der Theorie der Unendlichkeit", *Kodikas/Code. Ars Semeiotica* 11: 127–47.
Behler, Ernst (1989). *Unendliche Perfektibilität: Europäische Romantik und Französische Revolution* (Paderborn: F. Schöningh).
Behler, Ernst (1993). *German Romantic Literary Theory* (Cambridge: Cambridge University Press).
Blasco Pascual, Francisco Javier (1981). *La poética de Juan Ramón Jiménez: desarrollo, contexto y sistema* (Salamanca: Universidad de Salamanca).
Blasco, Javier, and Francisco Silvera (2007). "Juan Ramón Jiménez: El hilo del Laberinto", *Cuadernos Hispanoamericanos* 685–6: 7–44.
Blasco, Javier, and Teresa Gómez Trueba (1994). *Juan Ramón Jiménez: La prosa de un poeta. Catálogo y descripción de la prosa lírica juanramoniana* (Valladolid: Grammalea).
Blasco, Javier, and Teresa Gómez Trueba, eds. (2000). *Juan Ramón Jiménez prosista* (Huelva: Diputación provincial).

Bousoño, Carlos (1970). *Teoría de la expresión poética (I-II)* (Madrid: Gredos).
Bürger, Peter (1974). *Theorie der Avantgarde* (Frankfurt am Main: Suhrkamp).
Cardwell, Richard A. (1977). *Juan R. Jiménez: The Modernist Apprenticeship, 1895–1900* (Berlin: Colloquium Verlag).
Cardwell, Richard A. (1990). "Mirrors and Myths: Antonio Machado and the Search for Self", *Romance Studies* 16: 31–42.
Cardwell, Richard A. (1992). "'Vano fantasma' y 'Ley misteriosa': la verdadera herencia becqueriana en la poesía española moderna", in *Actas del congreso "Los Bécquer y el Moncayo": celebrado en Tarazona y Veruela del 6 al 8 de septiembre de 1990*. Edited by Jesús Rubio Jiménez (Zaragoza: Institución Fernando el Católico), 38–57.
Cardwell, Richard A. (1997). "Espejo y sueño: la práctica simbolista en España", in *La metáfora en la poesía hispánica (1885-1936)*. Edited by Hans Lauge Hansen and Julio Jensen (Sevilla: Alfar), 19–35.
Cardwell, Richard A. (2005). "Juan Ramón Jiménez y el modernismo: una nueva visión de conjunto", *Ínsula*, no. 705: 9–12.
Cassirer, Ernst (1955). *The Philosophy of Symbolic Forms, vol. 2: Mythical Thought* (New Haven: Yale University Press).
Cirlot, Juan-Eduardo (1988). *Diccionario de símbolos* (Barcelona: Labor).
Coke-Enguidanos, Mervyn (1982). *Word and Work in the Poetry of Juan Ramón Jiménez* (London: Tamesis Books).
Cole, Leo R. (1967). *The Religious Instinct in the Poetry of Juan Ramón Jiménez* (Oxford: Dolphin Book Co.).
Crowe, Benjamin D. (2008). "On 'The Religion of the Visible Universe': Novalis and the Pantheism Controversy", *British Journal for the History of Philosophy* 16, no. 1: 125–46.
De Man, Paul (1984). *The Rhetoric of Romanticism* (New York: Columbia University Press).
Derrida, Jacques (1973). *Speech and Phenomena and Other Essays on Husserl's Theory of Signs* (Evanston: Northwestern University Press).
Díaz-Plaja, Guillermo (1958). *Juan Ramón Jiménez en su poesía* (Madrid: Aguilar).
Díez-Canedo, Enrique (1944). *Juan Ramón Jiménez en su obra* (México: El Colegio de México).
Domínguez Caparrós, José (1999). *Diccionario de métrica española* (Madrid: Alianza).
Domínguez Caparrós, José (2005). *Elementos de métrica española* (Valencia: Tirant lo Blanch).

Eliade, Mircea (1959). *The Sacred and the Profane: The Nature of Religion* (New York: Harcourt, Brace & World).
Eliade, Mircea (1974). *The Myth of the Eternal Return, or, Cosmos and History* (Princeton: Princeton University Press).
Expósito Hernández, José Antonio (2005). "Problemas en la edición de la obra en verso de Juan Ramón Jiménez", *Ínsula: revista de letras y ciencias humanas*, no. 705: 23–7.
Font, Maria Teresa (1972). *Espacio: autobiografía lírica de Juan Ramón Jiménez* (Madrid: Ínsula).
Foucault, Michel (1984). "What Is an Author?", in *Modern Criticism and Theory: A Reader*. Edited by David Lodge (New York: Longman), 197–210.
Frank, Manfred (1979). *Die unendliche Fahrt* (Frankfurt am Main: Suhrkamp).
García Font, Juan (1995). *Historia y mística del jardín* (Barcelona: MRA).
Garfias, Francisco (2002). *La idea de Dios en Juan Ramón Jiménez* (Moguer: Diputación Provincial de Huelva).
Gentile, Emilio (2001). *Politics as Religion* (Princeton and Oxford: Princeton University Press).
Gombrich, Ernst H. (1960). *Art and Illusion: A Study in the Psychology of Pictorial Representation* (New York: Pantheon Books).
Gómez Trueba, Teresa (1995). *Estampas líricas en la prosa de Juan Ramón Jiménez. Retratos, paisajes y recuerdos* (Valladolid: Universidad de Valladolid).
Gómez Trueba, Teresa (2005). "El editor en el laberinto (Problemas en la edición de la obra en prosa poética de Juan Ramón Jiménez)", *Ínsula: revista de letras y ciencias humanas*, no. 705: 27–30.
Greimas, Algirdas J., and Courtés, Joseph (1982). *Semiotics and Language: An Analytical Dictionary* (Bloomington: Indiana University Press).
Gullón, Ricardo (1958). *Conversaciones con Juan Ramón Jiménez* (Madrid: Taurus).
Gullón, Ricardo (1960). *Estudios sobre Juan Ramón Jiménez* (Buenos Aires: Losada).
Habermas, Jürgen (1990). *The Philosophical Discourse of Modernity: Twelve Lectures* (Cambridge: Polity Press).
Habermas, Jürgen (1992). *Postmetaphysical Thinking: Philosophical Essays* (Cambridge: Polity Press).
Habermas, Jürgen (2006). "Pre-political Foundations of the Democratic Constitutional State?", in Joseph Cardinal Ratzinger and Jürgen Habermas, *The Dialectics of Secularization: On Reason and Religion* (San Francisco: Ignatius Press), 19–52.

Habermas, Jürgen (2008). "The Boundary between Faith and Knowledge: On the Reception and Contemporary Importance of Kant's Philosophy of Religion", in *Between Naturalism and Religion* (Cambridge: Polity Press), 209–47.

Hernández-Pacheco, Javier (1995). *La conciencia romántic* (Madrid: Tecnos).

Herrera Espinosa, Rafael (2006). "Ritmo en *Espacio*", in *Juan Ramón, Alberti: dos poetas líricos*. Edited by Diego Martínez Torrón (Kassel: Reichenberger), 186–95.

Jauss, Hans Robert (1982). *Aesthetic Experience and Literary Hermeneutics* (Minneapolis: University of Minnesota Press).

Jensen, Julio (1997). "Naturaleza y metáfora en Juan Ramón Jiménez", in *La metáfora en la poesía hispánica (1885-1936)*. Edited by Hans Lauge Hansen and Julio Jensen (Sevilla: Alfar), 87–108.

Jensen, Julio (2004). "The Face of the Author: A Sample of the History of the Humanities", in *The Object of Study in the Humanities: Proceedings from the Seminar at the University of Copenhagen, September 2001*. Edited by Julio Jensen (Copenhagen: Museum Tusculanum Press), 149–66.

Jofré, Álvaro Salvador (1981). "La dialéctica vestido/desnudo en la poesía de Juan Ramón Jiménez", in *Criatura afortunada. Estudios sobre la obra de Juan Ramón Jiménez* (Granada: Universidad de Granada), 195–213.

Juliá, Mercedes (1988). *El universo de Juan Ramón Jiménez: un estudio del poema "Espacio"* (Madrid: Ediciones de la Torre).

Kierkegaard, Søren (1954). *Fear and Trembling* and *The Sickness unto Death*. Translated by Walter Lowrie (New York: Doubleday).

Kierkegaard, Søren (1967). *The Concept of Dread* (Princeton: Princeton University Press).

Lacoue-Labarthe, Philippe, and Jean-Luc Nancy (1988). *The Literary Absolute: The Theory of Literature in German Romanticism* (Albany: State University of New York Press).

Lanz, Juan José (2007). "El legado poético de Juan Ramón Jiménez y la Modernidad", *Letras de Deusto* 37, no. 114: 205–24.

Lejeune, Philippe (1989). *On Autobiography* (Minneapolis: University of Minnesota Press).

León Felipe, Benigno (2005). "Las prosificaciones en Juan Ramón Jiménez: el proyecto de Leyenda", *Signa: Revista de la Asociación Española de Semiótica* 14: 145–62.

León Liquete, Carlos (2010). *Los puntos sobre las jotas. La ecdótica ante los archivos de un poeta contemporáneo: Juan Ramón Jiménez* (Valladolid: Universidad de Valladolid).

Litvak, Lily (1981). "Sensuality and Spirituality in the *Modernismo* of Juan Ramón Jiménez", *Renaissance and Modern Studies* 25: 83–103.

López Castro, Armando (1995). "Lo sacro en Juan Ramón Jiménez", *Cuadernos Hispanoamericanos*, no. 539–40: 23–42.

Löwith, Karl (1955). *Meaning in History: The Theological Implications of the Philosophy of History* (Chicago: University of Chicago Press).

Márquez, Miguel Ángel (2003). "Verso y prosa en la etapa americana de Juan Ramón Jiménez", *Rhythmica* 1: 149–81.

Martínez Torrón, Diego (2006). "El panteísmo de Juan Ramón. Poesía y Belleza en la obra juanramoniana", in *Juan Ramón, Alberti: dos poetas líricos*. Edited by Diego Martínez Torrón (Kassel: Reichenberger), 1–162.

Meillassoux, Quentin (2008). *After Finitude: An Essay on the Necessity of Contingency* (London: Continuum).

Mellor, Anne K. (1982). *English Romantic Irony* (Cambridge, MA: Harvard University Press).

Navarro Tomás, Tomás (1965). *Arte del verso* (Mexico: Compañía General de Ediciones).

Navarro Tomás, Tomás (1973). *Los poetas en sus versos: desde Jorge Manrique a García Lorca* (Barcelona: Ariel).

Novalis (1997). *Philosophical Writings*. Translated and edited by Margaret Mahony Stoljar (Albany: State University of New York Press).

O'Hara, Edgar (1987). "Un cielo hecho polvo: 'Espacio' de J.R.J.", *Revista chilena de literatura* 30: 155–70.

Olson, Paul R. (1967). *Circle of Paradox: Time and Essence in the Poetry of Juan Ramón Jiménez* (Baltimore: Johns Hopkins University Press).

Ortega y Gasset, José (1948). *The Dehumanization of Art, and, Notes on the Novel*. Translated by Helene Weyl (Princeton: Princeton University Press).

Ortega y Gasset, José (1957). *Obras completas*, vol. 3 *(1917-1928)* (Madrid: Revista de Occidente).

Ortega y Gasset, José (1963). *Obras completas*, vol. 2. *El espectador (1916-1934)* (Madrid: Revista de Occidente).

Palau de Nemes, Graciela (1957). *Vida y obra de Juan Ramón Jiménez* (Madrid: Gredos).

Palau de Nemes, Graciela (1971). "Tres momentos del neomisticismo poético del 'siglo modernista': Darío, Jiménez y Paz", in *Estudios sobre Rubén Darío*. Edited by Ernesto Mejía Sánchez (Mexico: El Colegio de México), 536–52.

Palau de Nemes, Graciela (1974). *Vida y obra de Juan Ramón Jiménez: la poesía desnuda* (Madrid: Gredos).

Palau de Nemes, Graciela (1982). *Inicios de Zenobia y Juan Ramón en América* (Madrid: Fundación Universitaria Española).
Paraíso de Leal, Isabel (1991). "La germinal poética romántica de Juan Ramón Jiménez", in *Poética e historia literaria: Bécquer, Antonio Machado, Juan Ramón Jiménez, F. García Lorca, Rafael Alberti. XI Cursos de Verano, Seminario de Autores Andaluces "José Cadalso", San Roque, 1990.* Edited by R. Reyes Cano and M.J. Ramos Ortega (Cádiz: Universidad de Cádiz).
Paz, Octavio (1973). *The Bow and the Lyre* (Austin: University of Texas Press).
Paz, Octavio (1981). *Los hijos del limo: Del romanticismo a la vanguardia* (Barcelona: Seix Barral).
Paz, Octavio (1990). *La otra voz. Poesía y fin de siglo* (Barcelona: Seix Barral).
Paz, Octavio (1991a). *Children of the Mire: Modern Poetry from Romanticism to the Avant-Garde* (Cambridge, MA: Harvard University Press).
Paz, Octavio (1991b). *The Other Voice: Essays on Modern Poetry* (New York: Harcourt Brace Jovanovich).
Paz, Octavio (1994). *La casa de la presencia. Poesía e historia. Obras completas vol. 1* (Mexico: Fondo de Cultura Económica).
Pieper, Josef (1961). *Scholasticism: Personalities and Problems of Medieval Philosophy* (London: Faber & Faber).
Poe, Edgar Allan (1946). *The Complete Poems and Stories of Edgar Allan Poe* (New York: A.A. Knopf).
Prat, Ignacio (1982). *Estudios sobre poesía contemporánea* (Madrid: Taurus).
Predmore, Michael P. (1973). *La poesía hermética de Juan Ramón Jiménez. El Diario como centro de su mundo poético* (Madrid: Gredos).
Pujante Sánchez, José David (1990). "Proceso creador e imaginación romántica en Juan Ramón Jiménez, teórico y poeta (apuntes para una poética)", *Epos: Revista de filología* 6: 263–78.
Ramsden, Herbert (1981). "Depuración and poesía pura in the work of Juan Ramón Jiménez", *Renaissance and Modern Studies* 25: 121–54.
Recio Mir, Ana (2007). "El dios destino de la sensualidad hermosa", *Letras de Deusto* 37, no. 114: 253–64.
Ricoeur, Paul (1978). *The Rule of Metaphor: Multi-Disciplinary Studies of the Creation of Meaning in Language* (Toronto: University of Toronto Press).
Ricoeur, Paul (1981). "What Is a Text? Explanation and Understanding", in *Hermeneutics and the Human Sciences: Essays on Language, Ac-*

tion and Interpretation (Cambridge: Cambridge University Press), 145–64.
Ricoeur, Paul (1988). *Time and Narrative,* vol. 3 (Chicago: University of Chicago Press).
Ricoeur, Paul (1994). *Oneself as Another* (Chicago: University of Chicago Press).
Riffaterre, Michael (1985). "Prosopopeia", *Yale French Studies* 69: 107–23.
Río, Emilio del (1973). *La idea de Dios en la Generación del 98* (Madrid: Studium).
Salinas, Pedro (1970). "Sucesión de Juan Ramón Jiménez", in *Literatura española siglo XX* (Madrid: Alianza), 145–9.
San Juan de la Cruz (2002). *Cántico espiritual y poesía completa.* Edited by P. Elia and M.J. Mancho (Barcelona: Crítica).
Sánchez Barbudo, Antonio (1962). *La segunda época de Juan Ramón Jiménez, 1916-1953* (Madrid: Gredos).
Sánchez Barbudo, Antonio (1981). *La obra poética de Juan Ramón Jiménez* (Madrid: Cátedra).
Sánchez Romeralo, Antonio (1961). "Juan Ramón Jiménez en su fondo de aire", *Revista Hispánica Moderna* 27: 299–319.
Santos-Escudero, Ceferino (1975). *Símbolos y Dios en el último Juan Ramón Jiménez (El influjo oriental en Dios deseado y deseante)* (Madrid: Gredos).
Saz-Orozco, Carlos del (1966). *Desarrollo del concepto de Dios en el pensamiento religioso de Juan Ramón Jiménez* (Madrid: Razón y fe).
Segre, Cesare (1985). *Principios de análisis del texto literario* (Barcelona: Crítica).
Silver, Philip W. (2001). "Juan Ramón Jiménez and the Recovery of Romanticism", in *Prosa y poesía. Homenaje a Gonzalo Sobejano.* Edited by J.-F. Botrel, Y. Lissorgues, C. Maurer and L. Romero Tobar (Madrid: Gredos), 365–78.
Sørensen, Bengt Algot (1997). "Blomst og stjerne. Billedtyper og billedteorier i tysk litteratur omkring 1800", in *Billedsprog.* Edited by P.K. Hansen and J. Holmgaard (Aalborg: Medusa), 101–22.
Taylor, Charles (1985). "Language and Human Nature", in *Human Agency and Language. Philosophical Papers,* vol. I (Cambridge: Cambridge University Press), 215–25.
Taylor, Charles (1989). *Sources of the Self: The Making of the Modern Identity* (Cambridge, MA.: Harvard University Press.
Ulibarri, Sabine R. (1962). *El mundo poético de Juan Ramón Jiménez. Estudio estilístico de la lengua poética y de los símbolos* (Madrid: Edhigar).

Valente, José Ángel (1971). "Juan Ramón Jiménez en la tradición poética del medio siglo", in *Las palabras de la tribu* (Madrid: Siglo Veintiuno de España Editores), 89–101.

Villar, Arturo del (2002). "San Agustín, Juan Ramón Jiménez y los demonios", *Letras de Deusto* 32, no. 94: 9–28.

Wilcox, John C. (1987). *Self and Image in Juan Ramón Jiménez: Modern and Post-modern Readings* (Urbana: University of Illinois Press).

Wilcox, John C. (2005). "La prosa de Juan Ramón Jiménez en 'El otro costado': la confrontación estética con lo espantoso", *Ínsula: revista de letras y ciencias humanas*, no. 705: 18–20.

Xirau, Ramón (1980). *Dos poetas y lo sagrado* (México: Cuadernos de Joaquín Mortiz).

Young, Howard T. (1968). "Génesis y forma de 'Espacio' de Juan Ramón Jiménez", *Revista Hispánica Moderna* 34: 462–70.

Young, Howard T. (1980). *The Line in the Margin: Juan Ramón Jiménez and his Readings in Blake, Shelley, and Yeats* (Madison: University of Wisconsin Press).

Young, Howard T. (2005). "La prosa de Juan Ramón Jiménez", *Ínsula: revista de letras y ciencias humanas*, no. 705: 15–17.

INDEX

Abrams, M. H., 171n3, 191n13
Absolute subject, 4ff., 12, 25, 30, 32ff., 44, 47, 52, 61, 63, 86, 89, 106, 119, 121ff., 140, 147ff., 163ff., 169n10
Acillona, Mercedes, 177n20, 180n13
Aesthetic experience, 28, 33, 93ff., 108, 112, 121, 133f., 163
Aestheticism, 5, 186n5
Alberti, Leon Battista, 174n23
Alberti, Rafael, 182n7
Almas de violeta / Violet Souls, 13f., 26, 145, 173n18, 189n5
Anamnesis, 118ff., 186n7
Animal de fondo / Animal of Depth, 20, 22ff., 30, 48, 52ff., 83, 86, 122, 126f., 154ff., 163, 172n15, 173nn16–17, 174n1, 176n15, 177n17
Anthropomorphism, 68f., 72, 121, 153
Aquinas, Thomas, 2
Arias tristes / Sad Airs, 14, 96ff., 106, 113f., 145
Aristotle, 2, 177n22, 183n12
Aub, Max, 53
Aufhebung, 155
Augustine, 95f., 141, 181n3, 187n14, 191n13
Author, 4ff., 48, 60f., 71, 73, 75, 82, 87ff., 102, 105f., 136, 143ff., 170n3, 189n3

Autobiographical pact, 172n13
Autobiography, 152, 175n5, 190n10, 191n16
Avant-Gardes, 4ff., 38, 90f., 93, 163
Axis mundi, 72f., 179n7
Azam, Gilbert, 171n4, 173n17

Bad infinity, 156, 191n14
Baladas de primavera / Spring Ballads, 56
Barthes, Roland, 4, 90, 122, 145, 186n6, 189n3
Baudelaire, Charles, 39f., 124, 169n11, 176n8, 176n17, 186n8
Bécquer, Gustavo Adolfo, 174n1
Behler, Ernst, 170n2, 175n3, 191n14
Bejarano, Rocío, 176n16
Belleza / Beauty, 103ff., 149, 183n15, 190n6
Benjamin, Walter, 8, 182n6
Bildungsroman, 153
Blake, William, 113, 170n2
Blasco, Javier, 167n2, 172n11, 174n24, 181n23, 188n23, 188n25, 189n2
Byron, Lord George Gordon, 176n14

Calendar time, 130f., 142
Canción / Song, 149, 190n7

Camprubí Aymar, Zenobia, 16, 20, 49, 88, 120, 129, 144, 151, 172n12, 176n9, 179n10, 181n22, 185n3, 187n18
Cardwell, Richard, 27, 28, 46, 69, 170n14, 171n8, 172n11, 174n1, 181n23
Cassirer, Ernst, 12, 25, 27
Cernuda, Luis, 191n15
Christianity, 11, 55, 112, 165, 189n28, 191n17, 192n3
Cogito, 2, 52, 117, 125
Coke-Enguidanos, Mervyn, 170n14, 172n10
Condorcet, Nicolas de, 175n3
Connector, 130, 188n20
Cosmic eros, 39f., 45ff., 50f., 107ff., 176n7, 189n27
Cuadernos / Booklets, 149ff., 190n9
Curtius, Ernst Robert, 190n8

Dadaism, 4f.
Darío, Rubén, 171n6
de Man, Paul, 68, 178n3
Derrida, Jacques, 5, 118, 124ff., 186nn9–11, 187nn12–14, 187n17
Descartes, René, 2, 159, 161, 167n8, 169n13
Dialectics of Enlightenment, 193n5
Diario de un poeta recién casado / Diary of a Newlywed Poet, 16ff., 118, 129ff., 157f., 164f., 172n13, 187n19, 188n22, 188nn25–26, 189n27, 191n15, 192n2
Différance, 124, 126, 128, 187n13
Dios deseado y deseante / God Desired and Desiring, 53ff., 88, 127, 158, 172n15, 176nn15–16
Distentio animi, 141
Domínguez Caparrós, José, 104, 183n14
Duchamp, Marcel, 4, 6

Eliade, Mircea, 11, 171n5, 179n7
Empirical subject, 2ff., 12, 16, 24f., 29, 32ff., 44, 47, 51f., 63, 88, 95f., 119, 121ff., 134, 149, 151, 164f., 185n1
Espacio / Space, 20, 63, 73ff., 81ff., 101, 106ff., 163ff., 167n2, 176n14, 179nn9–10, 180n19, 181n22, 183n16
Éstasis dinámico, 31, 59, 184n22
Estío / Summer, 48ff., 138, 176n9, 185n4, 187n18
Eternal return, 8, 106f., 111ff., 134, 136, 140, 142, 164, 184nn19–20, 184n22
Eternidades / Eternities, 35, 63, 72ff., 105, 184n19, 184n22, 192n2
Eternal/eternity, 17, 19f., 31, 37, 47, 61, 72, 83, 102, 106, 112ff., 141f., 153f., 184n22, 189n28
Expósito Hernández, José Antonio, 189nn1–2

Fichte, Johann Gottlieb, 162
Fin de siècle / fin de siglo, 27f., 46, 55, 69, 98
Finitude, 7ff., 12, 26ff., 36, 45, 55, 94, 96, 101f., 106, 113, 121ff., 128, 137, 156ff., 162ff.
Font, María Luisa, 107, 180n19
Foucault, Michel, 3, 38, 144f., 189n3
Freud, Sigmund, 15

Galtier, Lysandro, 53
Garcilaso de la Vega, 132ff.
Garfias, Francisco, 171n4
Giner de los Ríos, Francisco, 146
God, 2ff., 21f., 37ff., 54f., 94, 166, 169n10, 171n9, 173n17, 175n4, 177n19, 178n1, 189n28, 191n13
Goethe, Johann Wolfgang, 4, 40, 155, 184n19
Gombrich, Ernst, 174n23

Gómez Trueba, Teresa, 167n2, 176n11, 189n2, 192n2
Good infinity, 156, 191n14
Greimas, Algirdas, 171n7
Guerrero Ruiz, Juan, 145ff., 188n19, 189n4
Gullón, Ricardo, 53, 144, 157f., 173n17, 176n15

Habermas, Jürgen, 3, 61, 90, 93f., 112, 124, 155, 165, 168n5, 168n7, 169n8, 169n10, 170n1, 175n2, 177n19, 184n21, 185n1, 186n9, 187n11, 187nn16–17, 191n17, 192n4
Hegel, Georg Wilhelm Friedrich, 4, 40, 155, 169n10, 191n14
Herder, Johan Gottfried, 40
Hernández-Pacheco, Javier, 176n12
Herrera Espinosa, Rafael, 183n16
Hume, David, 3, 168n5
Husserl, Edmund, 95, 125f., 159, 169n13, 181n5, 186nn9–11, 187n12, 187n14
Hölderlin, Friedrich, 191n13

Idealism, 4ff., 41, 77, 88ff., 161, 164, 168n5, 169n8, 173n19, 178n1, 179n13
Identity, 8, 117, 128, 131, 140, 145ff., 156ff., 163ff., 167n3, 169n12, 172n14, 181n4
Infinite longing, 8, 37ff., 41ff., 52ff., 69, 171n8, 174n1, 180n13
Infinite perfectibility, 37, 148, 175n3
Inner/subjective time, 95ff., 98ff., 103ff., 106ff., 125ff., 130f., 181nn3–4, 187n14, 189n28
Institutción Libre de Enseñanza, 178n1
Interiority/inner world, 5, 7f., 14ff., 40ff., 69ff., 121ff., 138ff., 154, 163, 168n8, 172n10, 173n17, 186n7

Isotopy, 15, 85, 99f., 104f., 111, 121, 127, 171n7, 175n6, 182n9

Jauss, Hans Robert, 186n8
Joyce, James, 4, 6
Juliá, Mercedes, 180n19

Kant, Immanuel, 2ff., 11, 15, 37, 41, 71, 94, 117, 124, 128, 159, 162, 168n6, 169n10, 170n1, 175n2, 175n4, 179n6, 181nn1–2, 185n1
Kierkegaard, Søren, 141f., 189n28, 191n17, 192n3
Krause, Karl Christian Friedrich, 178n1

La estación total / The Total Season, 34f., 173n20
Laberinto / Labyrinth, 119
Lacan, Jacques, 47, 174n1
Lacoue-Labarthe, Philippe, 60
Lanz, Juan José, 172n11
Leibniz, Gottfried Wilhelm, 162, 192n3
Lejeune, Philippe, 172n13
León Felipe, Benigno, 167n2, 183n16
León Liquete, Carlos, 189n2
Litvak, Lily, 26
Llansó, Joaquín, 176n16
López Castro, Armando, 170n14, 171n4
Löwith, Karl, 112, 184n20

Machado, Antonio, 174n1
Mallarmé, Stéphane, 5, 16, 124, 144, 169n11, 171n6
Márquez, Miguel Ángel, 183n16
Martínez Torrón, Diego, 170n14, 180n13, 181n22
Marx, Karl, 15
Meillassoux, Quentin, 168n6
Mellor, Anne, 172n9
Memory, 8, 20, 95, 107ff., 117ff., 143ff., 165

Merleau-Ponty, Maurice, 178n3
Metaphor, 25, 31f., 45ff., 68ff., 84, 100, 136, 139, 161f., 174n23, 183n12, 188n25
Metrics, 100f., 104ff., 111, 182nn7–8, 183n11, 183n14, 183n16, 183n18
Modernismo, 74, 171n6
Modernity, 3ff., 16, 40f., 63f., 73, 93ff., 124, 128, 131f., 155f., 161ff., 169n10, 192n3, 193n5
Monadic time, 8, 73, 94ff., 98ff., 103ff., 106ff., 117, 125ff., 130f., 136, 163f., 182n8
Mystical poetry, 54f., 177n19
Myth, 8, 11ff., 25f., 36, 39ff., 72f., 112f., 122, 163, 165f., 171n4, 174n25, 179n7, 193n5

Nancy, Jean-Luc, 60
Narrative identity, 117f., 181n4
Natura naturans, 41
Naturalization, 68ff.
Navarro Tomás, Tomás, 101, 182nn7–8, 183n11
Neoplatonism, 38, 124
New Criticism, 9
Nietzsche, Friedrich, 5, 15, 93ff., 112, 115, 164, 184nn20–21
Ninfeas / Water Lilies, 13f., 27, 29f., 118f., 145, 152, 157, 174n1, 189n5
Nominalism, 2, 168nn4–5
Novalis, 170n2, 171n6, 176n13, 179n6

O'Hara, Edgar, 87
Obra / Work, 8, 10, 12f., 82f., 102ff., 143ff., 164f., 177n23, 187n19, 190nn7–9, 192n2
Ockham, William of, 2, 168n4
Olson, Paul, 173n17, 177n21, 178n2, 182n8

Organic work of art, 4f., 147f.
Ortega y Gasset, José, 32f., 161f., 174n24

Palau de Nemes, Graciela, 49, 120f., 165, 172n16, 174n1, 185nn3–4, 187n18, 190n10
Panentheism, 178n1, 178n6
Pantheism, 6, 8, 41, 63ff., 73ff., 95, 100, 107ff., 135, 140, 157f., 163f., 178n1, 178n6, 179n13, 189n17
Paraíso de Leal, Isabel, 170n14
Pathetic fallacy, 16
Paz, Octavio, 11f., 38ff., 73f., 93, 107, 112f., 144, 163, 170n2, 179n9, 180n20
Piedra y cielo / Rock and Sky, 31f., 146f., 177n21, 190n6, 192n2
Pieper, Josef, 168n4
Platonism, 2, 118f., 124, 186nn7–8
Plotinus, 177n19
Poe, Edgar Allan, 28f., 139
Poesía desnuda/pura, 7, 33, 35f., 49, 73, 82f., 118ff., 130, 137f., 152ff., 163ff., 174n24, 185nn4–5, 192n2
Poesías escojidas / Selected Poems, 151f.
Poetic gaze, 132ff., 139f.
Poet-subject, 10, 11ff., 16, 24f., 33, 35f., 47f., 59, 71, 73ff., 81ff., 122, 132ff., 163ff., 167n2, 169n12
Poststructuralism, 9, 90, 192n4
Prat, Ignacio, 175n5
Predmore, Michael, 172n11
Proust, Marcel, 191n16
Pujante Sánchez, José David, 170n14

Queneau, Raymond, 14f.

Ramsden, Herbert, 123, 191n11
Religion, 11ff., 27, 37ff., 59, 71, 88f., 94f., 141f., 170n2, 171nn4–5, 177n18, 191n13

Renaissance, 38, 60, 161, 174n23, 176n7
Retornelo, 99, 182n8
Reversibility, 69, 178n3
Revueltas, José, 156
Ricoeur, Paul, 95, 117, 130f., 142, 159, 165, 167n1, 167n3, 169n13, 170n15, 181n4, 187n14, 188n20, 191n16, 192nn3-4
Riffaterre, Michael, 69
Rimas / Rhymes, 14f., 41f., 64ff., 189n5
Río, Emilio del, 171n4, 173n17, 173n19
Robbe-Grillet, Alain, 177n22
Romantic irony, 16, 35
Romanticism, 4ff., 11ff., 28, 38ff., 46, 52, 59ff., 71, 81, 93f., 107, 134, 163, 169n9, 170n14, 170n2-3, 174n1, 176n7, 186n7, 191n13
Rousseau, Jean-Jacques, 40
Roussel, Raymond, 4
Ruskin, John, 16

San Juan de la Cruz, 177n19
Sánchez Barbudo, Antonio, 88f., 172n11, 179n11, 187n15
Sánchez Romeralo, Antonio, 158, 173n17, 190n7
Santos-Escudero, Ceferino, 171n4
Saz-Orozco, Carlos del, 171n4, 178nn5-6, 179n13, 180n15, 181n23
Schelling, Friedrich Wilhelm Joseph von, 4, 169n10
Schlegel, Friedrich, 16
Schopenhauer, Arthur, 181n2
Segunda época, 12f., 16, 33, 49, 52f., 118, 157, 188n22
Self, 8, 117f., 128, 140, 145ff., 158f., 163ff., 177n19, 189n28, 191n13, 191n16-17, 192n4
Self-parody, 8, 15, 64, 75, 82, 86, 90, 162f.
Self-reflection, 30, 52, 74, 86, 89, 98, 106, 168nn7-8, 169n10, 174n2, 193n4

Shelley, Percy Bysshe, 81, 107, 176n7, 180n16
Silver, Philip, 170n14, 186n7, 191n13
Simon, Claude, 177n22
Sonetos espirituales / Spiritual Sonnets, 49, 53, 119ff., 130, 138, 146, 157, 176n9, 185nn3-4, 187n18
Structuralism, 9, 125
Surrealism, 5
Symbolism, 1, 5, 49, 93, 96, 171n6, 174n1
Synaesthesia, 5, 69, 84, 108
Sørensen, Bengt Algot, 176n7

Taylor, Charles, 2, 40, 169n9, 170n3, 181nn1-2
Textuality, 8, 25, 36, 56, 63f., 73, 87f., 91, 95, 100, 105f., 118ff., 123ff., 154, 163f.
Trace of the past (Ricoeur), 130, 139, 187n14
Transcendental subject, 2ff., 52, 90, 118, 125f., 168n8, 174n2, 185n1, 186n11
Tree of life, 72f.

Ulibarri, Sabine, 31
Universal analogy, 38ff., 47, 50, 63, 69f., 75, 77ff., 101, 108, 163, 180n20

Villar, Arturo del, 176n17
Vinci, Leonardo da, 174n23

Warhol, Andy, 4,6
Wilcox, John C., 167n2
Will to power, 112, 184n21
Wordsworth, William, 191n13

Xirau, Ramón, 171n4, 186n7

Yeats, William Butler, 38, 79, 180n14
Young, Howard, 167n2, 179nn10-11, 180n14, 180n16, 183n16